NORFOLK IN THE SECOND WORLD WAR

Graham Smith

COUNTRYSIDE BOOKS
NEWBURY, BERKSHIRE

First Published 1994
© Graham Smith 1994
Reprinted 1994, 1996, 1999, 2001

All rights reserved. No reproduction
permitted without the prior permission
of the publishers:

COUNTRYSIDE BOOKS
3 Catherine Road
Newbury, Berkshire

ISBN 1 85306 320 7

To view our complete range of books,
please visit us at
www.countrysidebooks.co.uk

The cover painting shows Mosquitos taking off from a Norfolk airfield
in the summer of 1944, and is reproduced from an original
by Colin Doggett

Designed by Mon Mohan

Produced through MRM Associates Ltd., Reading
Typeset by Paragon Typesetters, Clwyd
Printed by Woolnough Bookbinding, Irthlingborough

CONTENTS

Map of the Norfolk Airfields	5
Map of the targets	6
1 Setting the Scene · Bomber Command Fighter Command · Coastal Command · USAAF	7
2 Attlebridge	43
3 Bircham Newton · 4 Bodney	51
5 Coltishall	66
6 Deopham Green · 7 Docking · 8 Downham Market	75
9 East Wretham	91
10 Feltwell · 11 Fersfield · 12 Foulsham	99
13 Great Massingham	117
14 Hardwick · 15 Hethel · 16 Horsham St Faith	122
17 Langham · 18 Little Snoring · 19 Ludham	143
20 Marham · 21 Matlaske · 22 Methwold	156
23 North Creake · 24 North Pickenham	173

25 Old Buckenham · 26 Oulton	183
27 Rackheath	195
28 Sculthorpe · 29 Seething · 30 Shipdham 31 Snetterton Heath · 32 Swannington 33 Swanton Morley	201
34 Thorpe Abbotts · 35 Tibenham	238
36 Watton · 37 Wendling · 38 West Raynham	252
39 Civilians at War	273
Bibliography	285
Index	287

NORFOLK WORLD WAR II AIRFIELDS

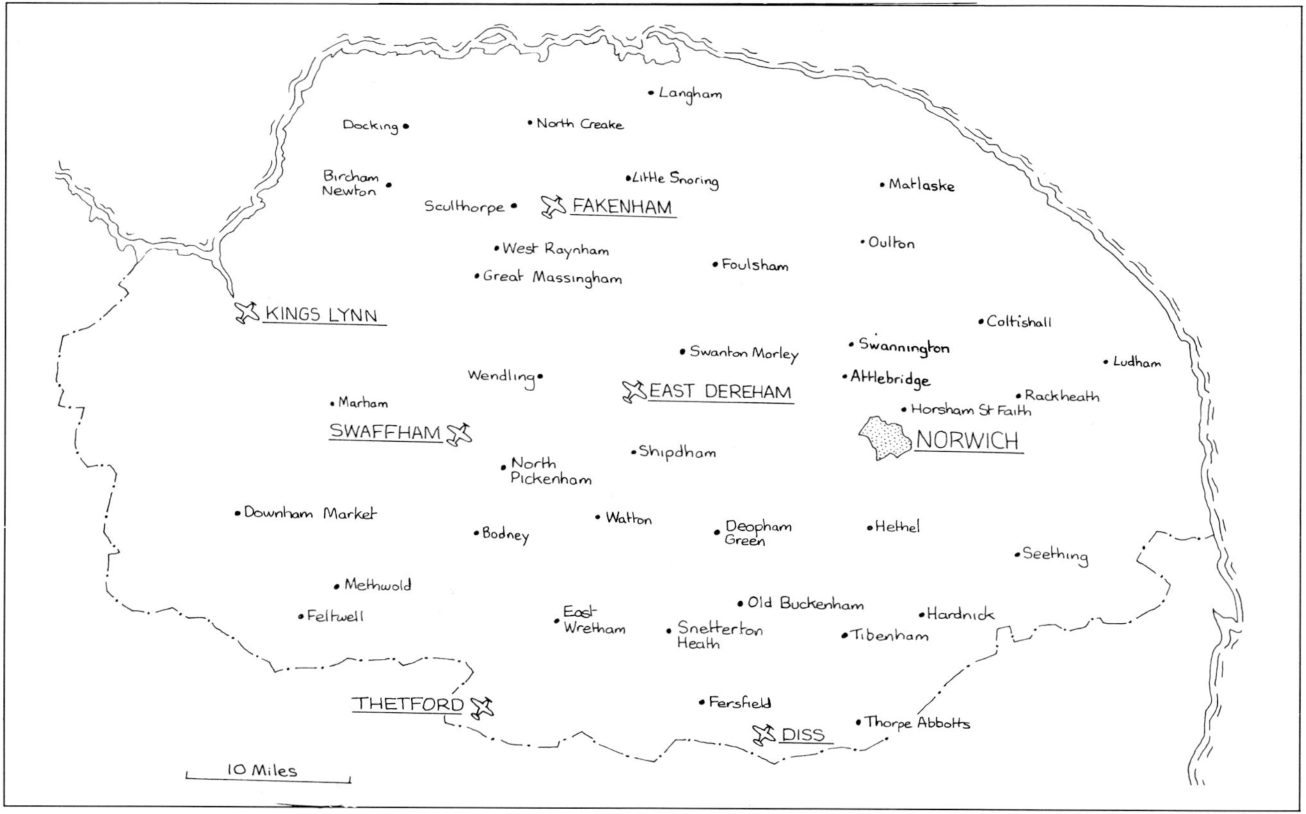

TARGETS OF R.A.F. BOMBER COMMAND AND THE EIGHTH AIR FORCE

1
SETTING THE SCENE

On the 4th September 1939, one day after war was declared, the Royal Air Force received a message from HM King George VI, 'The Royal Air Force has behind it a tradition no less inspiring than those of the older Services... you will have to shoulder far greater responsibilities than those which your Service had to shoulder in the last war; one of the greatest of them will be the safeguarding of these islands from the menace of the air. I can assure all ranks of the Air Force of my supreme confidence in their skill and courage and their ability to meet whatever calls will be made upon them.' Brave and stirring words, though a little daunting that so much was expected from such a relatively junior Service. But just how prepared was the Royal Air Force to face their sternest challenge?

At the outbreak of the war the RAF, as such, had been in existence for just 21 years, having been officially formed on 1st April 1918, from the Royal Flying Corps and the Royal Naval Air Service. Even during this short period it had been forced to fight strongly for its continued survival. Furthermore, it entered the war just three years after further reorganisation, having had barely enough time to settle down into its new role. In June 1936, the old Air Defence of Great Britain – a rather grandiloquent title – had been comprehensively dismantled and in its place the service was neatly divided into four separate and functional Commands: Bomber, Fighter, Coastal and Training – with the respective strengths of six, three, three and four Groups. Already it was thought that the German Air Force – the Luftwaffe – was bigger than the RAF; indeed Hermann Goering, the Luftwaffe's

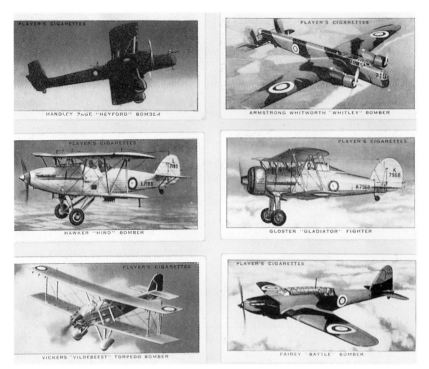

Some early RAF aircraft as portrayed on cigarette cards. Only the Heyford and the Hind did not see war service.

Commander-in-Chief, boasted that it was the strongest air force in the world, but most experts dismissed this claim as sheer bombast. Little did the RAF realise that the Luftwaffe was not only larger but was also growing at a far greater pace. Another disquieting thought was that with the Luftwaffe's participation in the Spanish Civil War, its aircraft were being tested in battle and its pilots were gaining valuable experience in the tactics of modern warfare. The RAF had always suffered from a lack of resources compared with the two other armed Services, so had a considerable amount of leeway to make up if, as it seemed likely, it was going to face a trial of strength with the mighty Luftwaffe.

The RAF of the 1930s was a small, select but highly professional service and was dubbed, somewhat unkindly, as 'The best flying club in the world'. Most of its officers had been recruited mainly from the public schools and they had graduated from the Service's own college at Cranwell. The RAF still bore the indelible imprint of Lord

Trenchard – the so-called father of the RAF and its first Chief of Air Staff. He had been responsible for the formation of a staff college and was adamant that if the Service was going to be small it would be of the highest quality. The vast majority of the ordinary airmen had served their apprenticeship at Halton and were later known in the Service as the 'Trenchard brats'! Both Cranwell and Halton inculcated a rigorous standard of discipline, perhaps it was a regime more suited to the regular Army than to the highly individualistic and imaginative tasks and demands that would be placed on RAF pilots and crews during the war years. Nevertheless it was these very officers and men that formed the backbone of the Service for most of the early war years and achieved amazing feats of valour against overwhelming odds.

This small and rather elitist Service was backed up by a number of auxiliary reserve squadrons manned by very enthusiastic 'weekend pilots', many of whom had learned to fly either at civilian airfields or whilst at university. Without question, whether regulars or reservists, all were utterly devoted to the Service. This dedication and fervour remained steadfast throughout the war years despite the quite intolerable and harrowing demands placed upon the aircrew and ground personnel. Even faced with quite crippling losses the RAF never once had to resort to conscription to replace their pilots or crews; throughout the war all were volunteers, such was the enthusiasm for the junior Service.

To understand the part these various Norfolk airfields played it is necessary to consider just how each Command pursued their war aims and objectives and to see how their different roles developed and changed during the progress of the war in the air.

Bomber Command

During the inter-war years the bomber pilots were considered the elite of the RAF; their squadrons outnumbered those of fighters by two to one. Their thunder was soon stolen by the pilots of Fighter Command, whose bright and glittering image was forever enshrined in the daring and valiant exploits of 'The Few' during the Battle of Britain, so much so that by the end of the war Air Marshal Arthur Harris, its Commander-in-Chief and almost the sole architect of

Bomber Command's assault on Germany, continually bemoaned the fact that his men had not received their deserved recognition for all the sterling and brave deeds they had achieved during the war.

The creation of the bomber crews as a privileged class had been largely brought about by Lord Trenchard's precepts of the Service. Lord Trenchard was utterly convinced that the main, if not sole, ethos of the RAF lay in the use of bombers as a strategic strike force. His view, expressed most categorically in 1928, was '... it is air power that can pass over the enemy navies and armies and penetrate the air defences and attack direct the centres of production, transportation and communication from which the enemy's war effort is maintained ... and it will be in this manner that air superiority will be obtained, and not by the direct destruction of air forces.' Allied to this unwavering conviction was his dismissive view of the role of fighters in an air war, which he considered would never be a match for a strong force of heavily armed bombers; the fighters therefore had been relegated to a minor role in the pre-war RAF. It was with this deeply engrained philosophy that heavy long range bombers would always reign supreme that Bomber Command entered the war. Two of Bomber Command's most famous chiefs – Sir Charles Portal and Arthur Harris – were willing disciples of Lord Trenchard and his theories, so it was quite unlikely that there would be any change of policy whilst they were in charge. Bomber Command's tardy appreciation of the Mosquito's great worth as a bomber can be attributed in some measure to the legacy left by Lord Trenchard.

In the three years before the outset of war, Bomber Command set out various plans for the provision of new twin and four engined heavy bombers that would meet the demands of a modern air war. Even if all the aircraft had been approved they would have taken considerable time to materialise from the drawing board to an operational aircraft. Their production was further delayed by a political decision, taken in 1938, that more of the country's precious resources should be devoted to building up the fighter forces rather than bombers, which with hindsight can be seen as a most wise, if not prescient, decision.

At least one policy decision was taken and positively acted upon in the immediate pre-war years and that was to move most of the Bomber Command's airfields away from southern England, where they had been sited to face a threat from France, to the eastern counties, those nearest to the new threat – Germany. It was as a direct result of this policy that Marham was reopened in 1937 and a

Vickers Wellingtons: the backbone of Bomber Command during the early years.

new airfield at Feltwell came into operation in the same year. These were quickly followed by Watton and West Raynham in 1939 and another two new bomber airfields were planned and approved for Horsham St Faith and Coltishall with the hope that they would both be ready to commence operations by 1940.

The first of the new twin-engined bombers that had been planned in the early days of Bomber Command came into service in 1938. It was the Armstrong Whitworth Whitley, followed quickly by the Handley Page Hampden. Then in the early months of 1939 the much beloved Vickers Wellington, which during the first half of the war would bear the brunt of most of Bomber Command's offensives, was supplied to several squadrons. These three new heavy and medium bombers joined the Bristol Blenheims and the single-engined Fairey Battles as the main bomber strike force for the early years of the war; this despite the fact that the Battles, and to a lesser extent the Blenheims, were already known to be severely outclassed and yet they were still being produced in great numbers even as late as 1940.

Thus at the outset of the war Bomber Command had just 33 squadrons, totalling some 640 aircraft of which probably no more than 600 were operational at the time. The majority were Battles and Blenheims with just a small number of the new twin-engined bombers. Most of the Battles were allocated to No 1 Group to form the Advanced Air Striking Force and were based in France. No 2

Group was mainly equipped with Blenheims and largely based in East Anglia – Watton, Marham and West Raynham all had Blenheim squadrons. No 3 Group operated Wellingtons with Feltwell being one of its prominent airfields, featuring in many of the Command's early operations. The airfields of No 4 and 5 Groups were spread throughout Yorkshire and Lincolnshire and the Whitleys and Hampdens became the precursors of the massive armada of bombers that flew from these airfields nightly during 1943 and 1944. Compared with the Luftwaffe forces the bombers were outnumbered by about four to one and they were likely to be faced with double their number of enemy fighters. Such odds do seem almost unassailable and it is a great credit to these pioneer aircrews of Bomber Command that many of them managed to survive their early operations.

The chief tasks of Bomber Command in 1939 were to attack the German Navy *at sea* and also support the British Expeditionary Force in France. However, it was almost grudgingly accepted that Bomber Command might attack 'definable military targets where there was no reasonable risks of bombs falling on civilians'! In those nervous and somewhat naive days the Chamberlain Government wished to avoid at all costs the threat of a large retaliatory air attack on British civilians. But the subsequent heavy German blitz on London in the late summer of 1940, and a change of Prime Minister, radically altered this humane policy.

During the remaining months of 1939 Bomber Command mounted several operations to attack German shipping in and around the Heligoland Bight and to drop propaganda leaflets over mainland Germany. The Chamberlain Government still thought that the German people could be persuaded to prevail upon their leaders to come to some peaceful agreement. Propaganda leaflets were still being dropped at various times right up to the end of 1944.

These first missions aimed at disrupting German shipping were really doomed to failure by the government's edict that no enemy vessel in harbour was to be attacked as civilians might be endangered. The raids were very costly in terms of aircraft shot down or badly damaged, but even more important was the tragic depletion of trained aircrews – all of whom were experienced and valuable pre-war regulars. Although many of the losses were as a direct result of enemy action – largely flak rather than fighters – some of the blame must be attached to the poor design of the bombers. For instance the fire-power of their guns was found to be woefully inadequate and unlike the Luftwaffe aircraft none of the fuel tanks was self-sealing, which tended to cause many serious fires. Also the aircraft were equipped with poor radio communications and with unsatisfactory heating and oxygen systems for the crews seriously impairing their operational efficiency.

Not only were the losses in aircraft and men unacceptably high but there was also a deep concern about the very disappointing bombing results. Certainly hasty and superficial briefings did not help the crews, nor did the lack of reliable weather information over the target areas. Nearly all of the crews experienced navigational and bomb-aiming problems of some kind or other, mostly due to the equipment but some were probably occasioned by the standard of pre-war training and established service routines that were not really suited to the vastly different war environment.

But perhaps the most disturbing and sobering lesson gained from these early tentative and probing operations was the folly of sending out bombers in close formations in daylight without adequate fighter protection. One particularly disastrous mission in December 1939 had such a profound effect on the mandarins of Bomber Command that almost overnight they abandoned their principle of daylight bombing. Henceforth no daylight operation involving heavy bombers in formation would be ordered without fighter support. After less than three months of operations Bomber Command became convinced that because there were no escort fighters, as yet, of sufficient range to penetrate into the heartland of Germany, then German industrial centres could only be destroyed by forces of unescorted bombers operating solely by night; a bombing strategy which survived for virtually the rest of the war. This night bombing policy was in direct variance with their American counterparts – the United States Army Air Force – when they entered the 'European Theater of Operations' in late 1942. The Americans were convinced that precision daylight bombing was the only way to operate effectively; but they, too, found how costly such a policy could be without strong fighter protection.

If Bomber Command's aircrews were finding great difficulty in bombing accurately by day, then how much greater would their task be at night? These problems needed to be solved before the Command's efficiency could be improved. And of course there were other difficulties associated with night flying in formation, not the least of which was navigational, and great improvements were essential both in training and the provision of other aids before

Bomber Command could become an offensive force to be reckoned with. This was to take almost three years to achieve.

The so-called 'Phoney War' – a term conjured up by an American politician to describe the apparent stalemate – was said to have lasted from September 1939 to April 1940; though the aircrews of Nos 1, 2 and 3 Groups would have said, with much justification, that as far as they were concerned the air battle had been anything but 'phoney'! Nevertheless with the start of the German offensive against France and the Low Countries on 10th May 1940, the war in the air changed very dramatically. It was on that day that the first RAF raid was made on mainland Germany and then just five nights later almost 200 aircraft attacked industrial targets in the Ruhr; a raid that signalled the start of Bomber Command's strategic offensive against Germany. This offensive, which would continue almost unabated for the next five years, started somewhat slowly and hesitantly before growing steadily in strength and severity until it became utterly devastating.

In May and June 1940 the Fairey Battles of No 1 Group, assisted by Blenheims from Norfolk airfields fought bravely and valiantly in France against overwhelming odds and much superior enemy aircraft. The Battles, particularly, suffered crippling losses and they were almost annihilated. This crushing defeat over the French battlefields ensured that the few surviving Battles were quickly

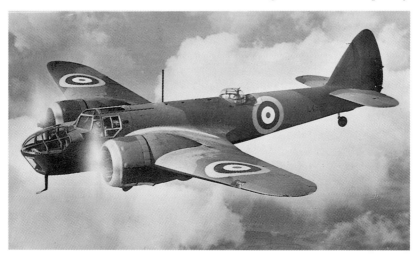

Bristol Blenheims of No 2 Group were heavily involved in early bombing offensives.

withdrawn from active service. Nevertheless this air debacle did produce the first air Victoria Cross of the war, it was posthumously awarded on 12th May to the crew of a Battle for a most bravely sustained attack on a bridge at Maas.

By the end of the month the Air Ministry had issued a new heavy bombing directive. Bomber Command's objectives were to be the destruction of Germany's industries especially the aircraft factories, and all oil installations must be considered priority targets; these operations would, of course, be conducted at night.

What was to become known as the Battle of Britain started with the first enemy bombs to be dropped on London on 24th August 1940. Bomber Command made its first raid on Berlin the following night. This operation was nothing more than a token act of reprisal largely undertaken for morale purposes; it was by no means a major raid – that would have to wait until January 1943. Nevertheless during the last quarter of 1940 19 German cities and towns were bombed – names that would become all too familiar to future aircrews of both Bomber Command and the USAAF. Daily the BBC News carried reports of Hamburg, Kiel, Essen, Bremen, Dusseldorf, Stuttgart, Cologne and Mannheim being 'attacked by strong forces of Bomber Command'. Although these raids were not that large nor indeed were they that effective they were particularly beneficial for public morale as they came at a time when the news in other war spheres was rather grim and bleak.

In February 1941 the first of the new four-engined bombers came into service. The Short Stirling arrived at squadrons, to be followed two weeks later by a small number of Avro Manchesters. Unfortunately this aircraft was soon found to be seriously under-powered, and continually beset with engine problems; most crews considered it a jinx aircraft and although it did fly operationally on many missions, it had a relatively short service life, being withdrawn after barely 18 months. Its main claim to fame was as the forerunner of the Lancaster. The following month saw yet another new heavy bomber make its entrance – the Handley Page Halifax – which quickly became dubbed the 'Hallibag' by aircrews. Nevertheless it proved to be a very successful and popular aircraft and until the Lancaster appeared on the scene, it spearheaded Bomber Command's raids on Germany. On one night in May 364 sorties were mounted, the largest number of aircraft used by Bomber Command in the war so far. Perhaps after all the tide was beginning to turn?

During the middle of the year Bomber Command switched its main

Avro Lancasters: the most famous of all RAF bombers.

bomber force to attacks on German shipping, in particular it targeted the French Atlantic ports, which not only harboured the U-boats but also some of the German navy's major vessels. These raids were most costly – the area was very heavily protected by enemy flak battalions – without producing many positive results. The bombs used for these raids were quite inadequate to cause other than superficial damage to the deep and strong defences of the U-boat shelters. Once again it was decided that the Command's resources would be better utilised against German industrial areas, so it was back to 'Happy Valley' as the Ruhr was ironically named by RAF crews.

The latter months of 1941, when Bomber Command was active almost every night, incurred some of its heaviest losses of the war. On some raids, to the Ruhr for instance, one in five aircraft failed to return and overall the losses of aircraft and men exceeded 10%; well over double what was considered an acceptable operational limit. Quite clearly no Command could sustain such crippling losses for very long and still remain a fighting force. But even more damaging was a report requested by the Air Ministry and based on two months' photographic evidence of bombed targets. It revealed that only one third of aircraft ever came closer than five miles of the primary target, and in raids over the Ruhr, where there was intense flak, this figure dropped alarmingly to barely one tenth. It was already known from debriefings that almost one third of returning aircrews admitted that they had not bombed the primary targets. Faced with such a damning indictment, serious questions were raised about the whole of the Command's strategic bombing policy, which was so very costly in men and machines for so few tangible results. Undoubtedly, at this stage of the war Bomber Command was at its nadir.

This serious crisis of confidence obviously did not filter down to the aircrews, or to the British public; both firmly believed the Air Ministry's confident and brash propaganda that heavy damage was being inflicted nightly on Germany, materially affecting its war efforts. Most of the senior officers in Bomber Command were also convinced of this despite the mass of evidence to the contrary! Oddly, when Bomber Command was at such a low ebb, a documentary film about one of its operations, *Target for Tonight* was released and quickly proved a resounding success. It graphically portrayed the bravery and dedication of the bomber crews and went some way to adjust the balance between them and the fighter pilots.

But matters were to improve for Bomber Command, in August 1942 the new GEE navigational device had been successfully tested and was to greatly aid future operations. Then in November the first de Havilland Mosquito arrived at Swanton Morley in Norfolk, though it would take a long time for Bomber Command to fully appreciate the worth and versatility of this amazingly successful aircraft. Finally on Christmas Eve the first Lancaster came into service and it quickly proved to be the outstanding heavy bomber of the war on both sides.

In retrospect 1942 can be considered as the watershed of Bomber Command. On 14th February the Air Ministry issued yet another bombing directive instructing that future operations should be 'focused on the morale of the enemy's civil population and in particular of the industrial workers'. Bomber Command was ordered 'to use the utmost resources at all times'. No longer were aircraft to be kept in reserve, the resolve now was an out-and-out air war pursued to the limits of Bomber Command's resources. Then just eight days later it received a new Commander-in-Chief, Arthur Harris, who was destined to direct operations for the duration of the war. He was undoubtedly the ideal man to carry out this strategy of outright area bombing. Quite unswerving in his commitment to this policy, he prosecuted it with a grim determination and, at times, unbridled ruthlessness. Harris was a born leader, gaining a fierce, total and undying loyalty from all the men under his command. They would have flown to hell and back on his orders and indeed most considered that they did precisely that every night!

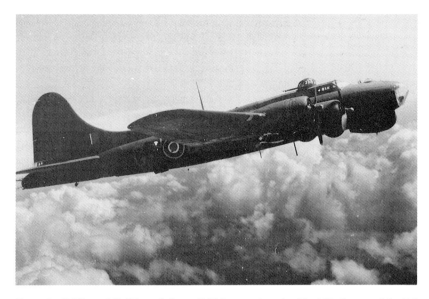

Even the RAF used B-17s mainly on RCM operations by No 100 Group. (No 100 Group/RAF Oulton Memorial Association)

Perhaps the attack on Old Lubeck on 29th March 1942 can be considered the Command's most successful operation of the war up until then, and it cannot be a coincidence that Lancasters were used operationally for the first time; henceforth they would become the main heavy strike bomber of Bomber Command. The old town was virtually destroyed and it was estimated that incendiary bombs caused almost six times the damage of high explosives. From now on the war in the air would become that of fire, and a new expression 'fire-storm' entered the vocabulary. This operation and a subsequent raid on Rostock caused the German High Command to make retaliatory raids on Bath, Canterbury, Exeter, York and Norwich – the 'Baedeker' raids, so named from the famous tourist guides from which the Germans had listed their targets; calling them 'Terrorangriffes' or terror attacks!

During May and June three '1,000' bomber raids were launched on Cologne, Essen and Bremen. Every possible aircraft was brought into the attack, including training flights and some aircraft were borrowed back from Coastal Command. These 'Greatest Air Raids in History' as the newspapers proclaimed them, did much to lift the morale of the British people, who felt that in the face of several military setbacks, Bomber Command was the only force taking the offensive. Harris put it much more succinctly, 'They have sowed the wind, now they will reap the whirlwind'. A most important step forward was taken in August when the first Pathfinder squadron was formed, despite Harris's scepticism as to its worth or need; indeed he disliked the thought of an elite group. Its task would be to mark the target areas in front of the main bomber force. This squadron was not overly successful in its early operations but it quickly developed into a potent force.

At the beginning of 1943 the major Allied conference at Casablanca came to an agreement on the Allied bombing strategy for the rest of the war. The directive known as 'Pointblank' ordered that 'the primary aim will be the progressive destruction and dislocation of the German military, industrial and economic system, and the undermining of the morale of the German people to a point where their capacity for armed resistance is fatally weakened.' It further listed the essential targets in order of priority – submarine yards and bases, the German air force and its factories, ball-bearing plants, oil and transportation. Air Marshal Harris felt that this changed nothing as far as Bomber Command was concerned, indeed he considered that 'it was ready and equipped for our strategic offensive'. Certainly 1943 was, as Max Hastings commented in his book *Bomber Command*, 'the most famous and bloodiest year of the British air offensive'.

What is generally known now as the 'Battle of the Ruhr' started in March and continued until July; it was a most ferocious and sustained bombardment of this important industrial complex, which was followed later in July by four devastating attacks on Hamburg. Then in November came the opening blows of the Battle of Berlin, a terrible onslaught that would continue well into 1944. In conjunction with this massive offensive were the much publicised other operations such as the famous Dambusters raid in May and followed in August by the very successful attack on the rocket research centre at Peenemunde. Also during the year were several spectacular low-level daylight bombing raids by Mosquitos. There was no respite for the embattled German defences or people as the growing strength of the USAAF in East Anglia carried out increasingly heavy and effective daylight raids over Germany.

An increasing number of navigational aids and radar jamming equipment and devices were brought into operation, many of these had been developed and tried by various squadrons based at Norfolk airfields. In November Group No 100 was formed at West Raynham to co-ordinate the various radio counter-measures as well as to carry out a long-range offensive against the German air defences.

Towards the end of 1943 a serious problem was foreseen – the very real threat of a V1 rocket assault on London and south east England. In December it was decided to devote considerable forces to attack the launching sites in northern France. The first serious raid took place on the 16th and was undertaken by No 617, 'the Dambusters' squadron led by Wing Commander Leonard Cheshire. The sites were numerous, small and well-hidden and required far greater bombing accuracy. Because they were so heavily defended they proved to be very costly in operational terms.

Both Bomber Command and the USAAF suffered heavily for their prolonged and sustained bombardment of Germany. On some raids, for instance to Berlin, losses exceeded 6% and those on targets further afield were closer to 8%. Such casualties could only be sustained because ample supplies of both aircraft and crews were forthcoming. Then on 30th March 1944 Bomber Command received a grievous setback during a single raid on Nuremberg; of the 795 aircraft despatched on the mission 110 failed to return or were fatally damaged – nearly 14% loss rate! This became the Command's worst disaster of the war. Somewhat fortunately for the aircrews just two weeks later the overall control of Bomber Command (and the USAAF) was passed to General Eisenhower, the Supreme Allied Commander in Europe, and much of the Command's resources were diverted to the preparations and support of 'Operation Overlord' – the invasion of mainland Europe. The targets now became the coastal defences and the hinterland of northern France.

Arthur Harris's firm conviction that Germany could be defeated solely by aerial bombardment had been proved wrong but nevertheless he stoutly maintained, right up to his death, that if he had been given a free hand in the summer of 1944 it could have been achieved, thus, he claimed shortening the war by many months. However, it is likely that he was about the only person in the RAF to hold such a view.

In August 1944 Bomber Command was back over Germany with their first daylight mission for over three years. This time they were heavily defended by Spitfires and all the aircraft returned safely. Then on 14th October over 1,570 sorties were flown on that day – a record never to be exceeded. On the last day of the year there was the famous and dramatic low-level attack by Mosquitos on Gestapo headquarters in Oslo, almost a replica of an earlier raid in October on a similar target at Aarhus in Denmark.

By January 1945 Bomber Command was at its zenith. With over 1,600 aircraft it was a highly technical and superb professional force with quite terrifying power. In the first four months of the year it conducted 36 major operations over Germany, dropping over 180,000 tons of bombs, which was a fifth of the total tonnage used throughout the war. But this final period of the war, when the two air forces dominated the skies over Germany, is almost solely remembered for their utter destruction of Dresden from 13th to 15th February, which has left an unfortunate stain on Bomber Command's wartime operations. Although the Air Chiefs declared on 16th April that all the objectives of 'Pointblank' had been achieved and thus the bombardment of Germany should cease, Harris, in an almost defiant and arrogant gesture, ordered an attack on Hitler's mountain retreat at Berchtesgaden. He followed it shortly afterwards with a final raid on Heligoland, where over five years earlier Bomber Command had suffered its first defeat. But now it all mattered so little as victory in Europe was assured and very close at hand. The last offensive action by Bomber Command took place on 2nd May and was undertaken rather appropriately by Mosquitos.

In the last 20 years or so much heated debate has been centred on Bomber Command's contribution to the defeat of Germany, and perhaps even more has been written on Air Marshal Harris's methods and use of the forces under his command. It has only been possible to outline briefly Bomber Command's operations and development during World War II and to merely hint at the controversy surrounding the area bombing of German cities and towns. Certainly the strategic bombing policy was very costly in human terms – 55,173 airmen killed, 8,403 wounded and 9,784 made prisoners of war. It is most sobering to reflect that Bomber Command's casualties amounted to one seventh of *all* British deaths by land, sea and air for the whole of the war. Of the 32 Victoria Crosses awarded to airmen during the war, 19 went to members of Bomber Command. The enormous sacrifice made by these men has probably been best remembered by their own commander 'Bomber' Harris, who wrote in 1947: 'There are no words with which I can do justice to the aircrew who fought under my command. There is no parallel in warfare to such courage and determination in the face of danger over so prolonged a period . . . It was the courage of men with long drawn apprehensions of daily "going over the top". Such devotion must never be forgotten.'

Fighter Command

On 14th July 1936 Air Marshal Sir Hugh Dowding arrived at Bentley Priory near Stanmore in Middlesex, the base of the newly formed Fighter Command, and found himself in control of a small, rather outmoded fighting force. There were just eleven fighter squadrons based at a handful of airfields and the fighters then in service looked decidedly old-fashioned for modern warfare. All were biplanes, all had open cockpits and all were armed with just twin machine guns. To the untutored eye they looked not very different to the fragile machines of the old Royal Flying Corps, seeming to belong more to the books of Captain W.E. Johns and his intrepid hero 'Biggles' than a modern fighting force! Somehow Dowding had to build and develop this force into an adequate air defence of the United Kingdom – which then seemed a rather tall order. But just four years later at the start of Fighter Command's greatest test – the Battle of Britain – Dowding had 50 squadrons at his command, all equipped with monoplanes, two of which were the supreme examples of fighter design – the Hurricane and Spitfire.

This aerial defence force was backed up by a chain of Radio

Spitfire II of the Battle of Britain memorial flight.

Direction Finding stations (RDFs), a well-trained and highly organised Observer Corps, a strong barrage balloon force, and an anti-aircraft defence system. It is to his everlasting credit and praise that Dowding had the vision and determination to bring Fighter Command into such a state of readiness that in the summer of 1940 it could seriously take on the might of the so-called invincible Luftwaffe and even achieve a famous victory.

From 1938 the Chamberlain Government radically changed its air policy; the new long range bombers so desired by Bomber Command would have to wait, fighter defence, the development of the radar stations and civil defence became the chief priorities. Thus Dowding entered the war with a far stronger Command than even he could have envisaged. There were 42 squadrons of Hurricanes and Spitfires, backed up by six Blenheim I squadrons to be used for night fighting and just two squadrons of Defiants. Fighter Command had been reorganised into four operational Groups – No 10 to cover Wales and the west, No 11, which was by far the strongest, was given the task of defending London and the south-east, No 12 covered East Anglia and part of eastern England, which left No 13 to patrol the north and Scotland. New fighter airfields were quickly set up and in Norfolk, Coltishall, which had been planned as a bomber station, was passed over to Fighter Command in May 1940 with nearby Matlaske prepared in the late summer as its satellite airfield. Horsham St Faith, which also had been planned for bombers, came into operation

Hawker Hurricane: the stalwart fighter of the Battle of Britain.

during May/June 1940 with a squadron of Defiants.

Fighter Command was rather slow to enter the war operationally and did not get too involved with the German advance into France and the Low Countries until May 1940, although in November 1939 a Spitfire from RAF Turnhouse in Scotland was credited with the first enemy aircraft destroyed over the British mainland. The Command's first major test came over the skies of Dunkirk. From 26th May to 3rd June 1940 32 squadrons were active, flying some 2,700 sorties. The losses were great with the Defiants suffering heavily and by the end of the evacuation Fighter Command had only 330 operational aircraft and a mere 30 or so in reserve. Fortunately the Command was allowed a short breathing space to regroup, and with fighters coming from the factories at a rate of about 100 per week, this precious respite enabled the squadrons to be brought back to full strength. On 18th June, Winston Churchill warned, 'The Battle for France is over. I expect the Battle of Britain is about to begin', and how right he was. The situation was critical: since the 10th May the RAF had lost 944 aircraft and of this total 386 were Hurricanes and 67 Spitfires. More distressing was the loss of 915 pilots, over half of whom were well-experienced combat fliers.

Early in July 1940 the Luftwaffe was ordered to attack British shipping in the English Channel with the dual purpose of inflicting damage to vessels and bringing Fighter Command into combat. The first attack came on 10th July, the first phase of the 'Battle of Britain'.

Hurricanes of No 242 Squadron during the Battle of Britain.

By the end of the month there had been countless attacks on Fighter Command's airfields and radar stations in which the enemy had lost 190 aircraft compared with 77 of Fighter Command. For a week or so there was a relative lull until 13th August when the Luftwaffe launched their 'Adler Angriff' or 'Eagle Attack' – their planned air offensive over England prior to the invasion, which they had code-named 'Operation Sealion'. But two days later the heaviest fighting of the whole Battle culminated in the loss to the enemy of 40 aircraft, mainly bombers, against 22 of Command's fighters. In the ensuing days more heavy raids were made on fighter airfields and the Defiants suffered such heavy losses that they were withdrawn from action. On 24th August some of the German bombers made a navigational error and dropped bombs on London, resulting in Bomber Command's raid on Berlin the following night and radically changing the future conduct of the air war.

By 1st September Fighter Command's losses had become desperate. New pilots were being sent into action with only 20 hours training and invariably were lost on their first sortie. Just five days later the command was stretched to its very limits not only by its losses in the air but also by the incessant attacks on its airfields. The Luftwaffe was now bombing London and Liverpool by night and the climax of the Battle came on 15th September when three separate heavy waves of enemy bombers attacked London. In these intensive raids the Luftwaffe lost 56 aircraft with the Command's losses amounting to half that number. The glorious exploits of 'The Few' on that Sunday are now celebrated as 'Battle of Britain Day'. Two days later it became known through intelligence sources that Germany had postponed 'Operation Sealion' indefinitely. Nevertheless the raids and the onslaught continued, with each side incurring heavy losses. It was not really until the middle of November that it could safely be said that the Battle was over. In the five months from 1st July Fighter Command had lost 1,268 aircraft and 975 pilots killed or seriously wounded against more than 2,000 enemy aircraft destroyed or seriously damaged. The only VC of the Battle was awarded on 16th August to a Hurricane pilot. It had been a narrow but very costly victory for Fighter Command. In November Dowding was relieved of his post, the efforts of the previous four and a half years had taken a toll on his health. He was sent to the USA as representative of the minister for aircraft production (1940-1942) and on his return he retired from the RAF. No man was more deserving of his long retirement. He died in 1970.

From now until the middle of May 1941 the provincial cities and towns would have to face an ordeal of night bombing, which to a large extent Fighter Command was powerless to prevent. The Spitfires and Hurricanes were not night fighters – although one Hurricane pilot did manage to make a number of kills. It was left to the few squadrons of Bristol Beaufighters, which had been hastily brought into service in September 1940, to provide some opposition to the seemingly incessant waves of enemy bombers. But in the hands of such experts as Group Captain John 'Cat's-eyes' Cunningham, they did begin to achieve some moderate success.

From the beginning of 1941 it became clear that a new role was needed for the Hurricanes and Spitfires and so they went on the offensive; they carried out combined operations across the Channel with light and medium bombers, flew individual sweeps over Northern France attacking airfields and transport systems, and patrolled the Channel for enemy shipping. These operations went under various strange names: 'Rhubarbs', 'Ramrods', 'Jim Crows' and 'Roadsteads'. Both types of aircraft were being refined and improved and with the addition of cannons were becoming formidable ground-attack fighters, the Hurricane especially being well suited to this role. With the use of extra fuel tanks their range of operations was extended. These operations proved to be quite costly in terms of men and aircraft and were reduced to just two or three a month. Also by this time a new German fighter had appeared on the scene – the Focke Wulf 190 – which proved to be a very fast aircraft, out-performing both the Spitfire and Hurricane and causing great concern until a more powerful Spitfire Mark was developed. The Hawker Typhoon which made its entry in mid-1941 had the performance to equal the Fw190 but unfortunately it encountered many early problems, which took rather a long time to resolve.

Perhaps it was the so-called 'Baedeker' raids of 1942 that demonstrated the way Fighter Command had fallen between two stools – defensive or offensive, though the Command's chiefs had always felt somewhat inhibited in the use of their fighters as an attacking force in case the Luftwaffe decided to mount another blitzkreig, especially considering Bomber Command's nightly onslaught of German cities and towns. The German raids of 1942 did take Fighter Command by surprise mainly because they were directed at cities and towns with few or no strategic targets and as such they had been lightly defended, and as the raids progressed it became almost impossible for Fighter Command to determine where

Focke-Wulf Fw190: the Luftwaffe aircraft that caused problems for Fighter Command.

the Luftwaffe would strike next. From April to July Fighter Command accounted for 67 enemy aircraft and of this number, the newly arrived Mosquito night fighter claimed almost one third of the victories.

The biggest task for Fighter Command since the Battle of Britain came on 19th August 1942 with the ill-fated raid on Dieppe. During the day the Command flew 2,339 sorties and claimed 91 aircraft destroyed with another 190 as probable kills. It lost 106 aircraft so that the Dieppe operation seemed quite a success, and the newspapers of the day claimed it as a great victory for Fighter Command, suggesting that at least one third of the Luftwaffe strength on the Western Front had been destroyed. In fact after the war it was discovered that the German losses were only 48 destroyed and another 24 damaged! So the Dieppe raid really amounted to a heavy defeat for Fighter Command and if its chiefs had known the true cost many grave misgivings would have been expressed at such losses for just one operation.

Fighter Command gave the impression of a fighting force that was still seeking some positive role in the air war over Europe. Increasingly the intruder missions and sweeps over the Continent were being undertaken by Mosquitos, which had proved to be better suited to the task and had produced far greater successes. It seemed most likely that the Command's fighters would become relegated to a pure bomber escort force, and in fact it was Spitfires that escorted the first mission of USAAF bombers in August 1942. Other fighter squadrons were also used more frequently to support and protect bombing missions over the near Continent as well as Coastal Command's anti-shipping strikes.

By June 1943 Fighter Command had reached the zenith of its power with no less than 102 squadrons – double its size at the outbreak of the war. However, all too soon it would lose many of these squadrons and in the process even lose its identity. In November a new Command was formed: the Second Tactical Air Force, an amalgam of light bombers, fighters and transport aircraft specially designed to provide close tactical support for the Allied armies in their invasion of Europe. *The Times* newspaper described the new force as 'the most significant reform made by the RAF since the war began.' What was left of Fighter Command regrouped and became known as the 'Air Defence of Great Britain' – a title which harked back to the days of the early 1930s.

Fighter Command's fears of a new German bombing offensive materialised in January 1944 when the Luftwaffe returned to night attacks on London. The first raid occurred on the 21st and continued intermittently until May. This series of attacks became known as the 'Little Blitz' and the Luftwaffe suffered grievously, losing over 300 aircraft, many falling to the Mosquito night fighter squadrons. One result of this crippling defeat was that Germany now concentrated its industrial efforts on fighter production for the final defence of the Reich and the development of V1 and V2 rockets for a last desperate bombardment of London and the south-east.

In June 1944 the fighter pilots once again found their true metier – single-handed combat – but this time it was against unmanned V1 rockets or 'divers' as the pilots knew them. Between 13th June and early September Fighter Command shot down 1,771 rockets. The most successful fighter at this type of combat was the Hawker Tempest, then the fastest aircraft to see service in the Second World War, accounting for over 630 of the total. In August yet another new fighter was in action against the 'divers', the Gloster Meteor Mk1, which became the first jet aircraft to see service in the RAF – a bright sign for the future of Fighter Command, which in October 1944 had regained its old designation.

The last operation by fighters took place on 4th May when Typhoons and Tempests along with Coastal Command aircraft attacked enemy aircraft and shipping in the Baltic. The men of Fighter

Command could feel very proud of their contribution to the air war. They had been called upon to carry out a hundred and one tasks and in the process lost 3,690 airmen. But, of course, their greatest hour had been in those few brief summer months of 1940 when they held the fate of the country and the outcome of the war in their hands. For that Battle they will never be forgotten.

Coastal Command

The third and last of the RAF's operational Commands was always considered and treated as the Cinderella of the service. It proved to be sadly ill-equipped for the important role it was called upon to play in the war. Although formed with three groups it was the smallest Command and could hardly muster 300 aircraft, operating from a handful of airfields, most of them in Scotland. More so than the other Commands it had prepared itself for a somewhat limited sphere of operations largely centred around the North Sea and this is why Bircham Newton in Norfolk had been developed into one of its major airfields. With the fall of both Norway and France in 1940 Coastal Command suddenly found its areas of operations greatly extended and its slender resources were stretched to their limits.

Coastal Command entered the war with just 19 squadrons to cover the whole coastline of the United Kingdom. Its main aircraft were Avro Ansons and Vickers Vildebeestes, both of which were considered obsolescent at the time, the Short Sunderland flying boat, which would ultimately become the mainstay of the battle against the U-boats, and just one squadron of the American Lockheed Hudson – the planned replacement for the Anson.

Three new aircraft had been planned in the pre-war years and they came into operation in 1940. Two of them were dismal failures; the Blackburn Botha was seriously under-powered and was withdrawn after barely six months of service and the Saunders Roe Lerwick flying boat was considered dangerously unstable and the project was abandoned after only 21 had been built. The only successful aircraft to come out of the pre-war plans was the Bristol Beaufort, specifically a torpedo bomber, which operated with some success in the early years of the war, though this aircraft was ultimately superseded by an improved version of the Beaufighter. Sadly missing in the

Air-Sea rescue was just one of Coastal Command's important tasks.

Command's armoury was a long-range aircraft able to deal with the growing threat of the U-boats, even the Royal Navy did not possess one anti-submarine aircraft and the old-fashioned but very hardy Fairey Swordfish, a biplane which had first seen service in 1936, was increasingly called upon to act as a torpedo bomber.

The main tasks of Coastal Command in the early war years were the protection of allied shipping, general reconnaissance and photographic work and air-sea rescue. Not until the full threat of the U-boat menace was realised and the Command had suitable aircraft with which to combat this, did its role become more offensive. As one Coastal Command pilot remarked, 'Regular, monotonous hours of flying over unbounded sea watching water with little to relieve the sheer drudgery – a constant need for alertness and concentration was required . . . 99% boredom interrupted by 1% heart-thumping action.'

From mid-1940 the Command mounted regular and extensive sea-area patrols from dawn to dusk and when the conditions favoured it – moonlight – patrols at night. Coastal Command never called off operations – many were conducted in atrocious weather conditions and often in very hostile circumstances – as can be judged by the four Victoria Crosses awarded to the Command's airmen during the war. Undoubtedly their aircraft played an important part in the Battle of the Atlantic, ensuring that the vital supplies of food and war materials reached a beleaguered Britain.

SETTING THE SCENE

In May 1940 it fell to a Bristol Blenheim of Bomber Command to sink the first enemy U-boat. Although about one seventh of the Command's aircraft were equipped with a basic ASV (Air-Surface-Vessel) radar device, this was rather rudimentary and neither reliable nor effective in locating submarines. The Command's record against submarines during the first years of the war was therefore extremely poor. In 1940 the authorities seriously considered transferring Coastal Command to the Royal Navy, as the Fleet Air Arm had been shortly before the outbreak of the war. However, the Command stayed with the RAF and was even enlarged with the formation of another Group – No 19 – to be based in the south-west to cover the Western Approaches and the Bay of Biscay, where the French Atlantic ports housed and supplied the packs of U-boats. Also for the first time two Command squadrons were based in Iceland, as the convoys from America were now taking a more northerly route in an attempt to avoid the U-boats. Just a few months later operational control of the Command was passed to the Admiralty and in the same month, May 1941, the Command's aircraft played an important part in hunting and tracking the *Bismarck*, in fact it was one of its aircraft that first sighted the battleship.

Not until late in 1942 was the Command equipped with the necessary resources to be able to take a more positive attacking role. As it was estimated that it needed about 7,000 hours of flying time to destroy just one submarine, one can see just how much of Coastal Command's patrols were 'water watching'! In April 1943 it formed its first Beaufighter Strike Wing, which when closely supported by fighters proved to be very successful. One wing operated from Langham during 1944.

By 1943 Coastal Command had a variety of aircraft to tackle the U-boats – the Consolidated Catalina flying boats, Liberators, Fortresses and Wellingtons – all capable of very long-range operations. The doughty Wellingtons had been specially adapted with 'Leigh lights' to operate at night. This light, named after a Command pilot who had developed it, was effectively a large carbon searchlight and intended to illuminate the target following the initial ASV radar contact. All Coastal Command aircraft were now equipped with a greatly improved ASV device and its aircraft began to make serious inroads into the U-boats that were operating in the Atlantic. In the first six months of the year over 90 submarines were destroyed, and in just three days in late July Coastal Command accounted for six U-boats destroyed and another two seriously damaged. By the end of the year

Short Sunderland flying boat: a stalwart of Coastal Command in its battle against U-boats.

the Battle of the Atlantic had been virtually won, though the U-boats still continued to be a danger as they were forced constantly to switch their areas of operations. However, with a stronger Naval presence the Command managed to keep them on the defensive for the rest of the war. It was on the penultimate day of the war – 7th May 1945 – that the last U-boat was sunk, bringing the total which Coastal Command had destroyed, totally unaided, to 197.

Although the battle against submarines and enemy shipping was the main preoccupation of Coastal Command during the war, its Photographic Reconnaissance Unit, using Spitfires and Mosquitos, played a major part in providing detailed information on bombing targets, radar installations, landing sites for the invasion and the monitoring of enemy shipping movements. The Command was mainly responsible for the collection of meteorological data as well as being greatly involved in air-sea rescue work, mainly in the North Sea, where during 1943 it was responsible for saving almost 1,700 airmen, these were mostly bomber crews (both RAF and USAAF) forced to ditch on their return from Germany.

Coastal Command's operations throughout the war went very largely unpublicised and unrecognised, and even now very little has been written about their exploits, at least compared with the wealth of published material on the other two RAF Commands. Over 8,700 of its aircrews were missing or killed in action and it could be argued that its contribution to the victory in Europe was equally, if not more, vital than that of Bomber Command.

The United States Army Air Force

The United States was much slower than its European allies in recognising the potential of the aeroplane as a powerful military weapon. In 1918 the American Air Service in France had been compelled to use British and French aircraft as there was not a single American military aeroplane available. Even during the twenties the Air Service was a very poor relation of the American Army, it had no independent voice on the General Staff and was considered as little more than a support for the Army. Indeed General 'Billy' Mitchell

5 Grand – the 5,000th B-17 built by Boeing and completely covered by signatures of Boeing assembly workers. It served with 338th Squadron of 96th Bomb Group. (Via G Ward).

who commanded the American airmen in the First World War, became so vociferous in his advocacy of the heavy bomber as an offensive weapon that he was court-martialled for his outspoken views. In 1926 his will prevailed when the Army Air Service was upgraded to the status of a Corps, but largely because of the United States' firm isolationist foreign policy the bombers were starved of resources in favour of purely defensive aircraft.

The Army Air Corps was dedicated to high altitude bombing to be undertaken by strongly armed fast bombers and in 1935 the Boeing B-17 made its entrance. Faster than any American fighter then in service it earned the name of the 'Flying Fortress'. But this concept of high altitude bombing, where the dangers of pursuit fighters and anti-aircraft fire would be limited, required two essentials – a satisfactory oxygen system for the aircraft and a precision bomb-sight.

In 1928 a new liquid oxygen system had been devised and developed; this proved to be very advanced and with some refinements was used in all the American heavy bombers throughout the Second World War. Then four years later C. Norden developed a quite amazing bomb-sight for the United States Navy aircraft and its potential was quickly appreciated by the Army Air Corps. Now everything was in place to pursue the Corps' bombing policy except the will and the resources to build a strong bomber force. By September 1941 the Army Air Corps still had only 23 B-17s in service.

The badge of the 'Mighty Eighth'

B-24s of the Second Air Division.

During 1941 it was decided to increase the strength of the American air forces and the first step was taken on 20th June 1941 when the Army Air Force was created with Major General 'Hap' Arnold as its Commander-in-Chief. However, by the time of Pearl Harbour – 7th December 1941 – the Army Air Force had less than 500 combat aircraft. But from now on the development of the United States Army Air Force during the Second World War must be considered as phenomenal. By June 1944 it had become the largest air force in the world, operating with great strength and power on three separate war fronts – Europe, North Africa and the Pacific.

Two American Air Forces served in England during the Second World War, the Eighth and the Ninth. It was solely the Eighth Air Force's groups that occupied the 18 Norfolk airfields. Known as the 'Mighty Eighth', a sobriquet that was fully justified, it was the mainstay of the USAAF in Europe. First formed in January 1942, it would, at its peak, operate from 58 airfields situated in East Anglia and the East Midlands.

The Eighth Air Force comprised three Bombardment Divisions (later renamed 'Air'), each was virtually an air force in its own right. Each division was divided into a number of bombardment or fighter wings, which were made up of three bomb groups or two fighter groups, each of which had its own airfield. To cope with such a massive influx of men and aircraft suitable land had to be swiftly found and airfields were constructed at a very rapid rate. Some existing RAF airfields were transferred to the Eighth and many that were planned and under construction were allocated to the USAAF. It needed a construction programme on a monumental scale, shattering the peace and tranquillity of the English countryside well before the arrival of the masses of men and their heavy bombers.

The Eighth Air Force was dedicated to a high altitude and precision bombing offensive conducted in daylight by large and close formations of heavily armed bombers. Unlike Bomber Command it eschewed the concept of area bombing and mainly concentrated its formidable forces on precise strategic targets – aircraft factories, ball-bearing works, communication centres and additionally oil refineries and installations. The two aircraft used for these operations were the Boeing B-17 Fortress and the Consolidated B-24 Liberator. They were escorted on their missions first by Republic P-47s, Lockheed P-38 Lightnings and later by the North American P-51 Mustangs. The main medium strike bomber was the Martin B-26 Marauder but all of these were transferred to the Ninth Air Force when it was reformed in England in October 1943 to provide tactical support for the Allied armies in Europe.

The first American Army Air Force involvement in the European war came on 29th June 1942 when one American crew joined No 226 squadron at RAF Swanton Morley for a raid on Northern France. It was not until the middle of August that the Eighth Air Force mounted their first mission, when twelve B-17s attacked a railway complex at Rouen and on this operation they were escorted by RAF Spitfires.

The build-up of the Eighth Air Force in England was quite slow and it was not until the New Year that it launched its first operation to Wilhelmshaven, Germany; on this occasion three aircraft failed to return. By the end of February 1943 the Eighth had lost 22 aircraft out of its effective strength of 84 – a loss rate of 26%. Despite these sobering statistics, during the next few months the Eighth became more active, mounting missions to Bremen, Rouen, Rotterdam and Paris, but their losses were still quite high and the planned strengthening of their force had received a serious setback with several of the Bomb Groups intended for service in England being either diverted to North Africa or the Pacific.

In the last five months of 1943 the Eighth Air Force was to suffer some of its most crippling and traumatic losses of the war. Mission after mission exacted a terrible toll on both men and machines. At the end of July 22 out of 77 aircraft failed to return from a raid on Magdeberg, and then on 17th August 376 aircraft were despatched to the ball-bearing works at Schweinfurt and also the Messerschmitt factories at Regensburg; 60 aircraft were destroyed and many more badly damaged. Even worse was to come in October when at the end of just one week's operations 148 aircraft had been shot down and some 1,400 men were lost. It was at this time that the whole policy of daylight bombing came under very serious consideration and the future of the Eighth Air Force was in the balance.

One of the problems was the lack of long-range fighter escorts; the existing P-47 Thunderbolts, even with extra fuel tanks, could only provide a restricted cover for the bomber formations and not until the appearance of the longer-ranging P-51 Mustangs did things gradually improve for the Eighth. Even in the early months of 1944 the Americans still continued to suffer unacceptably high losses. In February the Eighth launched a week-long offensive on key aircraft factories, and although considerable damage was inflicted the costs were high. In the following month the Eighth's 'Operation Pointblank', another week-long attack on key aircraft factories, was effective but again at a high cost. In the following month two missions were despatched to Berlin – the first time the Eighth had attacked the capital. But as the Luftwaffe fighter squadrons were now suffering it had become a matter of sheer attrition with the enemy losing on average 50 fighters every time the Eighth embarked on a major mission. By now the Eighth had exceeded the size of Bomber Command and with 50 heavy Bombardment Groups operating from English airfields it had truly become the 'Mighty Eighth'.

Along with Bomber Command the Eighth had all of its forces diverted to support the Allieds' invasion of Europe. General Doolittle, who had taken command of the Eighth in January 1944, issued a message to all his aircrews, 'The Eighth Air Force is currently charged with a most solemn obligation in support of the most vital operation ever undertaken by our armed forces . . .' They were soon back over German targets and now working closer with Bomber Command. On 14th October there was a combined operation on Duisberg when nearly 2,300 bombers with 750 fighters attacked the city both by day and night. On this mission the Americans lost just six aircraft. The P-51s were having a very marked effect on the Luftwaffe fighter force; on one operation in November they claimed 114 destroyed. By the end of the year it was reckoned that the USAAF

American military cemetery and memorial at Madingley near Cambridge.

had accounted for 3,706 enemy fighters merely in daylight operations in addition to the untold damage inflicted on the aircraft factories. This factor, in conjunction with the Eighth's offensive against oil targets, almost ensured that the two heavy bomber forces faced little fighter opposition during the last months of the war, except for a final flourish by the Luftwaffe's new jet-fighter.

The Eighth Air Force's biggest undertaking of the last six months of the war was supporting the Ardennes campaign in late December. During this period they flew the highest number of sorties of the whole war. Early in 1945 they, along with Bomber Command, attacked targets near the Rhine to assist the Allied armies' advance into Germany. One of their last major operations of the war took place on 10th April 1945 when over 1,000 bombers attacked various German jet-fighter airfields and encountered hardly any opposition – what a change in just two years. The final mission took place from Grafton Underwood in Northamptonshire – the same airfield from which the Eighth Air Force had launched its first heavy bomber mission almost three years earlier.

Winston Churchill wrote in March 1946, 'Before the end, we and the United States had developed air striking forces so powerful that they played a major part in the economic collapse of Germany'. And

General Milch, the State Secretary of the German Air Ministry maintained that 'The British inflicted grievous and bloody injuries upon us, but the Americans stabbed us to the heart'. However, the USAAF paid a very high price for their operations over Europe. They lost 3,000 aircraft and 41,186 airmen either killed or missing in action. Of this awesome total the Eighth Air Force suffered over 26,000 airmen killed with another 21,000 taken prisoner. The superbly designed American Military Memorial at Madingley near Cambridge provides a most poignant but dignified memory to the ultimate sacrifice of all those young Americans. And throughout the eastern counties there are very many memorials to some 350,000 Americans who served with the 'Mighty Eighth' over 50 years ago.

The Airfields

An American pilot serving in Norfolk during the Second World War commented, 'I guess if you just switch off and glide in you'll find you're more likely to have gotten on an airfield than any other place'! In 1939 there were just five operational airfields – Bircham Newton, Feltwell, Marham, Watton and West Raynham – and by the end of the war there were 37.

During the Second World War Norfolk played host to the aircraft and men of all three of the RAF's offensive Commands continuing a tradition that can be traced back to the pioneer days of the Royal Flying Corps. Because each RAF Command had a presence in the county almost every aircraft that the three Commands used in operations could be seen flying in the Norfolk skies. Some of the RAF's most distinguished and illustrious airmen saw service at these airfields at one time or another – Douglas Bader, 'Sailor' Malan, 'Johnnie' Johnson, Stanford-Tuck, 'Cocky' Dundas, John 'Cat's-eyes' Cunningham, Max Aitken, 'Hughie' Edwards, Leonard Trent, the Earl of Bandon, 'Pick' Pickard, Ian Bazalgette and 'Mick' Martin among others. Also out of the 32 Victoria Crosses awarded to airmen during the Second World War five went to airmen flying on operations from Norfolk airfields. Either by design or pure chance the majority of the RAF airfields were situated in the north of the county with most of the USAAF bases sited in the centre and south.

Certainly from the end of 1942 Norfolk could really be considered

Working on concrete runways. (John Laing PLC).

'Bomber Country'. This was largely occasioned by the massive influx of the Eighth Air Force's heavy bombers – the B-17s and B-24s, although it was the B-24 Liberators of the Second Bombardment Division that figured so large at most of the 17 USAAF airfields in Norfolk. Out of the 14 Medals of Honor (equivalent to the Victoria Cross) awarded to American airmen, six were gained by those serving in Norfolk. Also 15 out of a total of 76 Distinguished Unit Citations were gained by groups operating from Norfolk airfields.

Most of the airfields constructed after 1940, and this applies to the majority of those in Norfolk, were provided with three intersecting runways. The main one was normally about 2,000 yards long with a standard width of 50 yards, and it was sited roughly SW/NE, which suited the prevailing winds. The other two runways were usually about 1,400 yards long. A concrete perimeter road connected the ends of the three runways and the concrete hard standings for parked aircraft. These dispersal points could number up to 55.

The most recognisable feature of a 'standard' wartime airfield was the control tower or watch-tower as it was known in the RAF. These were simple two-storied buildings built of concrete and supplied with a railed balcony. Several of these control towers can still be seen standing derelict and forlorn amidst the ploughed fields, although some at the American airfields have been splendidly renovated and are now used either as offices or for Air Group museums. All the airfields were supplied with two T-type (transportable) hangars and the odd blister hangar; just a few have survived and now serve as grain stores. The headquarters, workshops, technical stores, sick

Post-Expansion RAF architecture – the officer's mess at RAF Watton.

quarters and briefing rooms were most frequently constructed from precast concrete slabs of which perhaps the 'Maycrete' huts were the most familiar. The accommodation and mess rooms were normally just Nissen huts clustered in sites numbering from ten to a dozen, all set well away from the airfield, thus making a bicycle a most prized and essential possession! For obvious safety reasons the bomb and ammunition stores were also sited well away from the airfield, usually on the opposite side to the working and living quarters. Finally the firing butts were most often positioned at the furthest point of the airfield and quite near to the end of the main runway.

Of course not all the Norfolk airfields were built to this 'standard' basic design, although most of the American bases were very similar both in plan and construction. The pre-war RAF airfields and those that came into use during 1940 provided a very high standard of permanent accommodation and their buildings tended to be rather elegant in a style that might well be called 'Post Expansion RAF'! Bircham Newton, Coltishall, Feltwell, and Marham are very good examples of this type of service architecture.

The construction of airfields in Norfolk during 1941/3 was a massive building project in which most of the well-known construction firms were involved – John Laing, Taylor Woodrow and Richard Costain – as well as numerous smaller sub-contractors. The building of the concrete runways took on average about six months but the final completion of the 'standard' bomber airfield might take another twelve months or so. One of the more complicated aspects of the construction of these airfields was the supply of various essential services, especially that of telecommunications. All the airfields required a vast number of telephone and teleprinter lines and in particular those connected to either the Group or Division headquarters had to be of high security.

Sadly, many of the Norfolk airfields have long since disappeared under the plough or have been turned into industrial estates. A few of them are used for private flying and others like Coltishall, Marham, Swanton Morley, Watton and West Raynham are still in use by the RAF.

In relating the wartime stories of the individual Norfolk airfields it was not the intention to list in detail all the various squadrons that served at the RAF stations as that would require a much larger work. Furthermore many of the Norfolk airfields were allocated to No 2 Group, Bomber Command and therefore their squadrons were engaged on very similar duties, so the major operations mounted by this Group have been spread through the various airfields involved in these missions.

The American airfields posed particular problems mainly because of the Eighth Air Force's method of operations – most of the Bomb Groups were engaged on the same operations; therefore merely a few of each Group's more important missions have been highlighted to obviate too much repetition.

It is fully recognised that most of these Norfolk airfields would require a much larger work to do full justice to the immense contribution they and their airmen made to the air war in Europe.

2
ATTLEBRIDGE

It does seem somewhat strange that the first Norfolk airfield to come under scrutiny should be one that was planned and built for the RAF and yet very few British-built aircraft flew from Attlebridge. Perhaps its destiny was always to be closely linked with American aircraft and American airmen – it is most appropriate that today the old airfield is given over to rearing turkeys. The site is just to the south-east of the charming village of Weston Longville.

Attlebridge was built during the early months of 1941 and was intended to be a satellite field for RAF Swanton Morley, which itself had only come into use in the previous September. Most important airfields were provided with satellites, which were normally not expected to mount major operations, though because of the pressure for extra airfield space, most of them did and often later became fully independent stations. Attlebridge, along with its parent station, was allocated to No 2 Group of Bomber Command; this was the oldest Group, having been formed on 1st May 1936, several months before Bomber Command itself. For the first two years of the war the Group had virtually borne the brunt of the Command's bombing offensive. At first its squadrons specialised in daring daylight low-level operations, later turning to night intruder raids over enemy occupied territories and engaging in anti-shipping strikes. All these varied operations were conducted with great determination against overwhelming odds, and the highest courage was shown by the Blenheim crews, but many operations resulted in a frightening cost of aircraft and airmen.

Towards the end of July 1941 No 88 (Hong Kong) squadron arrived from Swanton Morley with its Bristol Blenheim IVs, a very doughty aircraft that had been the group's sole bomber since the sad demise

Martin Marauder: the 319th Bomb Group came to Attlebridge in October 1942.

of the Fairey Battles in the summer of 1940. When the Blenheim had entered RAF service in 1937 it was considered 'the wonder bomber' and was then thought to be the fastest in the world, but now its operational days were severely numbered, and No 88 squadron were preparing to receive a new light day-bomber – the American-built Douglas Boston III (or DB-7 as the Americans designated it). Much heavier and faster than the Blenheim, with a cruising speed of 280 mph and a bomb load of 2,000 pounds it appeared to be a formidable aircraft and, in fact, Bostons operated with great success with the RAF throughout the rest of the war.

For most of the remainder of 1941 the squadron was receiving sporadic deliveries of the new aircraft and was busy training on them as well as mounting operations with their 'old' Blenheims. The last Blenheim sorties were made on 26th October. By the new year the squadron was fully equipped with 20 Bostons and had been detached to Long Kesh in Northern Ireland for intensive training, especially in low-level flying as well as working on techniques to improve army support strikes. Back at Attlebridge in the first week of February the Bostons went immediately into action – a mixture of missions against French power stations, railway yards and stations, airfields and

Channel ports, docks and shipyards – really the bread and butter of the Group's bombing activities. During the next eight months the squadron mounted over 300 missions for the loss of just four aircraft – a very fine achievement. By the end of September 1942 the squadron left Attlebridge for Oulton, another Norfolk airfield some miles to the north.

The main reason for the move was that the airfield had been allocated to the USAAF, and at the beginning of October some of the aircraft of the 319th Bomb Group arrived. This group flew medium bombers – the Martin B-26 Marauders – of which very few had been seen in Great Britain. These twin-engined aircraft looked really impressive, very streamlined and every inch a classic design. So confident were the USAAF in this aircraft that over 1,000 were produced without the development of a prototype. Its high landing speed presented certain difficulties during training, but with a top speed of over 300 mph, a range of over 1,000 miles and a bomb load of 3,000 pounds its performance matched its looks. Pilots found it not easy to fly, and several fatal accidents quickly caused rumours to circulate that it was a 'killer' – some of the early names stuck with the aircraft, such as the 'widow maker' and the 'Baltimore whore'. Many of the faults were rectified and it was first brought into action in the Pacific in early 1942, but nevertheless it was still felt that the B-26s were best suited to conditions in Europe.

The first three B-26 Bomb Groups to arrive in England were quickly earmarked for the Twelfth Air Force then serving in North Africa, and the first Marauders used by the RAF came into service in the Middle East. After a short spell of reorganisation at both Attlebridge and Horsham St Faith, the 319th engaged in some low-level flights over Norfolk and the Wash before leaving for North Africa in mid-November. The Group's problems continued to dog them on their flight out, an error in navigation resulted in the aircraft straying over Cherbourg and two were shot down with another aircraft so badly damaged that it was written off. Unfortunately the Group's Commanding Officer was lost over France. Ultimately four Bomb Groups in England operated Marauders quite successfully over Europe until late 1944.

Once the 319th had left there was still much work to be done on the airfield and its runways to bring it up to the required standard for heavy bombers. In early 1943, there was so much pressure on valuable airfield space in East Anglia that it was brought back into operational use specially for a Free Dutch squadron that had been ousted from RAF Methwold. This squadron – No 320 – had been formed on 1st June 1940 solely from the survivors of the Royal Dutch Naval squadron, and not surprisingly they found themselves engaged on anti-shipping work with Coastal Command. With the arrival of these Dutch airmen at the end of March 1943 yet another American-built aircraft appeared on the runways at Attlebridge – the North American B-25 Mitchell (see Foulsham).

For most of the time the Dutchmen were at Attlebridge they were working towards operational readiness on their new aircraft and impatient to see action. On 29th July the airfield was visited by the Dutch prime minister to see just how his fellow countrymen were coping and to give them some encouragement. Some three weeks later they were allowed to go into action for the first time. Seventeen aircraft (6 from No 320 squadron) bombed Calais power station and then two days later it was the Poix airfield in northern France; they were now truly on the bombing trail. During most of August they shared the airfield with a squadron of Hawker Typhoons (yes, British planes!) which had arrived for a very brief stay to make regular east coast patrols in the hope of intercepting enemy aircraft that were making troublesome attacks on coastal towns and ports. By the end of the month both squadrons had departed and the airfield lay idle waiting for its American heavies.

Late in the year the 61st Station Complement squadron settled in to prepare the airfield for the impending arrival of an Eighth Air Force Bomb Group. Second Lieutenant McLaughlin set up a good working relationship with the local residents, for great tact and understanding were required on both sides. Several minor local roads had been closed because of the airfield but a very satisfactory compromise was reached. At Christmas 1943 the lieutenant arranged a special party for the children from a Dr Barnado's orphanage at nearby Hovingham Hall, not a unique occurrence as all the American groups in Norfolk developed close ties with the locals, still recalled by dedicated people involved in maintaining the memory of the young American airmen and the several Bomb Group museums in the county.

The first aircraft of No 466 Bombardment Group arrived at Attlebridge at the end of February. The Group was part of the Second Bombardment (later changed to 'Air') Division and placed in the 96th Combat Wing. Like all the Eighth's Bomb Groups it comprised four squadrons of aircraft and because it was in the Second Division they were equipped with Consolidated B-24 'Liberators', as were all but three of the American Bomb Groups in Norfolk. This four-engined heavy bomber proved to be the most versatile of all Second World War bombers – serving not only as a pure bomber but as a transport carrier and it proved particularly suited to anti U-boat duties. Even to its most devoted admirers the B-24 Liberator did not look a very elegant aircraft with its twin tails and rather slab-like appearance, but it did have a greater range and bomb carrying capacity than its close rival, the Boeing B-17 'Flying Fortress'. The B-24 in its various models served in 15 Allied air forces and in every theatre of war. The name 'Liberator' arose as a result of a competition held in the manufacturer's works in San Diego, California, although originally the name 'Eagle' had been thought more appropriate. The 466th Bomb Group acquired the name of 'The Flying Deck' in a similar manner from a competition held on the base and perhaps not surprisingly each squadron also took its name from a suit of cards – 'Hearts... etc.'

Unlike most new Bomb Groups the 466th was not allowed the luxury or comfort of a gentle introduction into operations because on 22nd March it was detailed for a mission to Berlin or 'The Big B'. Largely as a result of Bomber Command's operations against the German capital it had become the heaviest defended area in all Germany and quite rightly was feared by British and American crews alike. On this day the German flak batteries were fairly light but the Group did lose three aircraft. Two collided in thick cloud over Holland and a third was so badly damaged that it was forced to land in neutral Sweden where the crew were interned. Within five days the Group had lost six aircraft, not to enemy action but because of mid-air collisions.

The sheer number and proximity of Norfolk airfields, the increasing number of aircraft used by the Eighth during 1944 and 1945, the presence of new Bomb Groups and inexperienced pilots, all added to the problem, and despite precautions every group suffered losses through collisions.

On 19th May 1944, whilst on an operation to Brunswick the 466th experienced its sternest test so far. Things did not go well right from the start. Aircraft were an hour late taking off because of armament problems on the ground and as a result their formation was not as disciplined as it should have been, although whether this made any appreciable difference is doubtful. Then because wind speeds were different than forecast the B-24s arrived over the target area earlier than scheduled, way ahead of what should have been the accompanying force of B-17s. Waiting for B-24s were the renowned enemy fighter groups justly nicknamed 'The Battling Bastards of Brunswick'. They took a heavy toll of the vulnerable B-24s and the 466th lost six aircraft, their worst single day of operations throughout the war. One pilot recalled: 'They don't come any harder than the one we flew today,' and he was probably right.

On 17th August the Group celebrated its 100th mission in really fine style as indeed did all Bomb Groups. Such occasions were necessary to relieve the tensions of operational life. A baseball match was held near the control tower and the Glenn Miller band flew in to perform at the Group's dance held in one of the hangars. The band's aircraft had to slowly circle the airfield to allow the Group's B-24s to land from an operation. Glenn Miller himself led the band – a rare honour in those days – and it was said that he had agreed to appear in person because the Group had purchased more War Bonds than any other outfit in the Eighth Air Force! James Stewart, the famous film star, also attended the concert, he was a serving officer at a nearby base. When the Group passed their 200th mission target in early April 1945, a flight of P-51 Mustangs came from Bottisham to put on an aerobatic display. It became the normal procedure on such days for the officers to serve in the men's messes and then the Group was relieved from operations on the following day – a rare rest day!

Perhaps the sheer dedication of the young American aircrew is best illustrated by examining what were considered two 'normal' missions during the first week of September 1944. On the 2nd the Group attacked targets at Karlsruhe and encountered very heavy opposition from sustained and accurate ground fire, so much so that 13 aircraft were heavily damaged and another four could not make it back to Attlebridge and were forced to land at other airfields. And yet on the following day the Group were detailed to return to the same target, although this time they would bomb from about 4,000 feet higher, the theory being that they would be above most of the flak. It certainly worked because they survived with the loss of just one aircraft and its crew managed to escape by parachute, ending up safe but prisoners-of-war. But why were they ordered to attack at the lower altitude on the previous day?

The steady and continual build-up of daily missions took an intolerably harsh toll not only on the aircrews but also the ground personnel, who after all had to work long hours to keep the Group's aircraft flying. When the 466th had first arrived in England in early 1944 the Eighth Air Force losses were running at almost 25% and on

An attractive village sign presented by 466th Bomb Group Association.

Attlebridge control tower now used as offices for Matthews' Norfolk Farms.

some operations the figure was even higher. It was estimated that the average operational life of aircrews at that time was 15 missions and as 35 were needed to complete a tour, their expectancy of survival was not high. These figures did, of course, greatly improve during 1944 but nevertheless even in the last months of the war when the Eighth Air Force's losses were relatively negligible, there was always the constant nagging thought in the minds of all aircrews that perhaps today 'would be their turn to be unlucky'. It is therefore amazing to discover that one of the Group's squadrons – No 785 – managed to fly 55 consecutive missions up to 25th July 1944 without a single loss of aircraft or crews.

It was no doubt with considerable relief to all when the 466th completed their 232nd and final mission on 25th April 1945. By the middle of June most of the aircraft had left for the United States and the airfield was returned to the RAF. It was not sold until 1959. The old control tower has now been converted into offices and there is a roll of honour to the Bomb Group in All Saints Church. The very attractive village sign was donated by veterans of the Bomb Group and there is a memorial plaque to 'the 324 men killed in action from the airfield'. The old airfield is fairly easy to find by taking a minor road signed to Weston Longville, which is off the main A47 between East Dereham and Norwich.

3
BIRCHAM NEWTON

This airfield can trace its origins back to the days of the Royal Flying Corps, those heady and exciting times of pioneer flying. It was built in 1916 as a training school for fighter pilots but was soon overshadowed by the nearby and much older RFC airfield at Sedgeford, some three miles or so to the west. Bircham's early fame rests with its development as a heavy bomber station; in 1918 No 166 squadron was formed here with the express purpose of the long-range bombing of Germany, it was even thought that Berlin could be reached by the Handley Page V/1500 four-engined bomber known as the 'Super Handley'. Hand-picked pilots and observers were specially trained for the task but before any operations could be mounted the Armistice intervened. So the whole concept of long-range strategic bombing, which dominated the Service's thinking for well over a quarter of a century can be said to have originated at Bircham Newton.

From the early 1920s the airfield hosted most of the famous bombers of the time and many of the older squadrons of Bomber Command were based at Bircham. The airfield was greatly developed and expanded during the thirties becoming one of the jewels in the crown of the pre-war RAF, as is seen in the number of splendid and elegant neo-Georgian buildings still surviving on the site. Some of the most illustrious names in the service's history served at Bircham Newton – both Lord Portal and Lord Tedder commanded bomber squadrons there.

When the RAF was comprehensively reorganised in July 1936, Bircham Newton severed its links with heavy bombers and instead became part of Coastal Command. No 208, one of the first of the Command's new squadrons was formed at Bircham Newton with the task of training pilots for both Coastal and Bomber Command's aircraft. In December of the same year the airfield was placed in No 16 Group and 208 lost its training responsibilities to become a fully operational unit.

Despite the number and variety of different aircraft that used the airfield during the war years perhaps Bircham Newton is best known for just two aircraft – the Avro Anson and the Lockheed Hudson – the latter an American-built aircraft that replaced the Avon in Coastal Command.

The Anson was probably one of the best loved aircraft in the RAF because so many crews were trained on them. It was affectionately known as 'The Faithful Annie' and was the first monoplane to see service in the RAF under the Pre-War Expansion Scheme. Like its successor, the Hudson, it had been developed from a small airliner that flew with the Imperial Airways, and 208 squadron became the first to be equipped with them. Ansons served with Coastal Command until 1942 and were then used as trainers until 1968 – 32 years of sterling and 'faithful' service.

At the outbreak of the war there were two squadrons based at Bircham Newton, 206 and No 42 squadron with Vickers Vildebeestes, rather ancient biplanes and then the only torpedo bombers in Coastal Command; they lasted a few weeks before being withdrawn from operations. In the first week of the war some of the Ansons' crews (especially navigators) were loaned to Bomber Command for its first tentative operations over Kiel, but the main duties of the two squadrons were convoy escorts, coastal reconnaissance of the German and Dutch coasts in the interminable hunts for U-boats. On 5th September an Anson from 208 was credited with the first strike against a U-boat, which was sighted diving just off the Dutch coast. The Anson attacked almost at sea-level, and when its bombs were released, the water spout created by the explosion damaged its tail section. Unfortunately the crew's claim for the sinking – the first to be submitted by a Coastal Command squadron – was not accepted by the Air Ministry because of insufficient evidence of the destruction. The early wartime operations revealed another useful attribute of the Anson – the ability to float longer in the sea than it could fly! One aircraft survived ditching for five hours – half an hour longer than what was then considered its safe working limit!

The early hectic and generally rather abortive skirmishes of Coastal Command had highlighted not only the limitations of the Anson in combat and range but also the woeful inadequacies of the

Fairey Albacore.

Command's resources. The first problem was resolved by the slow but steady replacement of the Anson by the Hudson and the second problem was slightly improved with the transfer of four squadrons of Blenheims from Fighter Command. No 235 squadron at Bircham Newton received its first Blenheims in February 1940 and they were immediately in action over the North Sea. Just a month later the airfield saw the arrival of its first Hudsons to replace the Ansons.

The Lockheed Hudson had been developed by the American company from a very successful commercial airliner, hence the row of portholes along its fuselage. In July 1939 there had been a political uproar in Britain when it was announced that a contract had been signed for 200 aircraft to be delivered by the end of the year. Lockheed actually achieved the target by October and the Hudson became the first American-built aircraft to see service with the RAF. The decision to purchase the Hudson proved to be an excellent investment because it became a most successful reconnaissance bomber and almost 2,000 served with the RAF. It had a cruising speed of about 120 mph, an operating range of nearly 500 miles, and with a bomb load almost equal to one tenth of that of the Lancaster the Hudson became the backbone of Coastal Command for almost three years. In October 1939 it was a Hudson that claimed the first enemy aircraft to be destroyed, and by January of the following year the Hudson was fitted with the first IFF (Identification Friend or Foe) and ASV Mark 1 Radar, a boon to locating submarines either by night or in poor visibility.

The Hudsons of 220 squadron made regular daily patrols of the

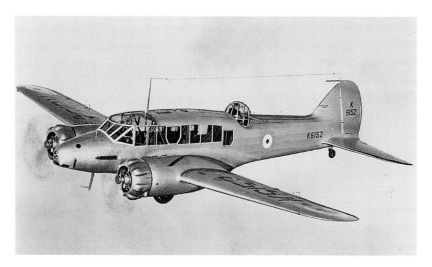

'The Faithful Annie', so beloved by RAF air crews.

French and Dutch coasts. Patrols from Dunkirk to Dieppe were known as 'Dundees', and the dusk to dawn flights from the Hook of Holland to Ostend were 'Hookos'; these patrols were conducted in addition to the regular sorties over the North Sea. The squadron also maintained a 'Battle Flight', which was on constant stand-by ready for an immediate take-off should a positive sighting of enemy shipping be made. Hudsons from Bircham Newton were directly involved in locating the *Altmark*, the infamous prison vessel. When intelligence sources suggested that the vessel was hiding in one of the Norwegian fiords, three Hudsons from 233 squadron went out to search and did finally locate it. The Blenheims provided cover for east coast convoys and various naval actions along the Dutch coast. They also provided fighter support for Hudsons when, in May 1940, they bombed targets at Bremen and Hamburg.

During April 1940 a detachment of Fairey Swordfish of 815 squadron of the Fleet Air Arm arrived to begin a series of magnetic mine-laying off the Danish coast. But it was 'Operation Dynamo' – the evacuation of the BEF at Dunkirk – that gave the Hudsons and Blenheims their most intensive period of action so far when they provided almost continuous daytime air cover for the armada of small vessels crossing the English channel. On 1st June Hudsons from 220 squadron attacked over 40 Junkers-87 dive bombers over Dunkirk and destroyed four before a group of Spitfires arrived on the scene to give a helping hand. Then during the evening of 3rd June three Hudsons went out to help some Fleet Air Arm aircraft that were under attack from Me109s. The Hudsons accounted for half of the enemy force without any loss – another role for the Hudson as a fighter? The squadron's crews had escorted 250 Dunkirk convoys without a single loss of aircraft and during the same period its crews had received 18 gallantry awards.

As Winston Churchill later commented, 'the only thing that ever really frightened me during the war was the U-boat threat...', and it was probably recognition of the Command's desperate battle fought against the U-boat menace that occasioned George VI to visit Bircham Newton in January 1941. He also undertook an investiture not only for Coastal Command crews but also for airmen from neighbouring bases. Notable amongst these were Squadron Leader Stanford-Tuck, who received a DSO to add to his DFC and bar. Another Coltishall pilot, Flight Lieutenant Van Mentz was awarded the DFC, unfortunately he was killed in action just a few weeks later. This visit proved to be an excellent morale booster for the station, as Coastal Command's crews always felt that they were the least regarded force compared with the more glamorous Bomber and Fighter Commands.

The aircrews serving at Bircham Newton during the early summer of 1942 little expected to be detailed for one of the '1,000 Bomber' operations mounted by Bomber Command during May and June, and this only came about because Air Chief Marshal Sir Philip Joubert, the Commander-in-Chief of Coastal Command, agreed to the loan of 250 aircraft from his precious squadrons that the '1,000' operations became at all feasible. There were two relatively new squadrons at Bircham Newton at the time – Nos 407 and 320. The first was a Canadian squadron and the second comprised airmen from the Dutch Naval Air Force. Both squadrons were very active in what were called 'Rovers', which were effectively low-level shipping searches with no specific targets in mind. They missed the first '1,000' mission to Cologne but joined in the next two – Essen and Bremen when just one Hudson failed to return.

With the departure of the Hudson squadrons in March 1943 the anti-shipping operations went somewhat into decline until late in the year when Wellingtons of 415 'Swordfish' squadron arrived to undertake sweeps over the North Sea and the Dutch coasts seeking E-boats. These Wellingtons were nicknamed 'Sticklebacks' because of the array of aerials along the top of their fuselages. The Wellingtons had proved to be excellent aircraft for Coastal Command work, they were equipped with the special 'Leigh' lights to illuminate targets once they had been located to enable either Beaufighters or Spitfires from Coltishall to move in for the attack. This squadron was very active in the days leading up to D-Day, mounting over 120 sorties over the northern reaches of the English Channel.

For almost three years from November 1941 Bircham Newton was greatly involved in Air/Sea rescue operations. Norfolk can claim the very first 'air sea rescue' operation when in June 1785 a Customs cutter from Great Yarmouth rescued an early balloonist from the sea off the Norfolk coast! Although the problems of rescuing aircrews from the sea was fully recognised before the outbreak of the war very little was done to improve the position except to increase the number of RAF high speed launches to 19. Only after a number of fighter pilots were lost in the English Channel during the Battle of Britain did Fighter Command decide to take independent action. They used a combination of RAF launches, Naval vessels and just 12 Lysanders (borrowed from the Army) to act as spotters. This operation was quite successful and finally received official approval with Fighter Command being made responsible for all air-sea rescues around the coast from the Wash to Wales and as far out to sea as 20 miles; beyond that range the operating unit losing the aircraft was responsible for launching any search for the lost crew.

Although the recovery rate of aircrew had risen to 35% it was still felt that more improvement could be achieved. A new Directorate for

Lockheed Hudson: the backbone of Coastal Command for nearly three years. (RAF Museum)

Sea Rescue was set up in January 1941 and the responsibility was passed to Coastal Command with the operational range extended to 40 miles. The Fighter Command units were immediately upgraded to squadron size and Air Ministry authority was given to form two new A/S Rescue squadrons – Nos 279 and 280 – both of which first came into operation at Bircham Newton during March and July 1942 respectively.

Many experiments had been carried out on a dinghy that could be dropped into the sea for crews ditching close to the enemy coast. Finally after considerable trials the Mark I Airborne lifeboat specifically designed for Hudsons was adopted, this despite the fact that Hudsons were in such short supply that Ansons were used in their stead! The first successful drop of a lifeboat by 279 squadron came in May 1943 when the crew of a Halifax was saved about 50 miles off the Yorkshire coast. During the same month the squadron was responsible for saving 156 men. One crew member described a rescue on 25th July: 'The crew of a B-17 [Boeing Fortress] had clambered on to the wings and were getting into the water. These were in one dinghy and the rest in another. When the dinghies started drifting apart we decided to drop the lifeboat, down it went landing like a leaf on the water... and as we left, they were chugging back to land with another aircraft providing air cover...' The squadron's most successful day by far came on 6th September when they saved 131 airmen, mainly from American bombers returning from Stuttgart.

The replacement for the 'faithful' Anson on air-sea rescue work was the Vickers Warwick. This aircraft had been designed as a heavier contemporary bomber to the Wellington, but unfortunately it proved to have a very disappointing performance and was transferred to Coastal Command. The first Warwick arrived at Bircham Newton in June 1943 to replace 280's Ansons and a Warwick Conversion Unit was established at the airfield to train the Command's crews. Throughout the war well over 10,000 persons were rescued by all the Air-Sea rescue services.

By the end of 1944 most of the airfield's operational squadrons had left and Bircham Newton was mainly involved in fitting specialised equipment into Coastal Command aircraft. It was known as the 'Special Preparation Pool' and many different types of aircraft used the airfield during the last six months of the war from Mosquitos (for the provision of rockets), Wellingtons, Beaufighters, Halifaxes and B-24 Liberators.

4

BODNEY

On a dark and cloudy night in late August 1943 a crippled Lancaster of Bomber Command was being nursed and coaxed home low across the North Sea. The captain and pilot, Flying Officer Bill Day, was coming to the end of only his third mission and on that night the target had been the big one – Berlin. The crew had not encountered any real problems on the long flight out and had just successfully bombed the target when the Lancaster was picked up by a 'master' searchlight and within seconds, or so it seemed, their aircraft was bathed in the blinding beams of literally dozens of searchlights. As one of the crew later recalled, 'We were caught like a moth in a brilliant flame – there was absolutely nothing the skipper could do.' In fact all Day's evasive actions proved futile and within minutes the Lancaster was attacked by three Fw190s, one of which the rear gunner managed to destroy before the aircraft went into a heavy and steep dive. Day fought desperately hard to bring the aircraft under control and after considerable effort succeeded in pulling it on to a level course. They were now flying very low over the outskirts of Berlin in a most sorry state indeed. The Lancaster had countless holes in its airframe, one engine was completely out of action and one of the others didn't sound very healthy, most of the instrument panel had been smashed and fuel was slopping around in the fuselage several inches deep. It seemed a miracle that the aircraft had not gone up in flames.

As the Lancaster neared the Norfolk coast, Day was making continual Mayday calls and was finally told by his base to try to make it home. But as that was still many miles away in Lincolnshire Day realised that he would not have sufficient fuel to get back safely. Day was one of those rare breed of airman – an American flying with

Fighter Aces of 352nd Fighter Group: Colonel J Mauden, Lt Colonel WO Jackson, Major CE Preddy, Colonel J Mason, Lt Colonel J Meyer. (R Smart)

Bomber Command – most of his fellow countrymen had already transferred to USAAF's Eighth Air Force. Day was only too aware that their only hope of survival was to crash-land somewhere and very soon. Then almost as if by 'an act of God', a row of bright lights suddenly blazed out beneath them, where they were they knew not but very thankfully Day made his tentative approach to the lighted runway. The landing was fairly rough and in the process the rear gunner was badly injured, but the consolation was that they had landed safely. Day's delight at their fortunate escape was further compounded by his utter surprise when he climbed down to be greeted by familiar American accents. Even more of a shock to Day was to find himself recognised by an old friend whom he had last seen in New York shortly before he left for Canada to join the RAF.

Day had landed at Bodney, the new home of 352 Fighter Group of the Eighth Air Force and Day's friend was now flying P-47D Thunderbolts with the Group. The 'act of God' was all due to a young American private who was manning the control tower when he had picked up Day's Mayday calls. Not knowing the correct procedure he had switched on everything that he could lay his hands upon! Day received the Distinguished Flying Cross for his skill and determination in bringing the severely damaged aircraft back and the injured rear gunner was awarded the Distinguished Flying Medal. Day and his crew's luck held because they later finished their tour of operations and four of them went on to complete a second tour.

Many Norfolk airfields were used for emergency landings by damaged aircraft and this incident, despite the high drama for all concerned, became just another statistic – 677 RAF aircraft crashed in Norfolk during the Second World War in addition to the countless number of USAAF aircraft that came to grief over the county.

Bodney's parent station was in No 2 Group of Bomber Command and in 1940 that meant its squadrons were equipped with either Fairey Battles or Bristol Blenheims. As the Battles had all been dispersed to the Advanced Air Striking Force in France, it was left to the Blenheim squadrons to support them from East Anglian airfields such as Watton and Bodney. Two squadrons of Blenheim IVs operated from the two airfields – Nos 21 and 82. Just before the outbreak of the war the Mark IVs had replaced the Mark Is, which were now mainly used as night-fighters although not particularly suited or indeed successful in that role, but there were no alternative aircraft available. The new Mark had been provided with superior crew accommodation but there was not a very marked improvement in the aircraft's performance. The most obvious difference was in appearance, the Mark I was short-nosed whereas the later mark was long-nosed.

The two Blenheim squadrons seemed to operate from either airfield though the aircraft of No 82 were perhaps more permanently based at Bodney, at least until mid 1942 when No 21 squadron settled in. During May and June 1940 the squadrons were active almost daily over France, in fact over the very battle fields of the First World War, in a vain attempt to bomb the rapidly advancing German armies. The crews were sent out to attack bridges, airfields and armoured columns and by the end of May the Group had lost 150 aircraft, almost equivalent to nine full squadrons. During 'Operation Dynamo' – the evacuation of Dunkirk – they were mounting daily attacks on the German armoured forces that were fast closing on the beach-head. After the fall of France the Blenheim squadrons turned their attention to targets in Holland, northern France and even as far afield as Norway. On one mission to Stavanger in July five aircraft out of the six despatched were destroyed within minutes and the Commanding Officer of No 21 squadron lost his life.

During the spring of 1941 the Group's Blenheims were engaged in attacks on enemy shipping, part of the 'Channel Stop' operation, which was an attempt to close the eastern approaches of the English Channel to enemy shipping. These involved daylight attacks normally in pairs, a slow dive from 5,000 feet through heavy flak with 250 pound bombs, which only had five second delay fuses, then trying to pull out of the dives in an attempt to avoid the ships' masts. Some did not make it and they either crashed into the vessels or the sea. One pilot recalled '... it was frightening. No ... on second thoughts ... it was bloody terrifying.' Most Blenheim squadrons were expected to take their turn at this most dangerous of operations.

During 1941 the heavy throb of the Bristol Pegasus engines was heard over the airfield marking the arrival of a detachment of Handley Page Hampdens of 61 squadron from Woolfax Lodge in Rutland. The Hampdens had come into service a year before war broke out and had taken part in most of the large bombing offensives mounted by Bomber Command, but they were to find their true forte as torpedo-bombers with Coastal Command and mine-laying with Bomber Command. The arrival marked an experiment by No 2 Group to trial night bombing operations when adequate cloud cover merited a mission. The first operation was launched from Bodney on 18th April when five aircraft went to Cherbourg but the mission was not particularly successful, especially as one aircraft crashed near Swindon. Several other sorties were made to Antwerp, Rotterdam and Emden but many had to be abandoned because of unsatisfactory weather conditions over the target areas. By the end of the month the Hampdens had returned to Rutland with nothing really achieved during their short stay.

The Blenheims from Bodney continued to operate a variety of daylight raids over northern France, anti-shipping strikes along the Dutch and German coasts and even night intruder missions over Germany. By 1942 it was clear that the operational days of the aircraft were nearly over. Towards the end of May one of its light bomber replacements began to arrive at the airfield – the American-built Lockheed Ventura (see Methwold). As with most new aircraft there were many teething problems and a long training and conversion programme with the result that the squadron did not become operational before it was moved to Methwold in October. The airfield had now become rather deserted with only a few Miles Master trainers of No 17 (Pilots) Advanced Training Unit keeping the airfield active, whilst it was being prepared for the Eighth Air Force and its fighters.

P-51D Mustang Pattie IV *of 328th Fighter Squadron. (R Smart)*

The first echelons of the 352nd Fighter Group arrived at Bodney in the middle of July 1943, even then there was insufficient accommodation for all their personnel and for a short time they had to be out-housed at Watton until extra Nissen huts were built. The Group had three squadrons – Nos 328, 486 and 487 – of Republic P-47D Thunderbolts. The P-47 was one of the most famous single-seat fighters of the Second World War, though it hardly looked the part, being variously described as the 'Jug' (short for 'Juggernaut'), the 'Flying Milk Bottle', or according to the RAF fighter pilots – 'The Flying Barrel'!

The first prototype had flown in May 1941 and was in service by September 1942, one of the fastest development and production programmes ever. The aircraft was noticeably different from contemporary fighters, for instance it was very heavy, almost twice the weight of the Spitfire but was to prove capable of sustaining and surviving heavy damage. For its weight it was very fast, especially at high altitudes. It was probably the heaviest armed fighter with the most devastating amount of fire-power. As one Luftwaffe pilot later recalled, 'The P-47 wasn't so bad, because we could out-turn and out-climb it initially. But that big American fighter could roll with deceiving speed and when it came down on you in a long dive, there was no way you could get away from it.' But the aircraft did suffer from restricted visibility over the nose so that its pilots had to weave to and fro when taxiing and they were described as moving 'like crabs'! Their biggest drawback as an escort fighter was their limited operational range and they only really survived in that role until a sufficient number of the longer range P-51 Mustangs became available to the Eighth Air Force.

As at first there were considerable problems in the supply of their aircraft the Group took rather a long time to become operational, going on their first mission on 9th September and like most new Groups found that their introduction to action was a relatively gentle affair, acting as escorts to a force of B-24 Liberators bombing several French airfields. Towards the end of the month the Group's pilots thought that they would get their first taste of action over Germany when the Group was detailed for a raid on Emden but because their drop fuel tanks had not yet arrived, they were relegated to a fairly harmless sweep over the Dutch coast.

Though later the Group was to become one of the highest scoring outfits in the Eighth Air Force, it was a couple of months before they achieved any success. On 1st December 1943 Lieutenants George Preddy and Bill 'Whizz' Whisner recorded their first victories, on the way to becoming two of the highest scoring fighter aces of the Eighth. The term 'ace' was a relic of the early flying days of the First World War. The French had first used the term and it was quickly taken up by both the British and Germans. During the Second World War the Americans and the Germans had quickly realised the promotional and propaganda value of fighter pilots, their exploits captured the imagination of the public and their successes were thought to be good for morale. American 'aces' required five positive victories in air combat, whereas the Luftwaffe pilots needed ten. Later on the Americans also counted aircraft destroyed on the ground when they realised just how dangerous ground strafing of airfields had become. The RAF officially refused to acknowledge 'aces' as such, because it considered the system was bad for team morale, nevertheless they were quite happy to publicise the victories of their most successful fighter pilots without actually calling them 'aces'!

During April 1944 the Group converted to the North American P-51 Mustangs, which had first seen service with the RAF. With new aircraft the Group's pilots soon made the superior qualities of the Mustang tell on their Luftwaffe opponents. But it soon became apparent that although they achieved more victories, the cost was far heavier, proving that the P-51s were unable to take as much heavy damage as the Flying Jugs.

On 8th May the self-styled 'Blue Nosed Bastards of Bodney' (so called from their blue painted propellers and nose cowlings) were escorting a force of B24s to Brunswick. The bomber formation was close to Hanover when they were attacked by a large force of about 200 Fw190s and Me109s. A fast and very furious air battle took place, which ended with the Group claiming 27 destroyed, two probables and another seven damaged, all for the loss of just one aircraft. Among the successful pilots was First Lieutenant Carl Luksic, who brought down five enemy aircraft to become 'an ace in a day'. For this most notable victory the Group was awarded its first Distinguished Unit Citation.

Like all Eighth Air Force units there was a maximum effort called for on 6th June 1944 – D-Day. On that day the Group's aircraft flew no less than nine missions, strafing airfields, railways, roads and even attacking the German fortifications at the Normandy beach-heads. But the day had started with a disaster. On the very first mission as the Group's fighters were taking off, four abreast, in light rain which had greatly restricted visibility, one of the Mustangs careered into the new control tower. Its pilot, Lieutenant Frascotti, was killed instantly, a tragic accident that marred the Group's enthusiasm for the rest of the day's operations. Later in the month the American Secretary of State for War, Henry Stimson, visited Bodney to acknowledge that the 352nd had fast become one of the most effective Fighter Groups in the Eighth.

Two weeks later the Group accompanied the various Bomber Groups that were despatched on the first of the 'Frantic' shuttle flights to Russia, which included bombing targets in eastern Germany en route to Russian airfields. The Group did not arrive back at Bodney until 5th July having covered over 6,000 miles and claimed ten aircraft for the loss of seven Mustangs. Soon they were back to normal operations notching up a large number of victories. On one day they claimed 21 enemy fighters of which George Preddy, now a captain, accounted for four. When he went on leave to the United States he had 21 victories to his credit and was then the leading fighter ace in the Eighth Air Force.

Just a couple of days before Christmas 1944 the Group were moved to Asche in Belgium. They had probably complained about Norfolk living conditions, but Bodney was a palace compared with what they found at this makeshift airfield. It was primitive in the extreme, bitterly cold, with tented accommodation, no running water and as if to emphasise their close proximity to the front line, slit trenches were dug around the perimeter of the airfield and each pilot was issued with a side-arm. The Group was engaged on a continuous patrol of the fronts, which meant that one squadron was always airborne. Even on Christmas Day there was no break in patrols and Major Preddy, now in command of the 328th squadron, was in action. He and his supporting wingman became separated from the squadron and as they were returning back over the front lines both were shot down by American anti-aircraft machine guns in the belief that they were enemy fighters, and Preddy was killed. At that time he had completed 143 combat missions and destroyed 27 aircraft, the second highest American fighter ace of the war.

In the early hours of New Year's Day the Luftwaffe mounted a large offensive against the advance Allied airfields in Belgium and France. The 487th squadron was just in the process of taking off when the Luftwaffe struck. In barely three quarters of an hour just twelve aircraft of the squadron accounted for 23 enemy fighters for only one damaged P-51. The squadron received a Distinguished Unit Citation for this combat, the first and only individual squadron to be so honoured. Lieutenant Colonel John Meyer and Captain Whisner were active on the day and finally ended the war with 24 and 15½ victories respectively.

The Group did not return to Bodney until 13th April and flew their last mission on 3rd May 1945, their 420th and virtually the last American foray over Germany. During their operations they had destroyed 520 enemy aircraft in the air with another 287 on the ground, losing 118 fighters in the process. Their aircraft stayed at Bodney longer than most and did not move out until August, whilst the ground crews stayed until late October.

The airfield was finally returned to its original owner – Major J. Mills – and turned over to farming. Some of the original accommodation units are still occupied by Army personnel using the Sandford Training Area. The ruined control tower still stands looking most forlorn amidst the ploughed fields. There is a roadside memorial stone near the airfield site, which can be located by taking the A1065 road past Brandon and Mundford then after some four miles turning right on to the B1108 to the village of Bodney.

5
COLTISHALL

For the majority of people Coltishall is best remembered for its association with Douglas Bader, that legendary figure of Fighter Command, despite the fact that he only served at the station for less than four months and for the majority of that time he and his squadron used Duxford for operations. Nevertheless Bader himself felt a very close affinity for Coltishall because on 27th July 1945, shortly after being released as a prisoner of war, he flew a Spitfire back to the airfield to be greeted triumphantly. Bader's short period of time at the airfield was closely followed by a number of other famous fighter pilots – 'Sailor' Malan, Stanford-Tuck, Max Aitken and John Cunningham.

The airfield was first conceived in February 1939 as a heavy bomber station and construction proceeded on that basis; this was at a time when it was fully accepted that Bomber Command would be all important in the coming air war. There is a story that some men from the Ministry were looking for likely airfield sites in Norfolk when they lost their way some miles north of Norwich. As they emerged from a wood they came across a large field full of potatoes and thought it would make an excellent site for an airfield – thus Coltishall was born!

The quite disastrous air battles over France in the summer of 1940 quickly brought about a radical rethink in the Air Ministry and the defence of the United Kingdom became the major priority. It was also realised that East Anglia, with its number of bomber airfields, would become a prime target for the Luftwaffe, and as then Duxford provided the only fighter cover for most of East Anglia extra fighter support was essential, and the new airfield at Coltishall exactly fitted the bill. It opened in May 1940 as part of No 12 Group of Fighter Command, which was then commanded by Air-Vice Marshal Trafford Leigh-Mallory.

On the 29th the first aircraft arrived on detachment from Watton, then being used as an advance landing field for Duxford. They were Spitfire Is of No 66 squadron commanded by Squadron Leader Rupert Leigh. The squadron had been active over the beaches of Dunkirk and had returned to North Sea patrols until it became drawn into the Battle of Britain. The Spitfire had been designed by R.J. Mitchell, the chief designer of Supermarine, who unfortunately did not live long enough to see the resounding success of his aircraft. The company had gained its reputation with seaplanes and the Spitfire was a direct derivative of their famous S.6B seaplane which had won the Schneider Trophy in 1931. The first prototype flew in March 1936 and with a top speed of almost 350 mph it was the fastest fighter in the world. Powered by a Rolls Royce Merlin engine and armed with four (later doubled) .303 Browning machine guns, it became a most formidable fighting machine and 20 different marks were produced during the war.

Coltishall became fully operational on 23rd June and on the following day No 242 squadron arrived; this had suffered heavy losses during its service in France during the early summer of 1940. It was mainly manned by Canadian pilots, who had joined the RAF before the war, and they were equipped with Hawker Hurricanes. This aircraft became the backbone of Fighter Command during the Battle of Britain. It was first devised as a private venture by Sidney Camm, the chief designer of Hawker, because it was felt that the RAF were only interested in biplanes as they considered monoplanes too new and rather 'risky'. The first prototype was flown in November 1935 and it took the Air Ministry another three months to decide to accept the aircraft. The first Hurricanes, powered by a Rolls Royce Merlin II V12 engine, entered the RAF in December 1937. Although slower than both the Spitfire and the Luftwaffe's Messerschmitt 109 it was a very steady, reliable aircraft, accounting for more victories in the Battle of Britain than its more famous rival. The 'Hurry', as it was fondly named, inspired great loyalty in its pilots and there was a keen debate on which was the better fighter – the Spitfire or the Hurricane. Unfortunately, at certain angles, it bore a strong resemblance to the Me109 and was often mistaken for this by friendly aircraft, hence the infamous so-called 'Battle of Barking Creek' of 6th September 1939 when two Hurricanes were shot down by Spitfires from a neighbouring station and one pilot was killed.

It was felt that 242 squadron required a strong commander to raise the pilots' morale and to help the squadron regroup and re-establish itself after the horrors of France. This officer was Squadron Leader Douglas Bader, who at the age of 30 was really considered too old to be a fighter pilot, irrespective of his artificial legs. Shortly after his arrival he had the squadron hard at work and from 27th June to 3rd July Bader led the squadron on twice daily training flights, especially developing the tactics of large formation fighter attacks. One of the squadron's young pilots – Dennis Crowley-Milling (later Air Marshal) – recalled the hard training but stoutly maintained that under Bader the 242 was the best squadron in Fighter Command: 'It was the first, last and all time the best'. Bader claimed his first victory, a Dornier 17, on 11th July whilst he was flying a single mission along the Norfolk coast. However, the first victory for a Coltishall aircraft had been claimed the previous day by a Spitfire from No 66 squadron. Whilst at Coltishall Bader and his close friend Rupert Leigh used their squadrons to practise wing formation flying. Bader was utterly convinced of the concept of the 'Big Wing', named 'Balboes' after the Italian airman – Marshal Italo Balbo – who first proposed the theory, and believed that the most effective method of attack was to use at least three squadrons as one complete force. Subsequently strike wings were used by all RAF Commands with great success. Fortunately Air Vice-Marshal Leigh-Mallory, the head of No 12 Group encouraged and supported Bader's ideas although his opposite number at No 11 Group was less than enthusiastic and the 'Big Wing' controversy caused a serious division between the two commanders. Bader was nicknamed 'Dogsbody', which was his call sign taken from his initials 'D.B.'. He commanded his 'Duxford Wing' throughout the Battle of Britain and its most successful day was on 5th September when eleven victories were claimed.

During September another squadron of Spitfires arrived at Coltishall, No 616, one of the many 'auxiliary' squadrons that had been formed from dedicated week-end pilots. Strange to relate all these auxiliary squadrons were first formed as light-bomber squadrons though most of them ended up in Fighter Command during the war. In July 1944, No 616 squadron was to be the first to receive jet fighters—the Gloster Meteors.

At the same time as the appearance of No 616 another famous Battle of Britain squadron arrived from Hornchurch, No 74, with its commander, Squadron Leader A.G. 'Sailor' Malan, the famous South African fighter ace. Both squadrons became heavily involved in defending London from the incessant Luftwaffe raids. On 27th

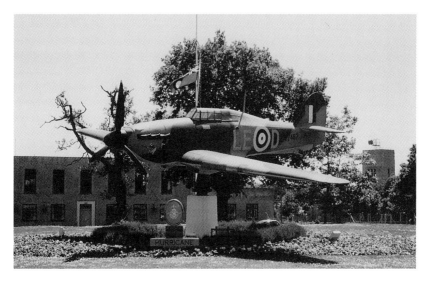

The replica Hawker Hurricane Mk I, as flown by Squadron Leader Douglas Bader DSO, DFC with No 242 Squadron, unveiled by Lady Bader, June 1989.

October Coltishall itself was attacked by a light enemy force but fortunately little damage was sustained. This raid was swiftly followed by another on 5th November when the control tower (or watch tower) was quite badly damaged. It was for such emergencies that Coltishall had a small satellite airfield at Matlaske.

Bader and his squadron left Coltishall in October for Duxford but by the beginning of December the now familiar 'Hurrys' were back in the form of No 257 squadron, perhaps the most famous to operate from the airfield during the war. It was named the 'Burma' squadron in recognition of the financial support for aircraft received from that country. The squadron badge carried a motto in Burmese which when translated read 'Death or Glory' and its pilots tried to live up to it. They had been heavily involved in the Battle of Britain from four different airfields and just before the squadron arrived at Coltishall its Hurricanes had taken quite a toll on the first Italian raid on London, destroying eight and a half aircraft with another four badly damaged. The commander was Squadron Leader R. Stanford-Tuck DFC, one of the most famous of 'The Few'. The squadron was destined to stay at Coltishall for almost twelve months, an unusually long occupation, because normally fighter squadrons moved airfields with great frequency as operational demands changed.

The Hurricanes were fully engaged on escort duties (known as 'Kipper' patrols) for the North Sea fishing fleets, which had been receiving undue attention from the Luftwaffe. When the weather conditions improved in the New Year the Hurricanes were used for fighter sweeps over the Dutch coast attacking any likely target and the so-called 'Rhubarbs' (which were effectively individual low-level strikes over enemy occupied territory when there were satisfactory cloud conditions). Operating both by day and night the squadron proved quite successful; indeed on 9th April they claimed a Me109 in the day and a Junkers Ju88 at night. One of their most successful pilots was Flight Lieutenant 'Cowboy' Blatchford, who in February 1943 was to return to Coltishall as a Wing Commander. On 21st June whilst on a patrol off the Dutch coast Stanford-Tuck was attacked by three Me109s. He shot down two before his damaged Hurricane crashed into the sea. Fortune shone on him that day as he was rescued by a trawler after less than an hour in the water, not many aircrew had such luck. When Stanford-Tuck left the squadron in the following month he was replaced as squadron commander by Blatchford.

At the end of July a brand new squadron of Hurricanes was formed at Coltishall and given the number 133. It became the third of the 'Eagle' squadrons to serve in the RAF, these were composed entirely from American volunteer pilots. The first 'Eagle' squadron had been established in September 1940 but No 133 was not destined to fly any operations from Coltishall as it moved to Duxford in August 1941. The three 'Eagle' squadrons were transferred to USAAF in September 1942 to form the Fourth Fighter Group at Debden, Essex, which became known as 'The Eagles Nest'. In total 244 Americans served in these three RAF squadrons before the United States entered the war. Indeed the Commander-in-Chief of Fighter Command said at the formal handing over of the squadrons and its Spitfires to the Eighth Air Force, 'We of Fighter Command, deeply regret this parting. In the course of the past 18 months we have seen the stuff of which you are made. We could not ask for better companions with whom to see this fight through to the finish... We shall watch your future with confidence . . .'

During the summer of 1941 a squadron of night fighters was based at Coltishall for the night defence of Norwich and the east coast ports. No 255 squadron, which had been operating Boulton Paul Defiants and Hurricanes in Yorkshire, arrived in late August to re-equip with Bristol Beaufighters. This twin-engined aircraft had originally been intended as a long range fighter but with the heavy night raids on

London in 1940 it was rather unceremoniously rushed into service during September 1940 as the best night fighter available to Fighter Command. Furthermore it was the only fighter capable of taking the heavily cumbersome Airborne Interception radar sets (AI). Immensely robust with an armament of four cannons and six machine guns and with a top speed in excess of 300 mph, the Beaufighter proved to be a most effective and versatile night-fighter. As its crews gained greater experience in the tactics of night-fighting, allied to improved AI radar sets the Beaufighter became a most able adversary and served Fighter Command with distinction until the arrival of the de Havilland Mosquito night fighter.

Unfortunately 255 squadron encountered numerous problems whilst converting to its new aircraft. On the day of their arrival at Coltishall one plane crashed on its approach to the runway and within the first fortnight there were five serious accidents, one of which resulted in the death of the squadron commander, Wing Commander D. Bennett, DFC. To cover the eastern sector whilst the squadron was working towards an operational standard, B Flight of 604 (County of Middlesex) squadron, which was based at Middle Wallop, was quickly drafted in. The top-scoring night fighter squadron in the Service, it was commanded by Wing Commander John Cunningham DSO, DFC, whose prowess at night flying had earned him the nickname 'Cat's Eyes'. Cunningham's young navigator, Pilot Officer R. Rawnsley recalled the Flight's duties at Coltishall, '... there was a fairly steady trade with bombers running in across the Wash on their way to raid the industrial towns of the Midlands... minelayers... enemy intruders, roving enemy fighters mingling with the streams of our returning bombers to spread confusion and destruction among the closely spread aerodromes of East Anglia.' During the Flight's short stay at Coltishall, Cunningham claimed at least two victories and on the second occasion the Station Commander, Group Captain R. Lees, was on board 'just for the ride and to see how the job was done'!

When 255 departed for High Ercall in March 1942 it was quickly replaced by yet another Beaufighter squadron – No 68. This was largely composed of Czech personnel and commanded by another famous Battle of Britain pilot, Wing Commander Max Aitken DFC. Aitken was the son of Lord Beaverbrook of *Daily Express* fame and had done sterling work as Churchill's Minister of Aircraft Production in 1940. During its first months of operations the squadron launched 83 patrols and in three nights accounted for five enemy aircraft and continued to build on these early successes. April and May 1942 saw several air raids on Norwich and Great Yarmouth and the squadron's aircraft achieved some moderate results with four positive kills.

Later in the year, as the Luftwaffe threat declined, the Beaufighters were mounting patrols over the east coast convoys and soon became more aggressive, launching 'night ranger' missions mostly in conjunction with Fairey Albacores from Bircham Newton. The intention was that the Albacores would seek out likely targets, especially E-boats; once located the Albacores would circle the target and light it with flares to allow the Beaufighters to come down to attack. These missions were called 'Operation Deadly' – a rather apt name for what proved to be a decidedly dangerous occupation! Wing Commander Aitken left Coltishall late in January 1943 and as Group Captain later became the Station Commander of RAF Banff in Coastal Command, where he brought his unrivalled experience of Beaufighters to develop a very effective anti-shipping strike force. Aitken's old squadron became the airfield's longest serving and did not leave until February 1944 when it could claim 70 aircraft destroyed during its time at Coltishall. The squadron did however return briefly in October 1944 when it was particularly engaged in seeking out Heinkel He111s, which were launching V1 rockets from over the North Sea, and on the 5th November it destroyed its first Heinkel.

Because of the airfield's proximity to the coast there were close links with the various Coastal Command units operating from Bircham Newton and Docking, and frequently fighters from Coltishall afforded escorts for the Command's Beaufighters. An Air Sea Rescue unit had also been established at Coltishall in July 1941 and later a new A/S rescue squadron, No 278, operated from Coltishall and its satellite field at Matlaske. When George VI visited the airfield in January 1942 he formally presented the squadron badge to 278, a considerable honour as it was the first time that a badge had been signed and handed over by a reigning monarch.

Besides regular bomber escorts for the Norfolk squadrons of No 2 Group, most of the operations conducted from the airfield were directed against enemy shipping activity. All the various Spitfire squadrons that came and went with a monotonous regularity were engaged in these missions, which were not very popular with the crews for obvious reasons, but were nevertheless considered essential to keep the country's shipping lanes open. No 118 squadron, although equipped with 'old' Spitfire Vbs were active on 'Roadsteads' (which were fighter mounted strikes against enemy

Bristol Beaufighter: an artist's impression of this famous night fighter.

shipping without bomber support). This squadron had gained a fine reputation whilst operating with Coastal Command in Cornwall and its badge featured an old sailing ship, which acknowledged its prowess in sinking ships. It was composed largely of Dutch and Free French pilots, who fast gained a fine reputation and even when they were engaged on purely bomber escorts, the pilots still managed to claim a fair share of Fw190s — hard won considering the inferior performance of their mark of Spitfires.

The challenge of the Luftwaffe's new Fw190, which outclassed the Spitfire in performance, resulted in the Supermarine's designers coming up with an improved model — Mark IX. This had a supercharged Merlin 61 engine which gave the aircraft a top speed in excess of 400 mph, and a much better performance at high altitudes. It was armed with two 20 mm cannons and became a most effective fighter with well over 5,000 being produced. Most of the squadrons that arrived at Coltishall during 1943/4 were equipped with this 'new' Spitfire. No 64 squadron, which arrived in September 1943, was the first to receive the new mark and along with 611 (West Lancashire) squadron operated very successfully.

One of the features of station life at Coltishall during the last twelve months of the war was the very strong presence of Polish pilots, four Polish squadrons served at the airfield. The first to arrive in April 1944 was 316 (City of Warsaw), followed quickly by a detachment of No 307, then based at Church Fenton. This had been the first Polish night fighter squadron and it brought the fabulous de Havilland Mosquito, which appeared at Coltishall for the very first time. But perhaps the most famous Polish squadron to serve at Coltishall was No 303, which had been formed in August 1940 and quickly brought into the Battle of Britain, fighting with great distinction — in fact more Polish pilots flew in the Battle of Britain than any other country, foreign or colonial. 303 was led with a certain elan by Squadron Leader B.H. Drabinski DFC and their aircraft were engaged on bomber escort duties for both the RAF and Eighth Air Force. On 5th September the Polish pilots claimed five Fw190s on one single mission.

303's operations were many and manifold, from attacking V1 rocket sites, seeking and destroying midget submarines operating from German North Sea ports and mounting day ranger incursions over Holland. Its Spitfires provided escorts to B-24 Liberators attacking 'Big Ben' sites (V2 rockets) and the squadron took part in 'Operation Market Garden', the airborne invasion of Holland. In April 1945 the squadron exchanged its Spitfires for North American P-51 Mustangs with the intention of providing long range escorts for bomber operations, and for this reason they moved to Andrews Field in Essex, but only completed two operations before returning to Coltishall for the last few weeks of the war.

6
DEOPHAM GREEN

The search for this airfield is best started from that most delightful of Norfolk villages – Hingham. Surely it is a perfect example of what most Americans would consider a typical English village? A small and neat village green with a charming market place surrounded by elegant Georgian houses; the whole scene dominated by a magnificent 14th century church, surprisingly large for the size of the village. If this is not sufficient, add the fact that it was from here, in the early 17th century, that Samuel Lincoln, the ancestor of the famous president, left for the New World to help to found a new Hingham in Massachusetts. Now a more recent historical link with America has been established with the simple memorial stone set in the church wall, dedicated to the men of 452nd Bomb Group that served at the nearby Deopham Green airfield just about two miles south-east of the village.

The American servicemen began to arrive at the airfield in the first days of 1944 and were allocated to the Third Air Division to become the third and last Group to serve in this Division in Norfolk. Unlike the Second Division's groups, the 452nd was equipped with Boeing B-17 aircraft – the famed Flying Fortresses – which will forever epitomise the USAAF in England during the war, due in no small measure to William Wyler's famous documentary film *Memphis Belle* and the classic war film of 1949 *Twelve O'Clock High*.

The first Boeing B-17 flew in July 1935 and as the first all-metal four-engined monoplane was a revolutionary aircraft at the time. The slender design made it visually elegant, which was an exception to the general rule for military aircraft in the thirties. Its several prominent gun turrets caught the interest of the press, who described it as being 'like a flying fortress' and the name stuck. By 1939 the

Army Air Force had a mere 39 B-17s in service, so when the RAF received their first Fortresses in 1941, the Americans watched their performance with great interest. Although the RAF were not very impressed with the aircraft, the Americans were not too concerned as they felt this was in part due to the way the RAF had used them operationally. Nevertheless certain technical weaknesses that had been exposed by these early operations were eradicated and the aircraft underwent some redesign, resulting in a very powerful heavy bomber. The B-17 became the backbone of the Eighth Air Force and led the American air assault on Germany, and was fondly admired by all its pilots and crews.

Deopham Green's B-17s went into action for the first time on 4th February 1944. Their target was Chateauroux, a town set deep in central France, and all the aircraft returned safe and sound. This happy state of affairs was not to last very long. On its third mission, just four days later, it lost its Commanding Officer Lieutenant Colonel Wangeman. The Bomb Groups' COs tended not to be desk-bound leaders, many went on frequent operations and quite a few lost their lives in action. The Group had the unenviable record of having the greatest number of Commanding Officers in the Eighth Air Force – nine in 17 months – and two of them were killed whilst leading the Group. One of them, Colonel Smith lasted only four days. Certainly the Group sustained heavy losses in their early operations, which were mainly directed against targets in the Ruhr. Missions to the large aircraft assembly plants of Brunswick and Kassel resulted in a harsh toll of men and aircraft. By the end of the war the Group was left with just one of its original aircraft *E-rat-icator*, which survived 100 missions.

The burnt-out remains of a B-17 of 452nd Bomb Group at Poltava airfield. (USAF)

In April, the Group went even further afield to Poznan just inside the Polish border and some 150 miles east of Berlin. The town housed an important aircraft components factory. On their flight out the cloud cover over Denmark was very thick, but when the three Bomb Groups arrived at Poznan they found perfect conditions and despite very concentrated flak they bombed the target with a very high degree of accuracy. It was, without doubt, the Group's most successful operation so far, albeit a most harrowing experience for its crews.

This all proved to be good experience and training for their next major operation to Berlin and beyond. On 21st June 1944 a massive RAF and USAAF attack was planned but the RAF had to pull out because of insufficient fighter support for their slower and less heavily armed bombers. The Eighth continued on their own with a force of 1,311 bombers and an almost equal number of fighters. The Deopham Green Group was in the leading formation and the North Sea route was preferred in order to minimise the flying time over hostile territory. The Berlin flak was again particularly intense and over 2,100 tons of bombs were dropped. The leading groups of B-17s swung eastward to land at three Russian airfields – Poltava, Mirgorod and Piryatin – all to the east of Kiev. No 452 Group landed at Poltava with relatively light losses, just five aircraft missing. Only about five hours after the Americans had landed, a force of German bombers attacked the airfield and wrought terrible damage. Forty-four of the 72 aircraft that had landed were destroyed and another 26 were badly damaged. In the preceding 24 hours the Eighth Air Force had lost 88 bombers and 22 fighters, a most costly exercise and probably the worst in its history. The one consolation to be gained from the whole debacle was that the Eighth had not lost too many of its valuable crews. Nevertheless the USAAF doggedly persevered with the 'Shuttle' operations and the Group returned for its second mission on 11th September, this time Chemnitz was bombed en route and the Group's aircraft later returned via Hungary and Italy without losing a single aircraft.

On 7th November the Group was part of a force directed to bomb heavily fortified German positions at Metz in the Moselle valley prior to an Allied offensive. It flew into a particularly heavy flak area when looking for secondary targets and three of its aircraft were severely damaged. One of the aircraft, *Lady Janet* was piloted by first Lieutenant Donald Gott with Second Lieutenant William Metzger as his co-pilot. Three of the engines were out of control, the intercom system was not operational and two of the crew were seriously

A fine shot of a B-17 – 452nd Bomb Group was one of only three Norfolk Groups equipped with B-17s.

injured. Gott ordered the crew to bale out and Metzger gave his parachute to one of the gunners because his was damaged. Unfortunately the radio operator was too badly wounded to leave the aircraft. Gott jettisoned his bombs prior to attempting a landing but when the aircraft was just about 100 feet from the ground it exploded killing the three airmen. Both Gott and Metzger were posthumously awarded the Medal of Honor – the Americans' highest gallantry award equivalent to the Victoria Cross. They had both but recently arrived at Deopham Green as replacement crews. Gott was only 21 years old and Metzger was just one year older. Indeed the *average* age of the Eighth Air Force crews was only 21 years, it was certainly a young Air Force in more senses than one.

Another pilot of the Group expressed the fears of all these young airmen when he wrote, 'After about the first four or five missions I began to get this savvy feeling that there was just so much you could do to stay alive, and the rest was luck. It had nothing to do with how much skill you had as a pilot, or whether you were a good or virtuous guy. It was about 87% luck ... You felt that your life was simply in the hands of fate. Everything was out of scale then ... 33 missions completed you returned home as some kind of hero when you didn't really feel anything of the kind...' Of course all crewmen who managed to complete a tour of operations automatically qualified for the Lucky Bastards club. After the war such certificates were, quite rightly, given pride of place either in the home or the office.

Just as the war was drawing to a conclusion the Group experienced a very rugged mission. On 7th April 1945 they were part of a thousand strong force directed against a range of fighter airfields, oil storage depots and arms factories and their primary target was Kaltenkirchen, a German jet fighter station. The formations had not been long over north-west Germany when they were faced by a large force of fighters including the dreaded Me262 – the turbo-jet fighters. At this late stage of the war it was a great surprise to realise that the Luftwaffe could still muster in such strength. The escorting Mustangs were able to cope with most of the attacking force but some of the enemy fighters still managed to get through to the bombers. As they were in the lead formation the Group suffered heavy attacks for almost 45 minutes and two of their aircraft were destroyed by Fw190s ramming them. In total the Group lost four aircraft but their gunners claimed 14 aircraft destroyed. For their determined and brave fight against overwhelming odds the Group received a Distinguished Unit Citation, an award granted for a highly meritous mission. This the 66th and last such award made during the war.

At the various debriefings after the operation the official view was that the ramming of the Group's aircraft was caused by the enemy pressing their attacks too closely and then losing control, but most of the crews were convinced that they had been faced by suicide fighters and later intelligence sources substantiated this view. In March 1945 Goering had called for volunteers for 'special operations', which turned out to be a 'suicide force' known as the 'Sonderkommando Elbe', thought to be about 120 strong. The mission of the 7th April was the only known time that this force was used against the Eighth, possibly because the majority of the 59 fighters shot down on that day were believed to have come from this unit.

Just two weeks later the Group flew its last mission, an attack on railway yards at Ingoldstadt far into southern Germany; all aircraft returned from this operation which was almost a replica of the Group's first. In the 16 months they had operated from Deopham Green the Group had flown 250 missions losing 110 aircraft in action and over 50 by other causes. This was a very high loss rate considering the relatively short time the Group had been in action and compared very unfavourably with their near neighbours 453rd

A memorial to 452nd Bomb Group.

Bomb Group at Old Buckenham, who had gone into action on the same day but had only half the casualties suffered by 452nd Group. By the end of July most of the Americans had left and the site of the airfield was sold in 1959.

In May 1992 a fine memorial plinth sited on the very edge of the airfield was dedicated to the men of the 452nd. If one stands at that very spot, as indeed I did on a cold February day, it is quite easy to visualise the B-17s coming in to land after another long and harrowing mission, a most strange and eerie feeling recalling the opening images of *Twelve O'Clock High*.

7

DOCKING

Just a few miles up the road from Bircham Newton is the village of Docking and it was here, only a few months after the outbreak of the war, that a small grass airfield was laid out on a site to the east of the village. This purely functional airfield was supplied with rather basic accommodation for less than 1,000 personnel so it was never likely to become a very important or, indeed, particularly active operational airfield. Its main function was as a satellite out-station for the much more important and very prestigious Coastal Command airfield at Bircham Newton.

Throughout Docking's short existence as a wartime airfield it was used mainly as an overflow base for Bircham Newton. Various squadrons and flights arrived regularly from the main station and at times they even took off for operations but all the ancillary support work, servicing and repairs were undertaken at Bircham Newton.

During the early months of the summer of 1940 the first aircraft were dispersed to Docking – the Bristol Blenheims of 235 squadron. The squadron quickly became involved in anti-shipping strikes mainly in the North Sea and they were also engaged in acting as escorts for east coast convoys, and for the next twelve months or so they were the only aircraft to be seen around the airfield. Slowly they were replaced by Lockheed Hudsons, and then by the end of 1941 a squadron of Wellington VIIIs of No 221 squadron made a very brief appearance. They had flown down from Coastal Command's new base at Reykjavik in Iceland, en route for operations in the Middle East rather like a flock of migrating birds just stopping on a long flight south! Most of the basic Coastal Command tasks and operations that were undertaken by Bircham Newton also took place from Docking but, of course, to a far lesser degree.

Perhaps the most singular contribution that Docking made to the Command's war effort was the gathering of meteorological data and information. Weather obviously played a major part in flying right from the pioneer days and with the commencement of air warfare it became one of the most critical factors in the planning of any offensive strike. Hitherto the Met Office had garnered most of the information on which their forecasts were based from merchant vessels and now, in wartime, these sources had virtually disappeared.

In 1940 Bomber Command had become increasingly concerned about the accuracy of forecasts generally and more especially those relating to the landing conditions at their airfields when the bombers were returning. As a solution three new flights were formed to be devoted solely to the task of obtaining details of cloud formation and other essential weather data. One of these, No 403, was based at Bircham Newton but it was quickly transferred to Docking. The weather forecasters needed regular daily information from specific points along a long sea track of some 1,000 nautical miles. The obvious aircraft to undertake such duties were the Hudsons but because they were in very short supply and desperately needed for Coastal Command's main operations, the ubiquitous Blenheims had to be used but this meant that there was an appreciable reduction in the range of the flights.

On 1st March 1941 Coastal Command were given the overall responsibility for all meteorological units then in operation. The Command immediately upgraded the flights, they renumbered them and No 1401 (Met) Flight came into operation at Docking. Besides the Blenheims, the Flight received a mixture of aircraft – Hurricanes, Spitfires and even some Gloster Gladiators. This aircraft had earned a special place in the history of the Service. They were the last biplanes to be flown in the RAF – not only the last but also considered the best. And they had gained everlasting fame for their valiant defence of Malta in June 1940 by just three aircraft, *Faith, Hope* and *Charity*. A truly remarkable aircraft, which had entered the Service in January 1937 and yet was still in operational use although looking more suited to the First World War than the Second. Gladiators could still be seen on the Docking runways right up to the end of 1942. All of the Flight's aircraft were engaged on what were called 'Thum' flights, which obtained temperatures and humidity readings at various altitudes. The Spitfires set off at dawn and were compelled to fly within very precisely controlled areas. The aircraft

A pre-war photograph of Gloster Gladiators: some were seen at Docking. (RAF Museum)

would first climb to 40,000 feet and then descend slowly taking readings at every 5,000 feet. These operations became known as 'Pratas' and were very onerous not only because of the length of the flight but also the exactness of flying and navigation needed. They were, of course, flown daily irrespective of the weather conditions. Besides these regular flights, routine reconnaissance missions were flown from Docking along very set and regular patterns. The aircraft flew out diagonally over the North Sea to a point just south of Norway taking precise readings throughout the flight – these were called 'Rhombus' missions.

In August 1942 the Flight was made up to squadron strength and numbered 521 with Hudsons at long last replacing the Blenheims and a little later it was supplied with Hampdens, Mosquitos and a Ventura. These aircraft took on the most dangerous of all weather missions – the 'PAMPA' flights – despatched deep into enemy territory to gain vital weather information over the target areas. The first PAMPA flights had been made from Bircham Newton by Spitfires but when four aircraft failed to return, such missions were suspended until a more suitable aircraft emerged – another ready-made role for the amazing Mosquito! Although meteorology was a much belittled science in the RAF, by mid-1942 the Central Forecast Station at Dunstable was well established and Bomber Command's Met Officer one of the most important members of Air Marshal Harris's planning team. Ultimately by the end of October 1944 the Met squadron moved from Docking to Langham, Bircham Newton's other satellite airfield.

8
DOWNHAM MARKET

It can almost be said that this airfield came into existence by default. When the Air Ministry were seeking a suitable site for a new satellite field for Marham, Bomber Command's prestigious station, Barton Beamish, just a few miles due south of it, seemed to be the obvious choice as it had already been earmarked for development. On closer inspection, however, the site was not considered capable of accommodating the new heavy bombers. The search began for a more suitable situation and in late 1940 a site above the town of Downham Market was selected, but it was another twelve months before the contractors moved in and then the progress of work seemed to be anything but urgent.

Not until the first week of July 1942 was the new airfield fit for occupation and like its parent station it was placed in No 3 Group of Bomber Command. On 10th July the first Stirlings of No 218 (Gold Coast) squadron arrived from Marham. This squadron had served with the Advanced Air Striking Force in France during the fateful days of 1940 and on one single mission had lost eleven out of twelve of their Fairey Battles. In September 1941 whilst serving at Marham and being equipped with Wellingtons the squadron had been officially adopted by the Gold Coast territories and several of their aircraft were provided out of the 'Gold Coast Fund'. The squadron retained the designation throughout the war.

The Short Stirling was one of the series of heavy bombers designed to the famous specification B12/B36, which dictated the format of Bomber Command's early strike force. It was the first of the four-engined bombers to come into service in August 1940 but because certain operational limitations were discovered, most notably its poor ceiling height, its service life was relatively short – no more than four years. Nevertheless it still proved to be a most sturdy aircraft that could survive considerable damage. With an operational limit in excess of 2,000 miles the Stirling had the longest range of any RAF aircraft then in service and proved to be most versatile, acting as a troop transport, a glider tower and a pure freight carrier.

No 218 was active in many of the missions mounted by No 3 Group, varying from targets in the Ruhr, to Hamburg, Stuttgart, and Schweinfurt as well as cities in Italy – Milan, Genoa and Turin. The Stirlings were also employed on mine-laying or 'gardening' as the operation was known in RAF circles. Each sea area was given a codename, for instance 'Forget-me-not' for the Kiel Canal and 'Eglantine' for Heligoland. *Bomber Command*, an official paperback published in 1941, explained the procedure; 'It is not unusual for the mine-laying aircraft to fly round and round for a considerable time in order to make quite sure that the mine is laid exactly in the correct place. It calls for great skill and resolution. Moreover, the crew do not have the satisfaction of seeing even the partial results of their work. There is no coloured explosion, no burgeoning of fire to report on their return home. At best all they see is a splash on the surface of a darkened and inhospitable sea.' Mine-laying became a major Bomber Command offensive and is now recognised as one of its major successes of the war.

In August 1942, as a result of a small reorganisation of some Norfolk stations, Marham was transferred to No 2 Group taking Downham Market with it, but then in December Downham Market was granted full station status within No 3 Group. Although it was smaller than most bomber stations, having just one operational squadron, the procedure before any operation was very similar. The briefing for the crews would be made in the early evening and once roll call had been taken the doors of the briefing room would be locked and guarded by the RAF police. Then the Intelligence Officer would unroll the operational map normally to the ribald comments of the crews, such as 'Bloody Ruhr again . . . ******* Essen! . . .' Ignoring the good-humoured jibes the 'Gen' Officer, as he was known, would give full details of the target, the likely defences to be met, the forecasted weather and wind speeds and the precise timings of the operation. Normally the leader of the operation would explain the make-up of the force, the runways to be used, the take-off procedures and which flight would be leading. The aircrews cleared their pockets of any personal items – money, letters, etc, which were then placed in a personal bag to be returned after debriefing. A small

Avro Lancaster Mk VI: However Mark IVs were operated by 635 Squadron at Downham Market in 1944.

escape pack was handed out, which usually contained foreign currency, glucose sweets, a small compass and water purifying tablets. Letters from the crews were collected ready to be posted should they not return. They then went to their aircraft, which had already been serviced, fuelled, armed and loaded with bombs. It was then just a matter of waiting for the orders to taxi their aircraft into their position in the flight, wait and watch for the green light . . . take off . . . airborne on just another mission!

The airfield would then become strangely quiet for several hours although the control or watch tower, sometimes also referred to as the 'Black House' or 'Red Tower', was full of activity especially for an hour or so before the aircraft were due back. On their return before they could go to bed the aircrews attended a debriefing over coffee and sandwiches when they were questioned on the type of flak and enemy fighter opposition encountered as well as their bombing accuracy. Meanwhile the magazines of film had been removed from the aircraft and were quickly developed for transmission to Group headquarters. The aircraft's engines and turrets would be covered with tarpaulins and the following morning the ground crews would closely inspect the aircraft from top to tail, oil and fuel consumptions were checked against the pilots' logs, tyres pumped up, all controls checked and any repairs or maintenance completed ready for the next night's operation. And so it would start all over again...this routine was carried out every day at the countless bomber airfields throughout England.

In August 1943 the strength of No 3 Group was increased by the formation of a new squadron, No 623, from a Flight of No 218 squadron, and four aircraft went out on 10/11th August to bomb Nuremburg. The new squadron had a very short existence, being disbanded in December 1943 after flying its last operation on 4/5th when just one Stirling laid mines near Kiel. During its brief life the squadron flew 150 sorties against a variety of targets and lost ten aircraft in the process. These operations showed the vulnerability of the Stirlings to enemy flak, they suffered far heavier losses than either the Lancasters or the Halifaxes, largely because of their lower operational altitude where they were more vulnerable to flak. On just one mission to Berlin on 31st August 1943 when the Command's overall loss was 7.6% (itself unacceptably high), 17 of the 106 Stirlings taking part failed to return – a 16% loss! With such casualty figures the operational days of the Stirling were numbered.

On the night of 12th August 1943 aircraft from 218 and the new 623 squadron were detailed for a mission to bomb the Fiat works at Turin. Amongst the crews that night was Flight Sergeant Arthur Aaron DFM of 218 squadron, the captain and pilot of one of the Stirlings. *The London Gazette* of 5th November 1943 relates the story of Aaron's last mission. 'When approaching to attack, the bomber received devastating bursts of fire from an enemy fighter. Three engines were hit, the windscreen shattered, the front and rear turrets put out of action and the elevator control damaged, causing the aircraft to become unstable and difficult to control. The navigator was killed and other members of the crew were wounded.

'A bullet struck Flight Sergeant Aaron in the face, breaking his jaw and tearing away part of his face. He was also wounded in the lung and his right arm was rendered useless. As he fell forward over the control column, the aircraft dived several thousand feet. Control was regained by the Flight Engineer at 3,000 feet. Unable to speak Aaron urged the bomb aimer by signs to take over the controls. Course was then set southwards in an endeavour to fly the crippled bomber to Sicily. Flight Sergeant Aaron was assisted to the rear of the aircraft and treated with morphia. After resting for some time he rallied and mindful of his responsibility as captain of the aircraft, insisted on returning to the pilot's cockpit, where he was lifted into his seat and had his feet placed on the rudder bar. Twice he made determined attempts to take control and hold the aircraft to its course but his weakness was evident and with difficulty he was persuaded to desist. Though in great pain and suffering from exhaustion, he continued to help by writing directions with his left hand.

'Five hours after leaving the target the petrol was beginning to run low, but soon afterwards the flare path at Bone airfield was sighted. Flight Sergeant Aaron summoned his failing strength to direct the bomb aimer in the hazardous task of landing the damaged aircraft in the darkness with the undercarriage retracted. Four attempts were made under his direction; at the fifth attempt Flight Sergeant Aaron was so near to collapsing that he had to be restrained by the crew and the landing was completed by the bomb aimer. Nine hours after landing Flight Sergeant Aaron died from exhaustion...In appalling conditions he showed the greatest qualities of courage, determination and leadership, and though wounded and dying, he set an example of devotion to duty which has seldom been equalled and never surpassed.' Flight Sergeant Aaron was posthumously awarded the Victoria Cross.

The biggest change for Downham Market came in March 1944 when the airfield passed into No 8 Group – the Pathfinder Force. The Stirlings departed and in their place came three flights of Avro Lancasters, which were formed into a new squadron, No 635. Downham Market was ideally placed in what became known as 'Pathfinder Country'. The Pathfinder Force had been formed on 15th August 1942 with its headquarters at Wyton in Huntingdonshire and was commanded by Group Captain D.C.T. Bennett, who was promoted to Air Vice-Marshal when the Force was upgraded to a

Short Stirling of No 218 Squadron.

Group in January 1943. Originally composed of five squadrons, one from each of the Command's operational Groups, by the end of the war it had grown to 19 squadrons. The Pathfinder Force was effectively an elite corps of crews of high technical and navigational expertise. From its inception it led the main bomber forces to all targets right up until the end of the war. The losses tended to be heavier than other squadrons because of their operational methods and the gallantry of its pilots and crews became legendary in the RAF. Undoubtedly the Group's contribution to the strategic bombing offensive was massive and critically important.

The Avro Lancaster, developed from the rather ill-fated Manchester, was the most famous of all RAF bombers and had a wonderful war record. Its first mission took place on 10/11th March 1942 over Essen, merely the start of an almost non-stop offensive by these heavy bombers. The Lancaster had the largest bomb capacity of any Allied bomber used in the Second World War and was the only aircraft able to carry the 22,000 pound 'Grand Slam' bomb. Lancasters took part in most of the famous bombing operations of the war and they had the lowest percentage rate of loss of any aircraft. By 1945 there were 56 squadrons of Lancasters, making it the most significant aircraft in Bomber Command.

No 635 squadron went out on its first operation on the night of 22/23rd March to Frankfurt, followed by many missions. On 4th August the squadron was detailed for a daylight 'marking' mission to a V1 rocket storage depot at Troissey St Maxim in northern France. One of the lead aircraft was piloted by acting Squadron Leader Ian Bazalgette DFC, who was the 'Master Bomber' for the operation. As he approached the target area his aircraft was crippled by heavy flak, two engines were put out of action and the starboard wing and fuselage burst into flames. The bomb aimer was badly wounded and the mid-gunner overcome with fumes. Despite the appalling state of the Lancaster Bazalgette managed to regain control and he accurately marked and bombed the target. He continued to fly on for another 30 miles before ordering the crew to bail out at 1,000 feet. Bazalgette attempted to land the aircraft in a field but the aircraft exploded as it touched down, killing him and the other two crew members. One year later Bazalgette was posthumously awarded the Victoria Cross; the citation reads, 'His heroic sacrifice marked the climax of a long career of operations against the enemy. He always chose the more dangerous and exacting roles. His courage and devotion to duty were beyond praise.'

No Pathfinder Force's airfield would have been complete without a Mosquito squadron and in the first week of April 1944 one was formed at Downham Market to become part of the Group's 'Light Night Striking Force' – later renamed the 'Fast Night Striking Force'. The new squadron – No 571 – began its operations from nearby Gravely airfield. It was not until August that Mosquitos appeared again at Downham with the reformed 608 (North Riding) squadron. When one Mosquito went out on 6th August to bomb Wanne-Eickel it was attacked by four enemy fighters and chased for over 15 minutes and although seriously damaged managed to escape but crash-landed when coming in to land at the emergency field at Woodbridge. The squadron completed their last mission to Kiel on 3rd May 1945 having completed over 1,700 sorties to Berlin, Frankfurt, Hanover, Essen, Nuremburg, Emden and Kiel. The squadron was part of the FNSF and perhaps their most famous operations were their 36 consecutive night raids made on Berlin in the early months of 1945, which became known as the 'Berlin Shuttle'.

During July and August 1944 No 635 squadron received four very special Lancaster Mark VIs for operational trials. Only four were used on operations and one was lost on its third sortie but another managed to survive 25 missions. Ultimately the aircraft was further developed and came into the RAF after the war as the Lincoln.

Another famous airman who served as a 'Master Bomber' with 635 squadron was Wing Commander Dennis Witt, DSO, DFC, DFM, who completed 35 sorties with the squadron, and on a raid to Duisberg in November 1944 he notched up his 100th mission. When he was awarded the DSO it was said that, '. . . he has displayed the highest standard of skill and bravery setting an example of a high order.' Witt had started his RAF career as a sergeant pilot and when he retired in 1959 he had reached the rank of group captain.

The squadron's last operation was on 25th April 1945 when four aircraft went to bomb gun batteries on Wangerooge Island and another 14 were part of the large force that bombed the SS barracks at Berchtesgaden, Hitler's famous mountain retreat. This proved to be Bomber Command's last major operation. Both squadrons were disbanded by September and the airfield was closed to flying in October 1946. Sadly little has survived of this quite remarkable airfield that saw the award of two VCs – a fine record.

9
EAST WRETHAM

Outside the council offices in Thetford is a memorial plaque honouring those men who served with the 359th Fighter Group at East Wretham during the years from 1943 to 1945. Most appropriately this memorial stands very close to the statue of Thomas Paine, Thetford's most famous son. Paine's thoughts, ideas and words did much to influence the American constitution and are immortalised in the 'Declaration of Independence'; he even coined the name 'The United States of America'. The airfield at East Wretham had a most cosmopolitan flavour, which would have greatly appealed to Thomas Paine; besides the Americans, Czech airmen and the British served there, and after the war it was used as a transit camp for Polish personnel. However, only the American servicemen have been commemorated.

The airfield was situated near the village of the same name, which is about six miles north-east of Thetford and set on the very edge of the massive Stanford military training area. Thetford itself once had an airfield that was used by the Royal Flying Corps during the First World War. East Wretham was one of the many airfields rapidly constructed and rushed into use during the early months of 1940. It was planned as a satellite for Honington, Suffolk, about six miles south-east of Thetford. The light loamy soils and underlying chalk were considered ideal for airfields as they afforded good natural drainage, or at least that was the theory; that is why there were so many airfields dotted around the Brecklands.

In May 1940 the first few Wellingtons from No 9 squadron appeared somewhat desultorily at East Wretham despite the fact that the facilities at the airfield were very basic and therefore not yet ready for occupation. This squadron had taken an active part in the first months of the war and its Wellingtons received quite a battering in their first operations.

East Wretham did not really come to life until early September when it saw the arrival of its first Czechoslovakian airmen. These flyers had escaped from their homeland when it was over-run in March 1939 and finally arrived in England in early July via France. By the middle of the month 43 officers had been granted RAF commissions as well as their own bomber squadron – No 311 (Czech). This squadron was placed in No 3 Group, despatched to Honington and given a British commanding officer, Wing Commander Griffiths, who worked closely with the senior Czech officer – Wing Commander Toman – presumably because of the language difficulties.

The Czech squadron were to be trained on their Wellingtons at East Wretham and the task was given to Flight Lieutenant Pickard, a most experienced Wellington pilot, who was destined to become one of Bomber Command's most illustrious names. The Czech airmen were brave and fearless almost to a fault, brilliant fliers, sometimes erratic but all had a burning desire to attack the enemy at every available chance. They also had their own special code of discipline, which was often at variance with that of RAF aircrews. It was Pickard's job to meld these diverse talents into an effective bomber force, and he coped very well with them, earning the nickname 'Cowboy' from the high-heeled riding boots he wore to cope with the quagmire of thick mud that covered the airfield. Living conditions were primitive, just one wooden hut used for administration purposes and clusters of canvas tents for eating and sleeping. The airfield was likened to 'the Somme but without the trenches.'

By the middle of September some crews were thought ready for action and five aircraft were sent to bomb marshalling yards at Brussels. Then on the 23rd of the month three Wellingtons were included in a mission to Berlin, two returned safely but the third landed intact in Holland and was subsequently used by the Luftwaffe in an attempt to confuse RAF crews. Slowly more aircraft and crews were brought into operation although on one mission in November 1940 three aircraft failed to return and another six crashed on landing. There was a frightening occurrence one night in December when one Wellington bound for Mannheim attempted to land again because of engine failure but crashed just short of the airfield and all the bombs exploded causing a colossal explosion that was heard for miles around the airfield.

This unfortunate accident proved to be just a foretaste of what was to come in the early months of 1941 when the airfield suffered from a series of air-raids. On February 3rd over 20 bombs were dropped without inflicting too much damage. Then one month later just as the squadron was returning from a night mission, one of the Wellingtons was followed in by a Junkers Ju88, a night fighter/bomber, which succeeded in unloading ten bombs before getting away safely.

In June 1941 three Wellingtons from 115 squadron at Mildenhall arrived on detachment and flew on regular night missions. Nobody seemed to know what they were doing, except that it was all 'hush hush'; the crews were kept segregated from the rest of the station. It was later suggested that East Wretham had been deliberately selected for these exercises because it housed a Czech squadron, making 'careless talk' between the crews far less likely! What was actually being tested was 'GEE', a navigational aid based on a radio-pulse system, by which a navigator could fix his position by reference to three transmitting stations in England. It was believed that it would take the Germans about six months to devise effective jamming methods and by then the equipment would have been refined. A series of trials was undertaken, the first one over the North Sea, and the rest over enemy territory. This was a calculated risk because if one of the aircraft should be lost the security of the new device would be breached. On 11/12th August two 'GEE' Wellingtons operated over the Ruhr and with the new aid not only found their target – Münchengladbach – without any difficulty but released their bombs using GEE co-ordinates. As a result of the trials GEE was put into large-scale production and was generally introduced into Bomber Command squadrons in March 1942.

Like most of No 3 Group's squadrons 311 mounted operations over a variety of targets mainly in the Ruhr but they did go to Berlin on six occasions and even as far as Leipzig – so very close to their own homeland. One of their best-known pilots was Flight Sergeant Jo Capka, who had completed almost 52 missions by August 1941. He was awarded the Distinguished Flying Medal and the Czech War Cross. Capka later became a very successful night-fighter pilot serving for a time at Coltishall. In June 1944 whilst in a Mosquito squadron, he was returning from a sortie over France when he spotted a badly damaged B-24 Liberator. Capka moved in close with the intention of escorting the damaged aircraft back to England only to be immediately attacked by the B-24 gunners. His aircraft was severely damaged and as he attempted a belly-landing his aircraft exploded in flames and Capka was blinded and badly burned.

During the early months of 1942 Coastal Command forces were being strengthened for the desperate 'Battle of the Atlantic' and in April the Czech squadron was transferred to 19 Group. However aggrieved the Czech airmen felt at being withdrawn from what they considered was the front line, they quickly adapted to their new operations and within four months had claimed their first U-boat sinking.

When the decision was made that Mildenhall in Suffolk was to be provided with long concrete runways, an airfield had to be found for No 115 squadron and as East Wretham was not occupied at the time it seemed an ideal choice. On 21st November the distinctive sound of Wellingtons was heard once again over East Wretham. They stayed until the end of August 1943 when the doughty Wimpys were phased out as a main strike bomber. In their place came a Lancaster Conversion Unit with Lancaster Mark IIs, which had become everlastingly famous with the public as a result of the immortal raid on the Mohne and Eder dams in May of the same year. Unfortunately the training unit was not without its tragic mishaps; one Lancaster with an instructor and four pilots on board banked very steeply in front of the control tower narrowly missing it but in the process the wing-tip hit the concrete apron and crumbled to the ground bursting into such such fierce flames that none of the pilots could be rescued.

115 squadron was quickly into operations with its Lancasters, first mine-laying, then targets in France and towards the end of March to Berlin. The crews were no doubt fired by Air Marshal Harris's message,'Tonight you go to the Big City. You have the opportunity to light a fire in the belly of the enemy and burn his black heart out'! The three raids undertaken in March were not overly successful; the crews faced enormous operational difficulties – rain, hail, electric storms and icing – besides enemy searchlights, flak and night fighters. The latter were particularly numerous on the night of 29th when 115 took part. It would be the end of the year before the 'Battle of Berlin' began in earnest but by that time the squadron had left. East Wretham now awaited the arrival of the Americans and the 359th Fighter Group.

The Group had left the United States in early October 1943 and the three squadrons – 368, 369 and 370 – began landing at the airfield during the last week of the month. They were equipped with P-47D Thunderbolts exactly the same as their colleagues at Bodney, some eight miles almost due north across the military training area. The

359th Fighter Group operated P-47D Thunderbolts from East Wretham. (USAF)

locals had already become quite used to the noise and sight of these 'flying milk bottles' thundering their way low over the Norfolk countryside.

Just as at Bodney steel sheeting and matting was required to take the weight of the very heavy fighters. Members of the Group were not particularly impressed with their new home or its facilities. The Nissen huts were considered just barely adequate (they should have been there a couple of years earlier!) and as for breakfasts, '... if I may be flexible with the term... consisted of Brussels sprouts, powdered eggs and an eerie liquid which with unbounded imagination the English called coffee!'

The 359th became the eighth Fighter Group to join the Eighth Air Force and they launched their first mission on 13th December 1943. It was quite a formidable force of fighters that took to the air but the sheer number of aircraft taking part could not disguise the fact that the P-47s were not the most ideal of escort fighters, their designated role was that of a ground strike fighter. But until the long-range P-51 Mustangs were available in sufficient numbers the Thunderbolts would have to continue their main and almost sole task of escorting the Eighth's heavy bombers, or at least as far as their limited range would allow.

Besides lettering each Fighter Group had its own individual markings, 359's aircraft had bright green propellers as well as green side and bottom cowlings. When their escort duties would allow, the Group was also employed on ground strafing attacks on airfields in northern France. On 23rd April 1944 17 of the aircraft were fitted with bombs and sent on a dive bombing mission but the results were anything but spectacular. Only on the previous day Group fighters had been part of a massive 859 fighter support force to the marshalling yards at Hamm during which the Group claimed seven fighters destroyed for the loss of just one aircraft. Towards the end of the month their P-51 Mustangs began to arrive and the first few flew operationally on 3rd May.

Without doubt the North American Mustang was the most successful American fighter of the war. It had been originally designed and developed as a result of a British contract and the Mustangs were first used by the RAF in the summer of 1942. The RAF recommended that it be equipped with a Rolls Royce Merlin engine (similar to Spitfires) and from then on their performance as long-range escort and pursuit fighters was almost without rival. With a speed well in excess of 400 mph at 25,000 feet, a range of over 2,000 miles and with an endurance of eight hours, they single-handedly turned the tables as far as the Eighth's bombing offensive was concerned. When they finally arrived in force over the German skies the days of the Luftwaffe fighters were numbered and the Mustangs were only seriously challenged by the appearance in the latter stages of the war of the German rocket and turbo-jet fighters. Unfortunately, the aircraft did bear a strong resemblance to the Me109 and there were several instances of P-51s being shot at by 'friendly' bombers so white recognition bands were painted around the nose, wings and tail.

With an increasing number of P-51s coming on to squadron strength, May 1943 proved to be a very hectic month for the East Wretham Group, their fighters ranged over targets as far as eastern Germany and Poland – a distance of some 1,470 miles. They were also involved in several missions over France aimed at trains and other railway communications, these were appropriately called 'Chattanoogas'. On 23rd May the Group, along with their near neighbours 361 Group from Bottisham in Cambridgeshire, sent over 100 P-51s to bomb a railway bridge at Hasselt in Belgium. Seventeen tons of bombs were dropped for the loss of just one aircraft – a far, far cry from the early days of 1940 when the RAF Battles took such a heavy beating over the very same area.

By the evening of Saturday 3rd June, it was obvious to all at East Wretham that the invasion of Europe was imminent. Everybody was confined to the airfield and each aircraft was carefully serviced, fully armed and fuelled. Each was painted with broad black and white recognition stripes and then covered up to ensure that the secret markings would not be seen. Every Fighter Group was given a particular area to patrol and were told that not only would they provide escorts for the heavy bombers but they were also to fly patrols continually throughout the day. On the big day itself the greatest risk was not from enemy fighters but from collisions in the air because there were so many aircraft in such a relatively small air space. On the days following the invasion the Group flew endless sorties in support of the Allied armies in Normandy.

By late June the Group returned to normal duties and on 28th July it made the first positive sighting of the new German menace – Me163 – a rocket-powered fighter. The arrival of this new fighter was not too great a surprise as intelligence sources had already established their existence and indeed a silhouette drawing had been circulated to all Groups. Nevertheless the thought that the P-51s would soon be faced with an enemy fighter capable of a speed in excess of 500 mph did provide some speculation. In the following month the Group's fighters were over Leipzig when they sighted the distinctive thick rocket trails of the new fighter. One probable victory was claimed by First Lieutenant Cyril Jones. This brilliant young

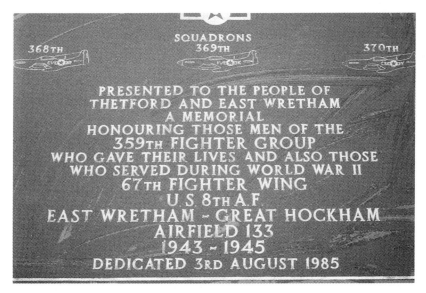

Memorial to 359th Fighter Group.

fighter pilot had claimed a victory on his very first mission but unfortunately he was lost on his 16th mission when he had six victories to his credit.

Unlike many Fighter Groups the 359th was not particularly noted for its fighter aces, except for Captain Roy Wetmore, who would survive the war with 22½ enemy aircraft to his credit, making him one of the leading fighter aces of the Eighth Air Force. Wetmore was promoted to Major in 1945 and given command of the 370th squadron. He flew a total of 142 missions and remained in the American Air Force after the war but was unfortunately killed in a flying accident in 1951.

The Group's greatest achievement came on 11th September when the Eighth Air Force's fighters were engaged in a massive air combat over southern Germany, which ended in an unprecedented total of 118 enemy fighters destroyed, and of this number the Group claimed 26 destroyed and many others damaged. For their part in this air battle the 359th was awarded a Distinguished Unit Citation. But November 1944 was to prove the critical month when four major fighter air battles were fought in the German skies. The Group's aircraft were active in all of them and on 26th November Captain Crenshaw of 359th became 'an ace in a day' with five Fw190s positively destroyed and a number of probables also claimed by him.

By the New Year the other new German 'secret' weapon – Me262 – a turbo-propelled fighter – was beginning to make its presence felt. It was not until February that the Group claimed its first Me262 and any victory over these aircraft was considered quite a considerable coup especially as they were much faster than the P-51s. The Group took an active part in the Arnhem landings, the battle in the Ardennes and also supported the Allied armies in the crossing of the Rhine. It flew its last mission on 20th April having then completed 346 and accounted for the destruction of 263 aircraft in the air with almost another 100 on the ground, for the loss of 106 aircraft and pilots. The Group did not leave for the States until the beginning of November 1945.

The airfield was then taken back by the RAF and later used as a Polish settlement camp. Much of the land was sold off in the late 1950s. The site of the airfield is off the main A1075 and some of the original huts are still being used by the military although the area is full of 'Out of Bounds' signs. On the war memorial outside the village church is another commemorative plaque to the 359th Fighter Group.

10

FELTWELL

Feltwell was one of only five pre-war airfields situated in Norfolk. It had been constructed in those early, heady days of the newly formed Bomber Command; a confident time when the Command's dogged belief in the omnipotence of heavy bombers still had to be tested in a war environment. Therefore right from the outset Feltwell was destined to operate as a heavy bomber station and was placed in No 3 Group as were the Command's other airfields in East Anglia.

When Feltwell opened in April 1937 the airfield quickly stamped its presence on the flat surrounding countryside, built as it was on the very edge of Norfolk's fenland. Pre-war permanent RAF stations were constructed to a very high standard of comfort and amenities, attention even being paid to their architectural merit! Most of the accommodation blocks were two storied and, along with the technical support buildings, were solidly constructed of brick; but they were not quite so grand or aesthetically pleasing as the officers' mess and headquarters building. The dominant features of the airfield were the five large and gabled 'C' type concrete hangars reaching over 50 feet high, making them the most prominent landmarks – or eyesores, depending on one's viewpoint – for miles around. But all airfields, old or new, shared the same unmistakable trademarks – a control tower, one or two tall and rather ugly water towers and the inevitable wind sock.

Within a few days of its formal opening Feltwell welcomed its first squadron – No 214 – along with its aircraft, the Handley Page Harrows. These aircraft were the first of Bomber Command's new heavy bombers. They were twin-engined with the then new innovation of powered gun turrets in both the nose and tail positions. At least they looked like modern bombers but although they had only recently entered the Service they were not destined to see much war action. By the end of April a new squadron – No 37 – was formed out of 'B' Flight of No 214, giving Feltwell its correct pre-war operational complement of two squadrons, each comprising twelve aircraft, though later the size of squadrons would increase to 16 and by 1944/5 to 20 aircraft. The two squadrons eagerly awaited re-equipment with yet another new bomber, which was slowly but steadily coming off the production lines – the Vickers Wellington. During that last summer of peace Wellingtons began to arrive at Feltwell.

For virtually the next three years Feltwell would be solely a Wellington station. This aircraft, designed by Barnes Wallis of the bouncing bomb fame, proved to be one of the most successful bombers of the Second World War rivalled only by the famous Avro Lancaster. It was produced in far greater numbers than any other RAF bomber – the Lancaster included. For the early years of the war it formed the backbone of Bomber Command and because it was featured in the famous documentary *Target for Tonight*, it became synonymous with Bomber Command.

The Wellington also proved to be a most versatile aircraft, it was adapted for a wide range of operational duties within Bomber Command, operated with great success as a U-boat seeker with Coastal Command, and as a freight and troop carrier and was used in experimental and development work. The aircraft was universally popular with all its crews, who fondly dubbed it the 'Wimpy' after J. Wellington Wimpy, a character in the early Popeye cartoons. With its most unusual and quite unique geodetic structure, derived in some measure from the airship R101, it quickly proved that it could survive considerable damage – an attribute that saved the lives of many a wartime aircrew.

At the outbreak of the war No 3 Group had six squadrons of Wellingtons and although some rather abortive sorties were mounted to seek out enemy shipping, it was not until December 1939 that No 3 Group's Wellingtons saw action and when they did it proved to be somewhat brutal. At the beginning of the month 24 Wellingtons from neighbouring airfields – Marham, Honington and Mildenhall – set out to attack German warships in the Heligoland Bight, which resulted in a German AA battery being bombed by accident and this was considered to be the first British bomb to fall on Germany in World War II. All the aircraft arrived back safely thus giving Bomber Command's chiefs an encouraging but very false sense of security.

So, on 14th December, a further twelve Wellingtons were ordered to attack the German cruisers *Nurnberg* and *Leipzig*, which were thought to have been damaged and making slow progress back to port. This second operation was an utter disaster, no damage was inflicted and five aircraft were shot down with another crashing on landing at Newmarket airfield. But even this somewhat abortive mission did little to dent the Command's confidence, as they felt the losses had been due to flak rather than enemy fighter action although the Wellingtons had been engaged in fighting off repeated attacks by Me109s!

Then on Monday morning of 18th December orders came through for yet another attack and this time No 37 squadron at Feltwell would be involved. The news of the first mission quickly spread around the airfield, 'They've found the German navy and we're going to Wilhelmshaven to attack them . . .' The operational orders were very precise: '. . . to attack enemy warships in the Schillig Roads or Wilhelmshaven at a height of at least 10,000 feet [believed to be beyond the range of effective flak]. Great care is to taken that no bombs fall on the shore, and no merchant ships are to be attacked. Formations shall not loiter in the target areas and all aircraft are to complete bombing as soon as possible after the sighting signal has been made.' Such instructions now seem rather naive!

At precisely 9.30 am six of Feltwell's Wellingtons took off and joined 18 others from Honington and Mildenhall but soon two (not from No 37 squadron) had to return to base because of engine trouble, leaving just 22 droning over the North Sea at a steady speed of about 190 mph. By 12.30 they were in sight of the German coast, it was a clear and cloudless day, perfect for the bombing mission. But the enemy fighter squadrons were waiting; the aircraft had been

Wellington IC – 1941.

picked up by the two German experimental 'Freya' radar stations on Heligoland and Wangerooge (there is a 'Freya' aerial on view at the Imperial War Museum at Duxford). About 45 minutes later the warships were sighted but as they were considered too close to the land Squadron Leader Kellett ordered his crews not to bomb. The whole mission was beginning to assume the mantle of a tragic farce. The Wellingtons managed to survive a quite heavy flak attack and were just turning to return home when they were set upon by a large formation of Me109s and Me110s. Because No 37 squadron were holding the rear of the formation they were the first to be attacked. The first real air battle of the war took just 30 minutes, which says much for the stubborn resistance of the Wellingtons and their gunners, but by the end of the enemy's attack twelve Wellingtons had been shot down with 13 enemy fighters destroyed – the air gunners had done exceedingly well. Soon the surviving Wellingtons passed beyond the German fighters' range and when they were some distance off the Norfolk coast two aircraft ditched in the sea and another one crash-landed at Coltishall. All six of Feltwell's Wellingtons failed to return and just a few of their crews survived as prisoners-of-war. This disastrous operation is now considered one of the most significant aerial combats of the war. It virtually brought to a halt daylight missions by heavy bombers without fighter escort and it exploded the long-held myth of the invincibility of heavy bombers operating in close formation. The lessons learnt in December became a major consideration in determining Bomber Command's ultimate offensive strategy – night bombing.

By coincidence, whilst I was researching this operation, the deaths were announced of two old and famous airmen – one British and the other German – both of whom had been greatly involved in these early operations. Flying Officer (later Group Captain) Ken Batchelor flew Wellingtons with No 9 squadron from Honington and he took part in the very first mission of the war (4th December) as well as two operations in December. On the German side was Johannes Steinhoff (later General), who was an early Luftwaffe fighter ace, and was credited with at least one of the Wellingtons shot down on the fateful raid on 18th December. Steinhoff later became Chief of Staff of the Luftwaffe (1966-70). Both men died in February 1994 within two days of each other.

Fortunately for Feltwell's rather beleaguered squadrons the severe weather of January and February 1940 greatly curtailed all air operations but then as the weather conditions eased the crews were employed in dropping propaganda leaflets or 'Nickel' raids as they were code-named, though the aircrews called them 'confetti throwing' and some were even less complimentary. As these operations were conducted at night they were considered very good training enabling the crews to gain valuable experience at night-flying – indeed sometimes the flights lasted up to ten hours. The so-called 'targets' were as diverse as Hamburg, Brunswick, Luneburg, Berlin, Prague and even Warsaw and these cities were showered with tons upon tons of these 'bomphlets' as *Punch* magazine insisted on calling them. They were, according to Winston Churchill, designed 'to rouse the Germans to a higher morality'! By the end of the war it was reckoned that no fewer than 30 leaflets had been dropped for every *single* man, woman and child in Western Europe. The costs in printing and despatching such a massive amount of paper were colossal and quite outweighed the propaganda value.

In the first months of 1940 there arrived at Feltwell a Flight of New Zealand airmen with their Wellingtons, and by April this Flight was formed into a new squadron in its own right – No 75. Both New Zealand and Australian pilots and crews made a massive contribution to Bomber Command throughout the war. With the opening of the Norwegian campaign, in April, Nos 37 and 75 squadrons became very active in attacking targets in Denmark and Norway. They were involved on 12th April in a raid directed on Stavanger harbour, which proved to be the RAF's biggest operation of the war so far and on this occasion just one Feltwell aircraft failed to return. On several other missions they were not so fortunate and each squadron suffered quite heavy losses. On just one operation the New Zealanders lost four aircraft to enemy fighters and five more crashed on return to Feltwell.

The 37th squadron, affectionately known as '37th Foot' was taken off operations in November 1940 to prepare itself for transfer to the Middle East and Malta in particular. Swiftly in their place came No 57 squadron equipped with the faithful Wellingtons and they were almost immediately transferred to Feltwell's satellite airfield 'just up the road' at Methwold. Early in the New Year the squadron became fully operational making several missions to the Ruhr and then on 23rd March they suffered heavy losses during a raid on Berlin.

One of the most famous New Zealand pilots to serve at Feltwell at this time was Flight Lieutenant Fred 'Popeye' Lucas. During June 1940 he had been on missions to Bremen, Hamburg, Lubeck, Gotha, Dusseldorf and Aachen and yet somehow managed to survive! By the middle of September he had completed 40 operations – quite an amazing feat especially at that time of the war. He was then taken off active duties to become an instructor on Wellingtons but returned to Feltwell later with the rank of Squadron Leader and was involved in the famous raid on Brest in July 1941. Because of the high standard of bombing accuracy required this was a daylight attack carried out by 79 Wellingtons on the two Germany heavy vessels *Gneisenau* and *Prinz Eugen*. The Wellington force encountered heavy and accurate flak over the target area as well as being attacked by a strong number of enemy fighters. Ten aircraft were lost and over half the remainder were severely damaged. Lucas survived this mission and indeed finished a second tour, ending the war as a Wing Commander.

The one New Zealand pilot from No 75 squadron to gain lasting fame was Sergeant James Ward, who arrived at Feltwell on 13th June 1941 and was appointed as co-pilot to Squadron Leader Widdowson, a very experienced pilot and pre-war regular officer. On the night of 7th July 1941 the target was Munster in western Germany and Widdowson's aircraft was one of the ten Wellingtons detailed from Feltwell for the mission. On the return flight the aircraft was repeatedly attacked by a solitary Me110, which Sergeant Box, the rear gunner, managed to destroy. But quite severe damage had already been sustained by the Wellington, its hydraulics system was severed, the wireless equipment as well as the intercom had been shattered and the cockpit was filled with smoke and fumes. The major concern was a fire coming from a split fuel line to the starboard engine, quickly growing in intensity, its flames threatening to engulf the whole wing. Widdowson told Ward to tell the crew to get ready to bale out and added almost in passing 'and see if you can put that ****** fire out.'

Ward and the navigator, Sergeant Lawson, tore a hole in the fuselage with the intention of directing a fire extinguisher on to the blaze but the force of the aircraft's slipstream only resulted in the liquid splashing back in their faces. Ward then decided that the only way to deal with the fire was to crawl out on the wing! Despite all Lawson's efforts to dissuade him from such a foolhardy action, Ward was adamant that this was the only way to save the aircraft. A rope was attached around his waist, which was then anchored to Lawson. After removing the 30" diameter perspex astrodome, Ward managed to clamber on to the fuselage. Although the aircraft was flying at the lowest possible speed of some 100 mph, the force of the wind was terrifying, but Ward managed to scramble forward and lay flat on the wing with his feet secured by the toe-holes he had kicked in the fuselage fabric. After many abortive attempts Ward finally succeeded in stuffing a canvas top into the fire, which was just sufficient to divert the flames from the engine. Although the fire had not been extinguished it had been considerably reduced and Ward had certainly prevented it from spreading any further. He battled his way back inch by inch until he was physically hauled back into the aircraft by Lawson. Ward collapsed in a state of complete and utter exhaustion, quite unable to speak or move. Although the brakes and flaps were not operating Widdowson managed with great skill to land the crippled aircraft at Newmarket airfield, needing the whole of the runway to do so, and the aircraft was finally brought to a halt only by the wire perimeter fence.

The crew arrived back at Feltwell by nine o'clock in the morning and after the debriefing Ward's only recorded comment was that it had been 'a dicey trip'! Widdowson and the squadron commander recommended Ward for the Victoria Cross for his quite incredible feat of bravery, all the more admirable as it had been undertaken with calm deliberation and not in the heat of battle. The award was approved at all levels and appeared in the *London Gazette* on 5th August. Two days later a grand celebratory dinner was held at Feltwell. Ward was given his own crew and aircraft and was soon back in action. Sadly, on 15th September, whilst engaged on a mission to Hamburg his aircraft was caught in searchlights and shot down, only two of the crew escaped. Ward and three of his crew are buried in Ohlsdorf cemetery in Hamburg.

The last big operational missions mounted from Feltwell took place during late May and June 1942. Their Wellingtons formed just a small part of Air Marshal Harris's 'Operation Millenium' – the three 1,000 bomber raids. On 30th May, the date of the first raid on Cologne, 47 Wellingtons left Feltwell and as one eye-witness recalled, 'There was just a long queue of bombers, they took off two at a time at a fantastic rate ... one every six seconds, it was a wonderful sight ... but the noise was deafening ... ' One pilot later described the scene over Cologne, ' ... the traffic over the target area was something you had to go through to believe. There were so many aircraft that it was literally like rush hour in a three dimensional circus ... ' Two nights later it was Essen and then on the night of 25th June Bremen was subjected to this intense and terrifying bombardment. In the first two raids Feltwell had sent out more Wellingtons than any other Bomber Command station and although overall the losses were not that high – a total of 121 aircraft destroyed or just over 4%, the Wellington squadrons did suffer heavily and these three missions at last suggested that perhaps the operational life of the dear old 'Wimpys' was nearly over.

On 15th August 1942 when No 2 Group took over Feltwell and its satellite Methwold, the Wellingtons disappeared for ever from Feltwell (or so it was thought at the time) to be replaced by Lockheed Venturas – an American built light bomber. Feltwell again found itself becoming the home of New Zealand airmen when a new squadron was formed – No 487 – and this was followed a month later with yet another new squadron – No 464 – manned almost entirely by Australian airmen.

Towards the end of 1943 it was decided that No 3 Group's squadrons would at long last be supplied with Avro Lancasters as they were now coming off the production lines in sufficient numbers. A training and conversion unit was needed for the pilots and crews and the unit was established at Feltwell. So from December 1943 until virtually the end of the war the airfield was almost solely involved in Lancaster training, becoming known as the 'Finishing School'! Although its operational days seemed past they were never forgotten.

11
FERSFIELD

The secrets of Norfolk's most mysterious airfield have been swallowed up amidst the quiet and secluded countryside to the east of the Lophams in the far south of the county. The lack of surviving evidence might suggest that the airfield was deliberately constructed in such a cloistered backwater purely for its use for highly secret operations. But such prescience was surely lacking in the then desperate rush of airfield construction in 1942/3. The site was allocated to the USAAF in August 1942 and went under the name Winfarthing, but because of delays the airfield was not finished until a year later, by which time its name had changed to Fersfield. The Americans did not allocate it to a specific Bomb Group although it was built to the full specifications of similar Norfolk airfields. It was merely held in reserve and earmarked for 'special projects', which could really cover a multitude of sins.

Fersfield is now solely remembered for two secret projects and just one very special RAF mission. The first German V1 rocket (flying bomb) was launched on 13th June 1944. It was this opening shot of the so-called second Battle of Britain that really activated the Americans to bring their own 'guided weapon' into operational use. This was effectively using battle worn B-17s, removing all the extraneous material before fitting them with radio receiving sets and then packing the aircraft with ten tons of explosives. The method of operation was for the 'robot' aircraft to be flown manually by a two-man crew until radio contact was ensured with the 'guide' aircraft; the two men would then bale out to allow the robot to be directed on to the target – known V1 rocket sites – by control from the guide aircraft. The whole project was code-named 'Aphrodite' and the first trial flight was authorised for action on 23rd June.

The project had been given to 388th Bomb Group at Knettishall, just over the boundary in Suffolk. On 7th July it was agreed that RAF Woodbridge would be used for the launches as an extra large runway was required. But there was much concern about the increasing number of damaged aircraft that were using Woodbridge as a haven and the very real risk of a collision with one of the loaded robot aircraft, with disastrous results! Therefore the search was on for a quiet and isolated airfield from which to mount the operations and what better choice than Fersfield? The unit moved there on 15th July and with them came a special unit of the United States Navy who also wanted part of the action. The US Navy had also been working on robot weapons and their project was code-named 'Anvil'.

The first two 'Aphrodite' missions were launched on 4th August, the first went off well but the second malfunctioned and the robot bomber landed in a wood near Sudbourne Park in Suffolk with an almighty explosion leaving a crater over 100 feet in diameter! Further attempts were made the same day but without much success. Two days later another two launches were made but because of problems with the radio control both fell harmlessly into the sea.

The US Navy despatched its first robot – a Liberator – on 12th August, targeted to a V1 site at Mimoyecques. The robot aircraft was piloted by Lieutenant Joseph Kennedy, the eldest son of the ex-US Ambassador to Britain and brother of John F. Kennedy, the future President. The robot headed out towards Southwold and at an altitude of 2,000 feet it exploded killing Kennedy and his radio-control engineer. The wreckage was strewn over a wide area, and his body was never recovered, but his name does appear on the memorial wall of the American Cemetery at Madingley. The second and last 'Anvil' operation was made on 3rd September, this time, because the rocket sites had been captured by the Allied armies, the target selected was Heligoland. Everything went well until the radio operator mistakenly aimed for the wrong island! During October there were four more attempts from Fersfield, all of which failed to hit their targets, one even deviated so far off target that it landed in southern Sweden.

By November the 'Aphrodite' project and all its support team had left Fersfield and returned to Knettishall from where two more robots were despatched but again without a great deal of success. The following month Fersfield passed to the RAF and placed in No 2 Group. It was used mainly as a training base for its crews though some operational missions were flown by the Group's Support Unit using Mitchells. These aircraft, produced by North American

Lieutenant Joseph Kennedy. (US Navy)

Aviation, were one of the most successful light/medium bombers of the Second World War, and were used by both Air Forces, although the Americans favoured their designation as B-25s. The aircraft had been named after General 'Billy' Mitchell, one of the pioneers of American aviation.

Then in mid-March 1945, 18 Mosquitos from 21, 464 and 487 squadrons arrived at Fersfield for a special and secret mission; all three squadrons were then serving in Belgium and a British airfield was needed to mount the operation. The crews were briefed very carefully, the target was to be the Shellhaus building in the centre of Copenhagen, the headquarters of the Gestapo in Denmark which housed all their records of Danish resistance workers. Allied intelligence sources had uncovered an imminent mass arrest of the leaders and the object was to set fire to the building in order to destroy the records. The attack, which would require pin-point bombing accuracy, was led by Group Captain R.H. Bateson of No 21 squadron, who had led the first Mosquito raid of this type in April of the previous year to the Gestapo headquarters in the Hague.

The Mosquitos, accompanied by Mustangs of 64 squadron from RAF Bentwaters, took off on 20th March in perfect spring weather. By the time they had reached the Danish coast they encountered cloudy conditions. It was about noon when they flew over Copenhagen and the city streets were crowded with people. The leading aircraft hit the target very precisely and one of the crews reported seeing the bombs entering the building between the first and second floors. One aircraft flew so low that it crashed into a flag pole. The Gestapo building was set ablaze and many of the records were destroyed.

One of the Mosquitos, piloted by Wing Commander Kliboe, hit a bridge on its approach and the aircraft crashed into a nearby school. Tragically some of the following aircraft assumed that the explosion marked the target and bombed the school with their usual devastating accuracy causing many grievous casualties. Four Mosquitos and two Mustangs failed to return from the mission and one heavily damaged Mosquito flew back on only one engine and crash-landed in England. In August 1945 the RAF presented a cheque of 470,000 kroner (about £20,000) to the Crown Prince of Denmark as a contribution to the Danish civilians injured in the three Mosquito raids on Gestapo buildings in Denmark.

12
FOULSHAM

Foulsham was a perfect example of a wartime Norfolk airfield rushed into operational use well before it was fully prepared. It had been designed to take heavy bombers and was granted full station status in May 1942. Rather surprisingly the following month the airfield was allocated to No 2 Group, which implied that either the American built Douglas Bostons or Lockheed Venturas would be arriving, but as two new squadrons were being formed at West Raynham it was found that the Foulsham station was in no sense ready for operational flying; the airfield was choked with mud and the accommodation still very basic and incomplete.

But because of the serious congestion at RAF West Raynham, the new squadrons – Nos 98 and 180 – were nevertheless moved to Foulsham during the second week of October. Not flying Bostons or Venturas but yet another American built light/medium bomber – North American Mitchell IIs or B-25s – which were completely new to the RAF. The first aircraft had only arrived at Bodney in July and had quickly moved to West Raynham for the slow process of familiarisation for both the aircrews and ground personnel.

This twin-engined day bomber had first flown in late 1940 and came into service with the USAAF about six months later. It had been named after General 'Billy' Mitchell, one of the pioneers of American aviation and an early advocate of bombers as the main air attack force. It had a relatively low cruising speed between 180-230 mph, was well armed with six guns and had a bomb load of 4,000 pounds. Its drawbacks, which were later exposed in operations, were its relative slowness and its lack of manoeuvrability, at least compared with its rival the Douglas Boston. Although basically a land-based aircraft, the Mitchells gained early fame in April 1942 when General 'Jimmie'

Mitchell II of 180 Squadron, July 1943.

Doolittle led a formation from an aircraft carrier to bomb Tokyo for the first time. The Mitchell proved to be a quite successful light bomber with the RAF although No 2 Group only ever had five squadrons of Mitchells in operational use. But as the Group had to rely on American aircraft to continue their operations it is understandable why so many hopes were rested in the new Mosquito aircraft then slowly coming into operation.

The Mitchells were beset by teething troubles. The guns and turrets needed certain alterations and the engines required some modification. It was hoped that the two Mitchell squadrons from Foulsham would contribute to the Group's largest operation of the war so far – the attack on Philips Works at Eindhoven in December 1942 but they were still not ready for action. This proved to be a blessing in disguise as the Group planners had enough problems mounting the operation with a mixed force of aircraft all with different operational speeds, and using the Mitchells would only have further complicated matters. It is rather easy to forget the contribution made by the 'backroom' planners of Bomber Command's wartime operations; with different aircraft taking part the Eindhoven mission required tight and precise scheduling and close liaison was needed with the various fighter squadrons detailed to give escort support.

It was not until well into the New Year that the Foulsham squadrons set off on their first mission. On 22nd January six aircraft from each squadron bombed oil installations at Ghent in Belgium. Unfortunately three aircraft were lost on this raid including that of Wing Commander C. Hodder, the Commander of 180 squadron. This was a grievous blow as Hodder had worked tirelessly to bring his squadron up to an operational standard. During February and March both squadrons were actively engaged in air/sea rescue duties, flying well over 100 sorties during the period.

By the time the two squadrons were ready to move to Dunsford, Surrey they had completed over 250 sorties mainly over Holland and northern France – targets such as Flushing, Boulogne, Abbeville and St Omer airfields and the power station at Ghent. Like most of No 2 Group's squadrons the Mitchells had been moved into Fighter Command on 1st June 1943 to form part of the Second Tactical Air Force. The squadrons were preparing to join in 'Operation Starkey', which was intended to persuade the Luftwaffe to transfer forces from Italy and also simulate preparations for a 'phoney' invasion by making heavy attacks on enemy airfields and communication centres. This operation is now accepted as a dismal failure.

In the late afternoon of 26th July there was a full emergency alert at the airfield as a badly damaged B-17 from No 92 Bomb Group (then at Alconbury) made its very tentative approach. This aircraft named *Ruthie II* had suffered a frontal attack from a Fw190 over Hanover leaving its pilot mortally wounded and with most of the crew unconscious because the oxygen lines had been shattered. The second pilot – Flying Officer John Morgan – had with great skill and courage managed to keep the aircraft in formation despite the fact that the pilot's body was heavily slumped over the controls and the cockpit window had been shattered. Morgan landed the B-17 safely at Foulsham and for his remarkable feat of flying he was later awarded the Medal of Honor. Morgan, although he was a Texan, had volunteered and flown with the Royal Canadian Air Force for seven months before he transferred to the Eighth Air Force – hence his rank of Flying Officer rather than Lieutenant.

With the departure of Foulsham's Mitchells, the airfield was transferred to No 3 Group, which would at last bring some heavy bombers for which the airfield had been designed. On 1st September the first Avro Lancasters arrived to form a new squadron – No 514. The Lancasters, according to Air Chief Marshal Sir Arthur Harris, had been the greatest single factor in winning the Second World War in Europe. The Mark II Lancasters were powered by Bristol Hercules engines rather than the Merlin engines that were normal in the other Marks and were fairly rare, only 300 were produced compared with over 7,000 of the other Marks.

After a long delay the squadron were at last active on the night of 3/4th November when two aircraft were despatched to bomb the

Bylaugh Hall: headquarters of No 2 Group and later No 100 Group Bomber Command.

Mannesmann works at Dusseldorf, whilst another four Lancasters laid mines just off the German coast. The squadron had only time to mount a handful of missions before there were more organisational changes in Bomber Command, which resulted in Foulsham being hived off to become part of a new Group numbered 100. Thus, on 23rd November, the Lancasters left for Waterbeach, which became the squadron's home for the rest of the war.

Although the RAF had developed many jamming devices to disrupt the enemy's radio communications and radar signals over the previous 18 months, it was now thought necessary to centralise all the various operations into one Group. Such a move was essential especially as the Command was about to enter upon its most intensive period of bombing of the whole war. A new Group was formed – No 100 (Special Duties) to provide a co-ordinated effort as well as further develop and trial other counter measures and equipment. No 80 Wing, which had hitherto been responsible for the programme, was moved to West Raynham to form the nucleus of the new Group. By January 1944 the Group's headquarters moved to Bylaugh Hall, a Victorian country house near Swanton Morley, now alas in ruins.

The Group was ordered to give direct support to night bombing by attacking enemy fighters and their airfields. Its squadrons would use the various radio counter measures in existence in an attempt to deceive or negate enemy radar systems and radio signals. All the intelligence relating to the enemy's radar and signalling systems had to be examined, as well as the movement and use of their fighter aircraft, and methods devised to counter their efficacy. The Group's motto 'Confound and Destroy' succinctly summed up its activities.

Nine airfields, all located in Norfolk, had been allocated to the new Group and by mid-December 1943 it had received six squadrons and one flight equipped with vastly diverse types of aircraft from Ansons, Defiants to Wellingtons and Halifaxes with the odd sprinkling of Mosquitos. But by the end of the war there were less than 14 squadrons operating the many complicated jamming devices that had been developed. By the very nature of their operations it was difficult to judge how successful the Group became in achieving its objectives, but undoubtedly the Group made a valuable and very essential contribution to the Command's war effort.

Foulsham's first squadron arrived on 27th November from nearby Feltwell in Norfolk, which had been engaged for the previous twelve months on 'Elint' duties, the gathering of information by electronic means of the operation and performance of the enemy's electronic equipment – hence 'ELectronic INTelligence'. For this special task No 192(SD) squadron was equipped with a mixture of Wellingtons and Halifaxes and from Foulsham they continued their operations to Belgium, Holland, Denmark and even as far away as Norway. In April a few Mosquitos were supplied to strengthen the force and on several occasions they operated over Berlin plotting and identifying the enemy's radar installations around this prime target. During the summer the squadron became involved in more offensive action, bombing targets in northern France and it lost just one Mosquito, and this to 'friendly' fire. Indeed during the squadron's service in the Group it had a very safe operational record.

In April a new Bomber Support Development was established at Foulsham with the express purpose of developing and trialling all the new equipment and the tactics which figured large in the Group's operations. The unit later moved to another 100 Group airfield – Swanton Morley. Then in the last days of December a RAAF squadron of Halifax IIIs – No 462 – came directly from RAF Driffield, although previously all its war service had been in the Middle East and Italy.

The Handley Page Halifax was the first four-engined bomber to attack Germany in March 1941. Despite some early problems (it had a higher loss rate than other heavy bombers) it developed into a most sturdy and reliable aircraft, well-appreciated by its crews, who dubbed it the 'Hallibag'. These aircraft very effectively supported Lancasters as the main attacking force of Bomber Command.

In the New Year aircraft of No 100 Group acted as 'window' carriers in various bombing operations as well as taking a light bomb load to be dropped in the first wave. 'Window' was bundles of metallic strip and proved to be the most simple and yet most effective countermeasure used by Bomber Command. It effectively created false radar signals, stimulating the same response as that of a large attacking force. There were at least twelve different types to be used against certain specific frequency bands.

Towards the end of the year FIDO (Fog Identification and Dispersal Operation) was installed along the airfield's main runway, which greatly enhanced the safety of operations during unfavourable weather conditions. Fog was dispersed by a parallel path of burning petrol cans along the runway; this proved most effective but pilots felt that it was like flying into 'the mouth of hell'. Normally only one airfield in an area was so equipped and Foulsham was the only Norfolk airfield to be supplied.

On 2/3rd May 1945 the Mosquitos from 192 squadron went out to Kiel on their last operational mission and the previous night the Halifaxes had been active on a 'spoof' raid to Flensberg. With these Foulsham's operational days came to a close. Many of the old wartime buildings can still be seen just east of the village off the A1067 road.

13
GREAT MASSINGHAM

A row of seven neat white headstones in a small country churchyard provides a moving and fitting memorial to the immense sacrifice made by so many young men who flew the Blenheims, the Bostons and the Mosquitos of Nos 2 and 100 Groups during the Second World War. That they stand in this quiet and secluded corner of Norfolk seems in some way appropriate as the two Groups they served were the Cinderellas of Bomber Command and the brave and daring exploits of their crews hardly ever reached public attention, the heavy bombers of the other Groups in the Command gaining all the attention and most of the acclaim.

The graves are to be found in Little Massingham's churchyard, close to the small wartime airfield that took its name from that most attractive of villages – Great Massingham. The airfield came into being during those dark days of 1940 as a satellite for nearby RAF West Raynham, which lay about two miles to the east of the grassed airfield. It was a bleak and chilly place perched above its eponymous village and it had the dubious honour of being the highest airfield in Norfolk, some 295 feet above sea level.

Its parent station was one of the major airfields of No 2 Group so it was inevitable that Bristol Blenheims would eventually appear at the airfield. During the beginning of September 1940 Blenheim IVs from No 18 squadron slowly began to arrive. This squadron had suffered severe losses during its time in France and later in the war it would acquire the unofficial title of 'Gloucester's own squadron'. By the time the aircrews were transferred to Great Massingham they were well experienced in attacking enemy airfields and had also been blooded over German targets. During the six months they operated from the satellite they mounted over 200 sorties despite the fact that

RAF graves in the churchyard at Little Massingham.

the winter of 1940/1 was one of the severest of the century. As the weather conditions eased in February the squadron mounted sorties over Hanover and its U-boat components factories as well as oil installations at Hamburg. But by April its crews had departed for the far greater comfort and elegance of Blicklington Hall, which accommodated the personnel of RAF Oulton.

The airfield had a quiet period until 11th May when the Blenheims of 107 squadron were brought down from Leuchars in Fifeshire, where they had been temporarily attached to Coastal Command. The squadron's reputation, until then, rested on the fact that five of its aircraft had attacked enemy shipping near Wilhelmshaven on 4th September 1939, which was the first bombing raid of the war. It had been commanded, until May 1940, by Wing Commander Basil Embry DSO, DFC, one of the most famous RAF commanders of the war.

On 13th May No 107 launched its first operation to Heligoland; twelve aircraft took off, two returned early but the rest bombed very successfully and for this mission the squadron received a commendation from Air Vice-Marshal A. Lees, the Air Officer Commanding of No 2 Group. When they returned to the same target about a week later, they attacked at low level and paid with the loss of one aircraft. The following month was a very active period with strikes over Dunkirk and the island of Sylt, just off the Danish coast, during which five aircraft were lost. On 4th July the squadron was part of the famous Bremen mission, which resulted in Wing Commander 'Hughie' Edwards gaining a Victoria Cross. On this raid two of the squadron's aircraft were shot down, one of which was piloted by the squadron commander, Wing Commander L. Petley, and unfortunately his successor only lasted another six days.

The second major operation in which the squadron was involved was No 2 Group's onslaught on the Knapsack and Quadrath power stations near Cologne on 12th August, when 58 Blenheims from various Norfolk airfields made a daring low-level and daylight attack. This mission was heralded by the Group as 'the operation of the war' and all the crews taking part had been buoyed up for over a week. The Blenheims faced ferocious ground fire and the short but terrifying attack proved to be highly effective, crews reported that they had seen 'bomb hits between rows of chimneys and clouds of heavy black smoke'. Ten aircraft failed to return – an acceptably high loss (17%), I think the Group planners had expected this to be much higher. The Great Massingham squadron lost just one aircraft but all the rest sustained damage from heavy flak. No 107 had one celebrated member – Pilot Officer 'Bill' Edrich, the England cricketer, as well as Flight Sergeant Kenneth Wolstenholme, later to become well known as a BBC sports commentator. Within a week of the Cologne raid the squadron was detached to Malta where even sterner challenges awaited its crews.

Earlier in the year considerable interest was aroused at the airfield with the arrival of a couple of Boeing B-17 'Flying Fortresses' from No 90 squadron at West Raynham. Although the small airfield was hardly suitable for this heavy bomber, it flew from there on several trial and test flights as well as mounting some operations during June until a more suitable airfield was found. For the whole sorry story of the RAF's use of these aircraft see West Raynham.

When 107 squadron returned from Malta it had been so thoroughly mauled that it had to be reformed and 1942 brought forth a new aircraft – the Douglas Boston. For the next 18 months the airfield was to reverberate to the throaty roar of the twin Wright double cyclone engines powerful enough to produce speeds in excess of 300 mph – quite a change from the slow Blenheims that were barely able to achieve 200 mph even with a strong following tail wind! It took the squadron's crews several months to get used to their new aircraft and it was not until the first week of March that they started a full programme of operations – airfields, docks, power stations and railway marshalling yards in both Northern France and Holland – and a silk factory in Calais appeared to feature as a favourite target. During the year it lost just 15 aircraft – a fine operational record.

Douglas Boston IIIs of 107 Squadron. (Via J Matthews)

Then in the late summer it was joined by another squadron – No 98 – which had returned from Iceland after a spell with Coastal Command. For this squadron's re-entry into Bomber Command it was equipped with another American aircraft – the North American Mitchell. However, quite soon the squadron moved out to its permanent station – RAF Foulsham.

Certainly the most memorable operation of 1942 was conducted on 6th December when nearly one hundred aircraft from No 2 Group attacked the Philips Radio and Valve works at Eindhoven. Twelve Bostons from 107 squadron took part in the raid and three aircraft failed to return including the squadron commander Wing Commander P. Dutton. The *Daily Telegraph* reported that it was '. . . a faultless operation . . . demanded a high degree of skill and accurate timing . . .' The squadron's crews received three personal awards including a DFC to Squadron Leader MacLauglin.

In the last few months before the airfield closed for redevelopment the squadron was joined by more Bostons from the Free French 342 squadron and it was they who flew the last Boston operations from Great Massingham in early September, after which they went to join 107 squadron at Hartford Bridge.

The airfield was ready for operations again on 17th April 1944 and it now possessed three concrete runways. It was also a full station in its own right and had been allocated to No 100 Group back in the previous December. The first two new units arrived in May and both turned out to be Training Flights for use of crews within the Group. The flights had a somewhat odd assortment of aircraft ranging from Ansons, Defiants to Beaufighters with a couple of Mosquitos thrown in for good measure. The two Flights operated regularly from the airfield but not without certain mishaps – two Beaufighters came to grief near the airfield during June and July and two Mosquitos crashed later in the same year.

Just a couple of days before D-Day, Mosquitos of 169 squadron arrived from RAF Little Snoring to continue their operations as a 'Serrate' force (see Little Snoring). Their first mission from Great Massingham was mounted on 5th June in support of the imminent invasion of Europe and just five days later the squadron commander – Wing Commander N.B. Bromley – recorded the first kill from Great Massingham. In July he also shot down the Group's 100th enemy aircraft, but unfortunately he was shot down and killed on 6th September whilst on a bomber support mission to Hamburg. When the squadron's Mosquitos operated from Little Snoring they had been actively engaged on night intruder raids, which continued until the late autumn. Then towards the end of the year the aircraft were fitted with 'Perfecto' devices, which were designed to trigger off the enemy's IFF (Identification Friend or Foe) radar and then provide a bearing on the transmission. The squadron's Mosquitos trialled the new equipment and although it was not instantly successful, after refinement it came into general use with 100 Group in January 1945.

No 169's last operation took place on 2nd May and was part of 'Operation Firebush', the firing of enemy airfields by using incendiaries and napalm. Unfortunately one aircraft was shot down on this final mission and on one of the last training flights from the airfield a Mosquito crashed near Brighton killing both crew members.

The two Training Flights were disbanded during June and July 1945 to be followed, in August, by No 169 squadron. By the end of August the airfield was passed over to the control of RAF West Raynham and some flying did continue for at least the next four years or so but it was now purely a satellite – the wheel had turned full circle. The airfield was finally sold in February 1958 for £23,500 and was one of the first wartime airfields in Norfolk to come under the hammer. Parts of the runways are still used for private flying but little remains now of the old buildings. What is left is to be found about a mile or so by road from the village along the minor road signposted 'to RAF West Raynham'. But undoubtedly the most lasting and poignant memorial to the airfield and its men can be found in Little Massingham's churchyard.

14

HARDWICK

The 93rd Bomb Group that occupied Hardwick for most of its time as an airfield had so many claims to fame that it almost seems to be an embarrassment of riches. Not sufficient that it was the oldest B-24 Group in the Eighth Air Force but it also mounted the highest number of missions of any Group, and all for an amazingly low loss of aircraft and men. During its time in England it became the most travelled of all Bomb Groups serving for periods of time in Algeria, Libya and Tunisia – thus its name 'The Travelling Circus'. Uniquely two of its squadrons were detached for short periods to operate with RAF Coastal Command and another one was selected to test new navigational equipment. But its greatest hour and fiercest test came with its participation in the famous raid on the Ploesti oil refineries, without doubt the most brilliant and courageous operation carried out by the USAAF throughout the whole of World War II.

However, before the illustrious 93rd arrived on the scene, Hardwick airfield, which had been specially constructed for American use, received its first aircraft in September 1942, Mitchells or B-26s of 310 Bomb Group. No operations were mounted during their short stay as the Group was merely preparing itself for service in North Africa, and by November most of the aircraft had left for nearby Bungay. In the first week of December a few B-24s of the 93rd began to arrive thus joining the 44th Group at Shipdham as the first Liberators to operate from Norfolk. They were just two of only six Bomb Groups then serving in England and really the whole viability of high altitude daylight bombing and the future fate of the Eighth Air Force lay in the hands of these pioneer Bomb Groups.

The Group, commanded by Colonel Edward 'Ted' Timberlake Jr, arrived in England in early September 1942 and was based at

Alconbury in Cambridgeshire. It had been placed in the First Air Division where it was somewhat of an anomaly with its B-24 aircraft, as the other Bomb Groups in the Division were equipped with B-17s. Within a month of its arrival the crew were in action, although the first mission on 9th October to a target in Belgium proved to be disappointingly inconclusive. Fourteen of the aircraft were forced to turn back either through mechanical failures or crews' errors and those who did manage to bomb the target did so in a very ragged manner largely due to their inexperience. Although only one aircraft was lost, many more were heavily flak damaged including one that had over 200 holes caused by enemy flak. One aircraft, *Boomerang*, returned in such a sorry state that it seemed doubtful whether it would every fly again, but it did and became the first B-24 to complete 50 missions.

Whilst still at Alconbury the 93rd were honoured with a visit from George VI, who made several similar trips to the embryo Eighth Air Force bases; these were to show the nation's appreciation of the American early costly involvement over Germany. The Eighth's Commanding Officer, Lieutenant General Spaatz who accompanied the King, still referred to his Command as 'a piddling little force'! His successor Lieutenant General Eaker, who took over the Eighth in

Lord Trenchard, 'Father of the RAF', at Hardwick with Colonel Ted Timberlake in the background. (USAF)

December, made the decision to centralise all B-24 Bomb Groups in the Second Air Division, which had its headquarters in Norfolk. And as a direct result of that policy the 93rd Group was transferred to the Second Division and moved to their new base – Hardwick.

During October two squadrons – 330 and 409 – were detached to assist Coastal Command, one in Hampshire and the other in Cornwall. Both were engaged on anti-shipping duties and hunting U-boats, for which of course the B-24s were amply qualified. Then in the following month a third squadron – No 329 – was detached to Bungay to undertake experiments with the RAF GEE navigational device and thus missed the first trip to North Africa.

On 6th December 1942, 24 aircraft set off for what was said to be a ten day detachment to North Africa, which was to stretch to almost three months. During this period the Group was attached to the Ninth Air Force. Whilst they were in Algeria they completed 22 missions, the pace of operational life was that much quicker than in England. Many of the operations entailed flying nine to ten hours at a stretch. Their last mission was directed on targets in Italy. During their time in the sun and sand they attacked airfields, ports and enemy convoys as well as giving tactical support to the British Eighth Army, all for the loss of a mere five aircraft. As a result of all these missions the Group was awarded their first Distinguished Unit Citation and was the first Eighth Air Force Group to be so honoured.

When they finally arrived back in England at the end of February 1943, they found themselves greeted as returning heroes. News of the exploits of 'Ted's Travelling Circus' had quickly spread; it was a time when the American press and public were desperate to hear some good news from Europe. The American public had little idea of how the mere handful of Bomb Groups were suffering in pursuit of the daylight bombing offensive. On 27th January the Eighth had launched its first operation against German targets and the Group was home in time to be included in the Eighth's largest mission to date.

On 18th March the Eighth Air Force despatched 97 aircraft to attack the Vulcan ship-building yards at Vegesack on the river Weser. The 93rd were able to provide 18 aircraft and all but one arrived back at Hardwick safely. The mission, the Group's first taste of action over Germany, proved to be a very rugged introduction to the hostile environment experienced over German targets. For almost two hours the crews had to fight off continuous fighter attacks and their gunners returned with claims of five positive kills and another eleven probably destroyed. The crews realised how different it was to their operations in the Mediterranean.

Several costly missions during April had somewhat reduced the Group's operational strength but nevertheless Hardwick still attracted considerable publicity. On the 6th they received a visit from Lord Trenchard, the 'Father' of the RAF. What he made of the more relaxed style of discipline that was operative in most American stations would have been interesting to know. He was followed three weeks later by Lieutenant General Frank Andrews, the overall Commander of the USAAF in Europe. He was killed just a week or so later when travelling as a passenger on board *Hot Stuff*, which was being flown back to the United States by the Group's first crew to complete its tour of operation. Cruelly the aircraft crashed into a mountain in Iceland killing the whole crew and General Andrews. Great Saling airfield in Essex, which was in the process of being constructed, was renamed Andrews Field in his honour.

In early June 1943 both B-24 Groups in Norfolk were taken off operations and found themselves daily careering across the Norfolk countryside, sometimes at heights less than 100 feet. They were later joined in this hazardous training by the new 389th Group, which had recently arrived at Hethel. The crews, of course, were not aware of the reason for this sudden and drastic change from high altitude flying for which they had been so carefully prepared. The object of the training was the mounting of 'Operation Statesman', a highly ambitious and daring air strike directed against the enemy's oil industry. The target was the massive Ploesti oil refineries in Rumania. Ploesti had, during the 1930s, become a boom area and its various refineries were said to supply almost 60% of Germany's oil. Undoubtedly this was a prize target but because of the distances involved it could not be reached by the Eighth's bombers from England. Even from airfields in North Africa it would necessitate a round trip of some 2,000 miles, which was almost the operational limit of a heavily loaded B-24. Furthermore most of the flying would be completed over enemy territory, which would give the enemy fighters ample time to group and attack the formation of bombers and there was no question of a fighter escort. The nature of the operation required low-level attacks over what were known to be strongly defended targets. Without question it was going to be a formidable and dangerous mission.

The three Norfolk Bomb Groups arrived in Libya at the end of June and they soon became involved with the Ninth's operations over

Shoot Luke *of 93rd Bomb Group being 'Bombed Up'. (USAF)*

Sicily and Italy. There were nearly two weeks of low-level training over the desert and even a model of Ploesti had been made in the sands. The operation was planned to take place on Sunday 1st August. The Commanding Officer of the Ninth Air Force, Lieutenant General Brereton who was to lead the mission, quite expected the losses to be heavy, 'in the region of 50%', and he also maintained, '... even though should we lose everything we've sent, but hit the target, it will be well worth it.' Ruthless words indeed; he didn't rate the chances of the crews' survival very high!

Out of the 173 aircraft that set out on the operation, the three Norfolk Groups supplied the lion's share – 103. The operation was to be led by a Ninth Air Force Group closely followed by the 93rd with their new Commanding Officer Lieutenant Colonel Addison Baker, heading his Group in a B-24 named *Hell's Wrench*. The other three Groups brought up the rear, with the newcomers from Hethel right at the back of the formation. Not surprisingly the close formation suffered somewhat during the long flight and by the time the two leading Groups were nearing the target they were well over ten minutes ahead of the main stream. The lead aircraft, belonging to the Ninth Air Force, made a slight navigational error and turned south too early, this would effectively take the bomber stream away from the primary targets. The 93rd followed suit until Colonel Baker realised the error and turned his aircraft to bring them into the target on a different approach, but this change brought the 93rd into a particularly heavily defended area.

As *Hell's Wrench* led the Group into the targets that had been allocated to two of the following Groups, their aircraft came under massive and withering flak, some of it heavy cannon fire. *Hell's Wrench* was almost immediately severely damaged and quickly became engulfed in flames. Nevertheless Colonel Baker continued to lead the aircraft on to the targets before his aircraft fell away and crashed with no survivors. For their bravery and dedication to duty the pilot, Major John Jerstad, and Lieutenant Colonel Baker, acting as co-pilot, were both posthumously awarded Medals of Honor. The rest of the Group's aircraft did manage to effectively bomb the target despite the intense enemy opposition but they lost seven aircraft. On the long return flight when all the surviving aircraft were damaged to some degree, two collided in thick clouds and another two were forced to land in Turkey, where the crews were interned for the rest of the war. Some of the returning crews had been flying for up to 14 hours when they finally struggled back to their North African bases. All Groups taking part in the Ploesti operation received Distinguished Unit Citations, which was the Group's second award.

As had been expected the cost of the operation was very high. Fifty two aircraft failed to return and one third of the crews taking part had either been killed, wounded or taken prisoner. Understandably the survivors of this operation were treated with the utmost admiration and reverence. The Ploesti mission has passed into the annals of the history of the USAAF and it ranks with the Dambusters raid as one of the epic air operations of the Second World War.

Perhaps anything the Group would achieve in their 'normal' operations over Germany would pale into insignificance compared with their exploits in August 1943. Along with their two other Ploesti veterans they found themselves back in North Africa during September to add support to the Ninth Air Force during the Allies' invasion of Italy and more especially the landings at Salerno. When they did finally arrive back at Hardwick in October, new aircraft arrived to replace their losses and with them replacement crews. Many of the old hands who survived the early days had completed their tours and departed for the United States, not many of the Ploesti veterans remained.

The new replacement aircraft B-24 H and Js were now equipped with power operated gun turrets in the nose, which replaced the old perspex domed nose, thus eliminating one of the aircraft's weak spots; the older B-24s had been very vulnerable to frontal attacks as the Luftwaffe fighters had quickly discovered. But these new aircraft were not universally popular with the crews. The design changes had somewhat reduced the aircraft's cruising speed as well as impairing its handling abilities, certainly at altitude. Furthermore the new gun turrets were anything but a tight fit and they allowed icy winds to penetrate the nose section especially, giving even further discomfort to the crews.

As the B-24 force in Norfolk increased dramatically during 1944, the 93rd continued its operations with the maximum of efficiency and the minimum of losses. It assumed the mantle of a very experienced and battle hardened Group that had seen it all during its time at Hardwick. It passed important milestones – its 200th mission was completed in July. And by the time it mounted its very last operation on 25th April 1945 the Group had completed 396, the highest total achieved in the whole of the Eighth Air Force. The Group only lost 100 aircraft in action, almost incredible considering that it had launched over 8,000 individual sorties. At the end of May the Group left Hardwick and although there are several wartime buildings still standing, the best reminder of 'Ted's Travelling Circus' is the fine memorial stone close to the old airfield, which was dedicated in May 1987.

A few years ago the site of the old airfield was under threat when Norfolk County Council applied for planning permission to establish a landraising waste disposal tip on the site. A Joint Parish Council Action Committee was quickly formed to contend the application. This committee took up a most catchy acronym 'RATS' (Residents Against Tip Site)! It launched an excellent campaign, including vigorous fund raising and ultimately it managed to obtain a public enquiry into the planning application. It is good to report that the RATS were successful in preventing the scheme going forward – it is not often that local residents manage to beat bureaucracy!

15

HETHEL

No Eighth Air Force Group received a sterner baptism of fire than the 389th, which when it arrived at Hethel in June 1943 became just the third B-24 Group to serve in Norfolk. Within days of their arrival the air crews had barely time to acclimatise themselves to their new home before they were engaged on an intensive training programme of low-level flying over East Anglia, though their original training had been in high altitude bombing. Most of the ground crews had not yet arrived and some detachments from Hardwick and Shipdham were brought in to adapt 389's aircraft to low-level flying by installing different bomb sights and making adjustments to the nose turrets. Their new Commanding Officer, Colonel Jack Wood, certainly kept them hard at the training, he was adamant that although they might be a new and inexperienced Bomb Group they were not going to let the side down. Unfortunately towards the end of the training programme (on 25th June) two aircraft collided killing both crews.

All this hectic preparation was for their participation in the epic and immortal Ploesti operation, though no amount of training would adequately prepare them for such a brutal and traumatic mission. By the end of the month 30 aircraft and their crews had exchanged their Norfolk airfield for the heat, dust and sand of an airfield near Benghazi in Libya, where the conditions were described as 'rugged'! Their first operational mission was conducted against targets on the island of Crete and with it came their first taste of air combat with Luftwaffe fighters in the shape of Me109s, a contest which mercifully resulted in the loss of just one aircraft. Along with their two Norfolk neighbours they formed the 201st Provisional Wing under the aegis of the Ninth Air Force, and along with the other two Bomb Groups carried out six more operations to various targets in Italy. At least the new Group had been blooded before their ultimate test – Ploesti.

The Group's B-24Ds were fitted with extra fuel tanks and for this reason it was given the longest route. Their target was to be Campina, some 18 miles north-west of the main oil refinery complex; it was also considered that this target had the lightest defences and thus more suitable for the inexperienced newcomers. There was, however, one distinct disadvantage with their new aircraft, a slightly slower cruising speed and thus thought to be more vulnerable to ground and air attack. Nevertheless the 389th had no difficulty in locating the target despite very heavy flak and strong fighter opposition and the accuracy of the bombing was such that they completely destroyed the target. It was later accepted that the Group's mission had been the most successful of the whole operation. They also suffered the lightest losses with just four aircraft shot down over Campina. One of these, *753*, was on its bombing run when a fuel tank was holed badly spraying petrol over the aircraft. Despite the imminent risk of the whole aircraft bursting into flames, the pilot – Second Lieutenant Lloyd Hughes, carried on to bomb the target just before flames engulfed the aircraft. Gallantly Hughes tried to land on a dry river bed but one of the wing tips touched a parapet of a bridge and the aircraft crashed. Three members of the crew managed to escape from the burning inferno but one died later. The pilot, who was only 23, was posthumously awarded the Medal of Honor.

During the return flight two aircraft were forced to land in Turkey and another seven in Cyprus. The Group was awarded a Distinguished Unit Citation for their part in the raid, it was the first time any Bomb Group had gained such an honour. Considering that the Group had only been in action for about three weeks it was an amazing achievement. The Group did not formally receive the ceremonial streamer from the hands of Lieutenant General Carl Spaatz, the overall Commander in Europe, until 9th May 1944 almost ten months later, when many of the crews that took part in the Ploesti operation had either been killed or had returned to the United States, having finished their tours.

All the crews that managed to make it back to their North African airfields were granted leave in Cairo. After this brief break from operations the crews were still not allowed to return to Norfolk, they took part in another three missions, including the raid on a Me109 factory at Wiener Neustadt in Austria. In the three missions only three aircraft were lost so when they finally arrived back at Hethel 17 aircraft remained out of the original 30 that had left Norfolk – this was far better than either the 44th or 93rd, their more experienced colleagues on the North African adventure. Beginner's luck or not the Group was so proud of their exploits in the desert that the crews coined a name for themselves – 'The Sky Scorpions', for which they were known for the rest of the war.

With barely enough time to enjoy the late English summer and the 'warm' English beer, they went out for the first time against a target situated in Germany (on 7th September) and returned relatively intact, only to find that they were on their travels again as they were ordered back to North Africa, this time to Tunisia. The crews found that they were engaged in a variety of operations over Italy, Sicily and with even a return visit to Wiener Neustadt for good measure. On this occasion their North African campaign was of quite short duration and by October they were happily settled back in Hethel, where they would stay for the rest of their time in England.

Towards the end of 1943 as the Eighth Air Force made deeper penetration raids into southern Germany, one of the operational problems they encountered, besides enemy action that is, was an acute shortage of fuel. On some of these long-range operations the fuel factor often became most critical and there was precious little leeway for any mishaps. The planning of such missions became quite a headache for the backroom officers in the Divisional headquarters. Usually the B-17s were the most vulnerable and parts of southern England became quite inured to seeing numerous B-17s crash-landing in the Kent and Sussex countryside, and RAF airfields such as Tangmere and Manston were frequently used for emergency landings. After one particular mission to southern Germany, so many parachutes were seen over Kent and Sussex that it was seriously thought this was an airborne German invasion! In theory the B-24s, because of their greater range, were less susceptible to such fuel problems but nevertheless on one December day the Group lost three aircraft which crash-landed in Kent because of fuel shortage.

During the third week of February 1944 the Eighth Air Force launched 'Operation Thunderclap', which was a massive offensive against the German aircraft industries; the week of operations later gained the name of 'The Big Week'. Perhaps the most momentous operation, at least as far as the Second Division Bomb Groups were concerned, was mounted on 24th February to what became known as 'dreaded' Gotha and its complex of aircraft factories. A most costly

The formal presentation of a Distinguished Unit Citation to 389th Bomb Group at Hethel on 9th May 1944. (USAAF)

mission for all the Bomb Groups that took part. Of the 239 B-24s that were despatched on the raid, 44 failed to return. Unfortunately the 389th suffered seven aircraft lost, more than their Ploesti losses.

During April 1944 identifying marks were given to all of the Division's B-24s. Each squadron in a Group was allocated two individual letters, which were painted on the fuselage. Then one month later new colour markings on the tails were introduced to aid easier identification at long range and perhaps help on formation. These new markings inadvertently caused some trouble on a major operation to Berlin on 21st June, when the Germans operated a captured B-24 properly marked in the Group's letters and colouring. On this mission the Group suffered their heaviest loss of the war so far with six aircraft destroyed over the target area and another two ditched in Sweden – although they were in good company, 13 landed there from the Berlin raid. Whether the abnormally high loss suffered by the Group on this raid was due to the 'rogue' B-24 in Hethel's markings will never be known. More certain is that several of the Groups taking part reported the incident and some crews claimed to have destroyed the 'rogue' aircraft – but did they get the right one?

One navigator with the Group vividly recalled that his 27th mission with 565 squadron '... was aborted, one engine out and a hydraulic leak. We turned back over Germany but we couldn't maintain altitude, we went down and down and would have become sitting ducks. And then three P-51 Mustangs showed up and escorted us to the Dutch border and one of them took us back up the Channel. He had *Linda* painted on his machine so it's no coincidence that my first daughter was called Linda because I wouldn't have been alive without that fighter!' He later recalled his feelings at the end of 30 missions in August 1944. He had only arrived in England on 1st May and went on his first mission on 13th, which shows how busy the Group must have been for him to complete a tour of operation in barely three months. As he explained, 'When you hit the runway at the end of 30 missions, it was heaven...sheer, sheer heaven. I remember thinking that this was the beginning of the rest of my life.'

In July the Group was once again involved in the Eighth Air Force's long, dogged and very determined offensive against oil targets. They became part of a 373 strong force of B-24s which the Second Division mounted against a variety of oil refineries and installations in central Germany. As the Group's aircraft were just passing over the Dutch coast two collided in heavy clouds with a total loss of life. Then as they were approaching Lützkendorf, the primary target, the leading formation was attacked by a mass of enemy fighters. Within minutes 20 aircraft were shot down, five of which came from Hethel. The day's mission cost the Group dearly, indicating that however experienced the crews were, any Group could sustain large losses on just one single mission.

Disaster could strike at any time as the 389th found out to its cost in April 1945. On the 7th they were leading the Second Division force on an operation to Duneburg where there was a large munitions plant. Just when the lead aircraft were within minutes of the target they were attacked by a formation of Me109s, one of which crashed directly into 389's leading aircraft shearing the nose as if it had been cut with a knife, this careered into the starboard wing of the second aircraft and both went spiralling down to the ground with no survivors. The second aircraft had the Group's Commanding Officer – Lieutenant Colonel Harboth – on board.

Just ten days later the 389th suffered an even worse accident. They were on what was considered 'a milk run' – bombing enemy batteries on the French Atlantic coast which were still tenaciously holding out again Allied forces. The flak was expected to be fairly light and certainly no fighter opposition was anticipated as the

B-24s of 389th Bomb Group preparing to take off. (USAAF)

Luftwaffe had been forced to pull back all their resources in a last ditch attempt to defend Germany. In this instance the intelligence sources were proved to be correct as virtually no opposition was encountered. But as the Group's aircraft were making their bomb run, a B-17 Group was making its second run from a higher altitude above them, and their bombs fell directly on 389's aircraft. Two immediately burst into flames and were completely destroyed with a total loss of the crews, another two were severely damaged but the pilots managed to fly them back to a French airfield and the fifth, though heavily damaged, struggled back to Hethel. Though not large such losses were all the more difficult to bear because of the unfortunate circumstances and the nearness to the end of the war when many operations were mounted without a single loss.

The Group completed 321 missions, of which 14 were undertaken whilst on detachment in North Africa all for the loss of 116 aircraft – a very creditable achievement. By the end of May the Americans had left and the airfield was passed over to Fighter Command, remaining a service airfield until early 1947. Now Lotus Cars Ltd own most of the site and parts of the old runways are used by the company to test their performance cars. The old control tower has been renovated and now acts as Lotus Sports and Social Club. The old airfield is quite easy to locate, just a few miles from Wymondham to the east of the A11 following the signs to 'Lotus Cars'.

16
HORSHAM ST FAITH

Horsham St Faith is only the second wartime airfield in East Anglia to have been developed into a modern international airport. However, unlike Stansted, 'St Faiths' as it was familiarly known, had a distinguished wartime career with both the RAF and USAAF. Defiants, Blenheims, Mosquitos, Marauders, Thunderbolts and Liberators all found a comfortable home at this airfield, which was situated so conveniently just three miles north of the city of Norwich.

The airfield was first planned before the outbreak of war and was formally opened on 1st June 1940 but already in the last months of 1939 some aircraft could be seen amongst the contractor's excavators and equipment; rather appropriately they were Bristol Blenheims, which were to figure large in Horsham's early wartime operations. The aircraft belonged to No 21 squadron, then based at RAF Watton, and they had been dispersed to the developing airfield because of fears of enemy air raids. Despite the fact that the airfield had been designated as a bomber station the first aircraft to use the grass runways were fighters – Spitfires – from two squadrons (Nos 19 and 66) then based at RAF Duxford. But perhaps the most interesting fighter to use St Faiths in the early summer months of 1940 was the Boulton Paul Defiant.

This could be truly considered a 'local' aircraft coming from the Norwich firm of aircraft manufacturers. The first prototype had flown in August 1937 and it was the first fighter to have incorporated a power-driven gun turret instead of the conventional weapons which only fired forwards. The Defiants came into service in December 1939, and A Flight of 264 squadron was detached to Horsham St Faith from whence it launched its first sorties on 12th May. By the end of the month 14 aircraft had been lost or put out of action. Although it

Boulton Paul Defiant: No 264 Squadron was equipped with this 'local' fighter.

operated well over the Dunkirk beaches, the early combats of the Battle of Britain exposed its weakness – a vulnerability to attack from underneath – and so many aircraft were destroyed that by August it was withdrawn from the Battle.

In June the airfield received its first squadrons of light/medium bombers – Nos 139 and 114 – and as Horsham St Faith had been allocated to No 2 Group of Bomber Command, these squadrons were equipped with the ubiquitous Bristol Blenheim IVs. The latter squadron, which had suffered heavily during its service in France, stayed only for a short time before moving on to Oulton, which had opened in July as a satellite for St Faiths. No 139 was destined for a longer stay at the airfield and in 1941 became known as the 'Jamaica' squadron in recognition of the immense contribution that island had made to the 'Bombers for Britain' Fund, which was sufficient to provide twelve Blenheims.

On 3rd July 1940 Group headquarters issued an operations instruction, 'The enemy are using airfields and landing grounds in France, Belgium and Holland to bomb targets in England ... The intention is to destroy as many aircraft as possible on the ground thus forcing the enemy to withdraw. Airfields are to be attacked by sections escorted by fighters or by individual aircraft using cloud cover ...' Horsham was allocated a sector covering Brussels and the coast from Le Touquet to Dieppe. Thus started No 2 Group's offensive against enemy airfields, which continued unabated for the duration of the war. The other major bombing policy was directed against the French channel ports and enemy shipping and by the end of June 1941 the Group's Blenheims had mounted over 1,000 sorties against shipping targets for the loss of 36 aircraft. On one of these shipping strikes the squadron lost their commanding officer.

By the middle of July No 18 Blenheim squadron arrived and within days it was detailed for an operation against Rotterdam docks, where a large Dutch liner, now in German hands, was the specific target. Eight Blenheims led by Wing Commander J. Partridge left Horsham to join other Norfolk Blenheim squadrons. The aircraft were armed with four 250 pound bombs and were ordered to attack the target at low-level. The squadron was to be the first over the target and thus were likely to face the stiffest opposition. As the Blenheims came in at a height of 50 feet they met very heavy flak and the squadron commander was shot down, shortly followed by another aircraft. However, the operation was considered a great success with over 22 ships being damaged for just four aircraft lost out of the original 36.

August 1941 proved to be a most auspicious month for the squadron, it had been detailed to take part in a large Group operation, mounted against the Knapsack power station and Quadrath generating station both near Cologne and believed to be producing a large amount of the energy used by the Ruhr industries. Power stations were always considered very worthy targets by No 2 Group. Most of the 54 Blenheims taking part came from Norfolk airfields and on this mission they would be escorted by fighters from a variety of airfields around London – most notably North Weald, Hornchurch and Biggin Hill. Nine Blenheims of 18 squadron took off from Horsham at 9.20 am on 12th August and were in the second wave to attack Knapsack. Before arriving at the target one Blenheim was lost as it hit high tension wires and another two disappeared shortly after completing their bombing. The two power stations were damaged, seriously reducing production for several months, but at a cost of twelve aircraft (over 20%), three of these from 18 squadron.

A signal had been received from the Germans requesting a spare artificial right leg for Wing Commander Douglas Bader, who had been shot down over St Omer airfield and had lost his artificial leg while freeing himself from his cockpit before baling out. The Germans offered a free passage for a Lysander to land at St Omer to deliver it. However, the RAF had a different idea and on 18th August a Blenheim of 18 squadron, piloted by Sergeant Nickelson, had on board a box containing the artificial leg. Whilst on a bombing mission to Gosnay power station, some 30 miles to the south of St Omer,

Bristol Blenheim IV: several Blenheim Squadrons operated from 'St Faiths' during 1940/41.

Nickelson dropped the box by parachute over St Omer airfield.

At the end of the month the squadron was detached to Manston in Kent to take part in 'Channel Stop' – the attempt to close the Straits of Dover to enemy shipping by day. Each Blenheim squadron in No 2 Group took their turn at these operations. Although the Blenheims were escorted by Hurricanes it was a rather savage and costly operation. On such operations the life of the squadron was not put at much more than two weeks as by that time the crews had become so depleted that the squadron was forced to retire, only to be replaced by another squadron and so on.

As No 18 squadron made their preparations to depart for the Far East, it was replaced by No 105 squadron from RAF Swanton Morley, which was the first RAF squadron to be supplied with the new 'wonder' aircraft – the de Havilland Mosquito. It had been first planned back in 1938 and was another example – like the Blenheim – of being developed by private enterprise rather than to an Air Ministry specification. The idea of a twin-engined, high speed unarmed wooden bomber was treated with disdain by the Air Ministry but despite the sad lack of official commitment Geoffrey de Havilland, the designer and manufacturer, had sufficient faith in the aircraft to carry on. However, the aircraft did have one dedicated official supporter – Air Marshal Sir William Freeman – who was the Air Member of the Air Council for Development and Production. He ordered the first 50 Mosquitos for the RAF against strong opposition.

Indeed in the early days of the project the aircraft became known as 'Freeman's Folly'!

The first flight was made in November 1940 and the trials were quickly rushed through in just three months. The first Mosquito arrived in the RAF in July 1941 and was used on photographic reconnaissance work. It was powered by two Rolls Royce Merlin engines and could claim speeds in excess of 350 mph. Although originally planned as a light bomber, a fighter version was developed, which first appeared in April 1942. The Mosquito was, without doubt, the most successful aircraft of the Second World War with well over 5,500 being produced during the war. It operated with equal facility as a high or low-level bomber, day or night fighter, an anti-shipping strike bomber and perhaps its greatest success was obtained with the Pathfinder Force. One of the most famous Mosquito pilots – Wing Commander Wooldridge DFC – said '[it] is, in every way, an outstanding aeroplane – easy to fly, manoeuvrable, fast and completely free from vices of any sort . . . it is a sturdy pugnacious little brute, but thoroughly friendly to its pilot . . .'

The new aircraft were rather slow to appear at Horsham. By 12th November 1941 the squadron had only five aircraft and five months later there were only two more but the squadron had 30 crews ready, trained and eager for the new and exciting aircraft. Certain problems had been experienced in equipping them with four 500 pound bombs, which were finally resolved by changing the size of the bomb fins so that they would fit into the aircraft's bomb bays. Perhaps their finest hour came on the night of 31st May 1942 when four Mosquitos from the squadron launched their first operational mission. It was to be a bombing and photographic sortie over Cologne after the first '1,000' bomber raid. Squadron Leader Oakeshott had the honour to lead the first Mosquito mission. He found smoke billowing to a height of 14,000 feet over the city, which made photography impossible. The aircraft did bomb the target but unfortunately one Mosquito failed to return. A similar mission was conducted after the Essen '1,000' raid with the Mosquitos going in about 18 hours after the main raid.

During June the squadron operated 16 successful operations, mainly photographing airfields in north-west Germany. But during the month the Germans claimed to have shot down a Mosquito and published a photograph in a newspaper as proof, so it would appear that the 'wonder' aircraft was no longer a well-kept secret although the RAF attempted to maintain the myth until October when it was officially unveiled to the national press! Just before the squadron moved to RAF Marham it received a new commander – Wing Commander 'Hughie' Edwards VC, DFC – a superb leader and brilliant pilot, and under his guidance the squadron would gain a fine reputation for its daring and very successful low-lying attacks. The early missions with the Mosquitos were not trouble-free, six had been lost out of 45 sorties and some cynics in Bomber Command were writing off this aircraft as a failure, but the squadron's operations from Marham proved them so wrong.

In September 1942 the airfield was handed over to the USAAF and in mid-November some Martin B-26 Marauders of the 319th Bomb Group arrived for a relatively short period before they left for service in North Africa. For all of the winter of 1942 the airfield lay dormant until April 1943 when the peace was shattered by the raucous sound of the Republic P-47C Thunderbolts. These somewhat ugly, ungainly fighters would gain a variety of unflattering sobriquets. They belonged to the 56th Fighter Group which was the first American Group to bring Thunderbolts to England. The Group's pilots had been busy training at King's Cliffe in Northamptonshire and had moved to Horsham to be closer to the action.

'The Wolfpack' as the Group became known, was most ably led by Colonel Hubert Zemke, who proved not only to be a fine fighter pilot in his own right but also was an acknowledged expert in fighter tactics. It was largely due to his inspiration and leadership that the 56th developed into one of the finest Fighter Groups in the Eighth Air Force.

The Group went on their first mission on 13th April and their first escort duty came on 4th May accompanying a B-17 force that was bombing Antwerp. Considering the Group's outstanding successes – it destroyed more enemy aircraft in air combat than any other Eighth Air Force Group – its pilots found victories hard to come by in the first few months of operations. Not until June did 'the Wolfpack' claim three kills – all Fw190s. The Group had the two highest scoring fighter aces of the war, Francis Gabreski and Robert Johnson, both of whom were credited with a total of 28 victories, an indication of the qualities of this most unlikely looking fighter. By 8th July the Group rather reluctantly left the comforts of Horsham St Faith for their new base at Halesworth in Suffolk. Horsham was to be closed to flying whilst three concrete runways were built in preparation for the Eighth Air Force heavy bombers.

Towards the end of January 1944 the first B-24Hs of the 458th Bomb Group arrived at the airfield. These were the latest model of this sturdy and dependable aircraft. The Group's crews were decidedly pleased with their new home, '... it was a good base – permanent with comfortable accommodation... and it was so close to town... we had no cause for grumbles..' In this respect the Group was rather fortunate as it was the only Bomb Group in Norfolk to occupy a permanent RAF station. It also became the first to be placed in the 9th Combat Wing and would be joined later by Groups from Attlebridge and Rackheath, who would come 'on stream' in March and April.

The first mission, on 24th February, was nothing more than diversionary whilst the Second Division's main force of B-24s went to the dreaded Gotha, which we will later see was a most disastrous mission. On 2nd March it was a different affair – Frankfurt. On the Group's return to Norfolk one aircraft crashed at Hellesdon on the outskirts of Norwich, which was directly under the airfield's flight path. The following day the target was the big one – Berlin – but there were several delays and the mission did not take place until the 6th when 27 B-24s from Horsham joined the large force of bombers, but this operation proved to be the Eighth's heaviest losses for a single operation throughout the war. Sixty nine aircraft were destroyed, 16 were B-24s and five of these came from the 458th. During the first full month of operations the Group lost nine aircraft.

During April the Group was involved in several missions to V1 rocket sites in Northern France. On the 9th the Group was despatched to another favourite target of the Eighth Air Force – Tutow – which was a Fw190 plant near the Baltic coast. Once again weather conditions over northern Europe caused problems and the crews were forced to bomb alternative targets. Four aircraft were lost. Certainly the Group's crews were not idle because on 27th April they mounted two missions in one day, a rare occurrence for Bomb Groups but it did give the Group a 'day off' operations on 28th.

Like all Bomb Groups the 458th was very active on D-Day, it launched three missions on the day mainly over shore installations. As one crew member recalled after he had finished his third mission, 'Instead of being excited, as we had in the morning we were just tired and worn out. Again we saw landing craft in the Channel; our target [Caen] was covered in clouds. We saw no flak or fighters.' Five days later twelve aircraft from 753 Azon squadron were detailed to join a force from the 96th Bomb Wing and lead the attack on an important strategic bridge – Blois-Saint-Dennis – over the Loire river. According to orders from headquarters this bridge had to be destroyed 'at all costs', which meant low-level bombing, and would be undertaken for the first time by American heavy bombers in the style of 'the Dambusters'. The mission turned out to be a conspicuous success, which elicited a citation of praise from Lieutenant-General 'Jimmy' Doolittle, who considered the operation '... an outstanding performance with extraordinary heroism...'

On 12th September the Group began its 'trucking' missions, to supply valuable fuel to General Patton's army in France and on the day the Group's aircraft delivered 13,000 gallons. Eleven of the Group's aircraft were specially modified to carry more of the five gallon cans. During the 13 days of these operations the 458th delivered over 700,000 gallons, but not without some cost because on the 20th one B-24 crashed near Horsham St Faith killing all the crew and one civilian in a terrace of houses that were severely damaged.

Another tragic accident occurred on 24th November, when, whilst returning from a practice mission Second Lieutenant Ralph Dooley piloting *Lady Jane* hit the flagpole of a church in Heigham Street, Norwich. The memorial plaque on the west side of this street recalls the sad circumstances, '... the pilot of the bomber as his last act avoided crashing on this and surrounding cottages, thus preventing the possible loss of civilian lives'. Dooley managed to land the damaged aircraft on waste-land but he and his crew were killed.

On 7th March 1945 the Group celebrated its 200th mission, no mean achievement considering that it had been in operation for barely twelve months. The momentous event was marked with dances and parties but all too soon the Group was back to the killing business – a full complement of aircraft bombed a railway viaduct in the Ruhr. Then towards the end of the month (24th) three missions were mounted on a single day. All of these were directed at the Luftwaffe's new jet fighter – the Me262 – which was causing great concern to the Eighth Air Force chiefs as they were beginning to appear in quite appreciable numbers. The Group's last mission took place on 25th April – the attack on railway centres at Salzburg and Bad Reichenhall near Berchtesgaden, where on the same day the RAF bombed Hitler's famous mountain retreat. The formation was escorted by P-51s from 479 Fighter Group at Wattisham. Very little fighter opposition was met although the 479th claimed the last Luftwaffe aircraft destroyed by the Eighth. The conditions were perfect for visible bombing and all of the primary targets were bombed and all the B-24s returned safely. This proved to be the last heavy bombing operation of the war for both the RAF and the Eighth Air Force. By the end of June virtually all the Americans had left and the airfield was passed back to the RAF, coming under Fighter Command's control.

17
LANGHAM

Langham was the most northerly of all wartime airfields in Norfolk and situated less than three miles from the coast, ensuring that once it came into operation it would be utilised by Coastal Command. Never considered a 'comfortable' posting because of the biting cold winds that came off the sea, the airfield could be a bleak and inhospitable place especially during some of those harsh winters that were a feature of the wartime years.

Built during the early months of the war as another satellite for Bircham Newton, it was ready for occupation in the late summer of 1940. In retrospect it is surprising just how under-utilised the airfield was in its first two years. But perhaps this situation only emphasises the desperate shortage of operational aircraft in Coastal Command certainly during the early war years. The odd aircraft from one of Bircham Newton's squadrons appeared at the airfield but really very little more. However, in late 1941 two flights of No 1 Anti-Aircraft Co-operation Unit arrived bringing their Hawker Henleys. These aircraft had been designed as a light bomber but the Air Ministry quickly became disenchanted with their rather inadequate performance, few were built and those that were became relegated to the mundane task of target towing. The aircraft had broad black diagonal bars to identify them as such and they became quite familiar sights towing their yellow drogue sleeves over the anti-aircraft ranges at Weyborne near Sheringham.

The Air Ministry had great plans for Langham, they visualised it developing into a major airfield and the first steps were taken in July 1942 when it became a full station in its own right. Whilst plans for its future development were being considered and approved, the Air/Sea Rescue squadron No 280 moved in. This squadron had been

Bristol Beaufighter of 455 Squadron. (RAF Museum)

initially formed at Bircham Newton and its Ansons were soon active patrolling the North Sea. In September the squadron was responsible for saving 56 men, mostly American aircrews returning to their Norfolk bases. Also a small detachment of Fairey Swordfish from the Fleet Air Arm came to mount anti-shipping patrols from the airfield. This quite remarkable little bi-plane had been in service since 1936 and was nearing obsolescence at the outbreak of the war. Retained for war service it operated as a torpedo bomber, anti U-boat aircraft, mine-layer, rocket projectile carrier and trainer. Though flying at not much above 140 mph, its squadrons operated with rare distinction throughout the war and it was fondly dubbed the old 'Stringbag'; it was the last bi-plane to fly operationally.

In October 1942 the airfield was closed for redevelopment and expansion and did not reopen until almost 16 months later in February 1944. It now boasted three concrete runways – one at 2,000 yards and two at 1,400 yards – and was well up to heavy bomber standard. No heavy bombers came but the airfield was about to enter a brief, glorious six months of operational action and this was in the shape of the rather ugly and pugnacious Bristol Beaufighter TFXs.

The Beaufighter, which had first entered the RAF in April 1940, had gained an early fame as a night fighter, but by now had been developed by Coastal Command into a most effective anti-shipping strike aircraft. It could carry a torpedo, rockets or bombs or a combination of these weapons and had become a most doughty bomber. It was a heavy aircraft, not particularly easy to fly but immensely strong and powerful and was the most heavily armed two-seater fighter/bomber in RAF use.

The concept of using a dedicated anti-shipping strike force within Coastal Command dated back to the early months of 1941. But the right aircraft were not available in sufficient numbers and many of the Command's most experienced aircrews were being drafted out to the Middle East, so the project had to be held in abeyance. It was not until September 1942 that the first Beaufighter Strike Wing was established at North Coates in Lincolnshire and although its early operations were far from successful the Command's chiefs were still convinced of its potential. They set about devoting more valuable resources to the programme with the ultimate objective of having three wings comprising ten squadrons of Beaufighters. By March 1944 Coastal Command had finally achieved the first part of their plan with the Strike Wings based at North Coates, Wick and Leuchars – a most effective and powerful attacking force.

During April 1944 the Leuchars Strike Wing was brought south to operate from Langham. This comprised two squadrons – No 455 RAAF and No 489 RNZAF – the 'Anzac' force had gained a fine reputation during the twelve months they had been operating from their Scottish base. Both squadrons had originally been equipped with Hampdens and had gained valuable experience using the aircraft as torpedo bombers. The Langham Wing went out on its first sortie on 6th May when 455 provided flak cover for the 'Torbeaus' (torpedo armed Beaufighters) of 489 squadron. On this occasion they located a heavy freighter off Borkum, a German island just off the Dutch coast, and a sustained attack enabled them to notch up their first Langham victory. Eight days later they achieved even greater success with an attack on another large merchant vessel and this was sunk along with an enemy mine-sweeper. The wings were expected to launch at least five strikes each month but most days when the weather conditions were suitable the squadrons were out patrolling the Dutch and German coasts searching for unsuspecting enemy shipping on which to use their 250 and 500 pound bombs.

On D-Day the two squadrons were moved on detachment to Manston fully armed with their torpedoes to be, in theory, closer to the action. Although the crews were maintained in a state of constant readiness much to their frustration they were not brought into the action. Not long after their return to Langham, a large enemy convoy was sighted late on the evening of 14th June, making its slow progress along the Dutch coast. Such a tempting target persuaded the Group to mount a large strike offensive against the German convoy and early the following morning 19 aircraft from North Coates joined forces with 23 from Langham. Ten Mustangs from 316 squadron at Coltishall were detailed to give the Beaufighter force support. The convoy was located off Schiermonnikoog, an island off the Dutch coast and it comprised two large merchant vessels protected by seven mine-sweepers and a number of R-boats (flak ships). The Beaufighters struck with devastating accuracy and power. The *Amerskerk*, a large vessel of 7,900 tons and the smaller *Nachtigall* were attacked with torpedoes and rocket projectiles and both sank, as did one of the mine-sweepers. Not a single aircraft was lost although some were damaged, including one that crash-landed at Langham. An operation of this power and success was a complete vindication of Coastal Command's faith in their Beaufighter Strike Wings.

During July and August especially, the Langham Wing continued to plunder shipping off the Dutch and German coasts. So effective were their attacks that the Germans were forced to move their convoys slowly by night and then retreat into the nearest port during the day for fear of attack. When it was discovered that much greater use was being made of the Norwegian ports and coasts Coastal Command chiefs rationalised their Strike forces with the effect that in October 1944 the Langham squadrons were moved back to Scotland. During their brief stay at Langham the Wing had accounted for 36 vessels and four U-boats destroyed with at least another 60 vessels damaged to some degree, a very impressive record.

To take their place came Wellingtons from Docking, which was suffering from water drainage problems. Then there was a brief appearance of a few Fairey Albacores of the Fleet Air Arm before they moved to Belgium. Both aircraft were torpedo bombers and really designed to be operated from aircraft carriers. The Albacores were almost at the end of their operational life and had been originally planned as the replacement for the Swordfish but in the end the sturdy 'Stringbag' survived it!

By the end of October the Meteorological squadron also arrived from Docking and henceforth Langham became one of the main airfields for weather reporting, a role it carried on after the war. In the early months of 1945 No 144 squadron arrived from Scotland with its Beaufighters and on 6th May 1945 they launched their final mission against enemy shipping in the Kiel area. It was expected that the airfield would become a two squadron fighter station but this did not materialise and the airfield was closed for flying in September 1947.

18

LITTLE SNORING

'Berlin was an orchestral hell, a terrible symphony of light and flares. An unpleasant form of warfare, but for those brave men – just a job.' These were the impressions of Ed Murrow, the very distinguished American reporter, who survived a trip to 'Big B' as a passenger in one of the hundreds of Lancasters that bombed Berlin in November 1943. This operation was just the beginning of Bomber Command's onslaught on Berlin, which is now known as the 'Battle of Berlin' and lasted for almost four months. During this battle over 9,000 aircraft were despatched for 'just' 500 losses 5.5% (but can one consider the blood-letting of almost 3,800 aircrew as tolerable?) With over 29,800 tons of bombs dropped, the Battle of Berlin was an awesome demonstration of the power of Bomber Command, which left Berlin in ruins, but whether the cost in terms of crews and aircraft lost justified all the operations has been debated ever since.

Some of the 'brave men' came from No 115 squadron, then based at a little known Norfolk airfield called Little Snoring. It had only opened in July 1943 and was intended as a satellite for RAF Foulsham but within a month it had gained full station status within No 3 Group of Bomber Command. All of the Group's airfields were situated in East Anglia and all but one of its squadrons were flying Short Stirlings – the one exception being 115 – which was equipped with Avro Lancaster IIs.

The mighty Lancasters first arrived at Little Snoring on 6th August and within days, or rather nights, were out on operations to the Ruhr. Not only was this squadron unique within the Group because of its Lancasters but they were Mark IIs of which very few were in operational use. Along with the squadron came a Conversion Unit (No 1678), the function of which was to train the aircrews of Stirling

Little Snoring airfield as it is today.

squadrons, who were in the process of changing to Lancasters as the Stirlings were now reaching the end of their operational life. The Unit had barely time to move in to Little Snoring before it disappeared off to Witchford in Cambridgeshire. The operational squadron stayed a little longer then it too departed in November after mounting its final mission to Berlin on the night of 26/27th November 1943.

This was the fourth operation of the Battle – 443 Lancasters were sent – some attacked Stuttgart as a diversionary raid. The weather over Berlin was quite clear and accurate marking had led to successful bombing. The crews' real problems began on their return to their home bases as most of eastern England was enveloped in heavy fog and the returning aircraft were diverted to other airfields in South Yorkshire and some even further afield. Many sadly came to grief and several crews were killed. Added to the 28 aircraft missing in action over 75 were severely damaged; a very costly operation. On the night 115 squadron escaped relatively lightly, losing just one aircraft over Berlin and another one on landing.

The reason for the squadron's relatively short stay at Little Snoring was that on 23rd November the airfield had been passed over to No 100 Group. This Group's units were vastly different from the Lancasters, being two fighter squadrons – Nos 169 and 515. The first had originally been a night-fighter squadron and it brought its Mosquitoes to the airfield on 7th December, followed just a week later by the Defiants and Beaufighters of No 515 squadron, which during the next few months would be exchanged for Mosquito VIs.

Both squadrons were engaged on similar tasks within the Group; day and night intruder raids, escorts for bomber offensives,

The honours and awards boards in St Andrew's church, Little Snoring.

minelaying and sorties to enemy fighter assembly points. No 159 squadron was selected to additionally undertake 'Serrate' patrols. As far back as October 1942 Air Vice-Marshal Harris had advised Fighter Command to place some fighters into the bomber streams to act as escorts. This tactic only really became possible with the development by the Telecommunications Research Establishment of an electronic device that enabled fighters to home in on German AI radar from as far away as 100 miles and so identify any intercepting enemy fighters. The equipment was said to have gained its name from the serrated image portrayed on the screens, and the device was first used in operations in June 1943. The squadron did not become operational until mid-January 1944 and achieved its first kill on a 'Serrate' mission on 30th January when Squadron Leader A. Cooper shot down a Me110 when the Mosquitos were acting as escorts for a mining operation of the Kiel Canal. The aircraft returned to Little Snoring with three positive kills – two Ju88s and one Me110. Then the following month the squadron moved to another airfield in the Group – RAF Great Massingham.

The other squadron – No 515 – proved to be very slow coming into operations and the reason for this becomes clear in a signal from Group headquarters to Bomber Command in February 1944, 'On taking over the Squadron [515] from Fighter Command... the training of the aircrew was found to be woefully inadequate. The squadron's aircraft had been standing in the open for two years and the state of serviceability was grave... The squadron's Beaufighter II aircraft were regarded as totally unsuitable for this role by the Group... 515 squadron should become a standard fighter squadron equipped with Mosquito VI aircraft.'

By the end of February, perhaps as a result of this *cri de coeur*, the squadron were supplied with just three Mosquito IIs but unfortunately they were found to be old and well-used aircraft with rather unreliable engines, resulting in a high percentage of aborted missions. Then towards the end of March the newer Mark VIs arrived and with them came one of the most famous Bomber pilots of the Second World War – Squadron Leader H.B. 'Mick' Martin. This highly decorated Australian airman was best known for his operations with No 617 'The Dambusters' squadron. When he was posted to 515 squadron, Martin had already completed 49 missions and by the end of the year he had doubled this number and had been awarded a second bar to his DFC. In the *Official History of the Bomber Offensive* he is described as 'Though not the most famous, was certainly one of the greatest bomber pilots who ever set course from British bases. His genius for flying was unsurpassed and his relentless determination in the face of any hazard was unquenchable...' 'Mick' Martin finally retired from the RAF in September 1974 as Air Marshal Sir Harold.

For a very brief period, during March 1944, four fighters from the American Eighth Air Force arrived at the airfield to work with the two RAF squadrons on night intruder missions. Two of the aircraft were P-51 Mustangs and the other two P-38 Lockheed Lightnings. The undersides of the aircraft were painted black and a yellow lightning flash stripe was the unit's insignia. Several missions were launched from the airfield but it was realised that both types of aircraft were quite unsuited for such operations and they were withdrawn.

In June 1944 No 23 squadron arrived at Little Snoring as a replacement force. During the following months both squadrons operated a mixture of sorties to enemy airfields, escort duties especially to V1 rocket sites and, of course, a fair number of day and night intruder raids. Whilst on a day intruder mission to Prague, aircraft from 515 squadron claimed nine enemy aircraft destroyed and another five damaged. Towards the end of the year the Mosquitos were equipped with ASH, an American Airborne Interception Radar which had been proved to be quite outstanding and very resistant to the use of 'window' metal strips. It was thought that this apparatus would be more suitable for the squadron's low-level strikes at enemy airfields that had become so much a part of the operations from the airfield. During April 1945 both squadrons were active with incendiary and napalm attacks on airfields. The last missions of the war were launched from the airfield on the night of 3rd/4th May and were directed against airfields at Hohne in central Germany and Flensberg on the German/Dutch border.

The two squadrons were disbanded at Little Snoring and by the end of September the airfield was closed to flying. During the 1950s it was reopened for flying and in more recent times it has played host to some amazing aerobatic flying. Not very far from the site of the airfield is the delightful village of Little Snoring with its charming 13th century church of St Andrew, which has a fine example of those round towers so unique to East Anglian churches. A plaque in the nave records that the RAF used the church during 1944 and 1945 and there are also Award and Memorial Boards that record lists of sorties, enemy aircraft shot down and the presentation of medals to the squadrons that flew from the nearby airfield. One of the original hangars is now used as a grain store and the control tower is still standing proudly flying a wind sock to show that 50 years later the airfield is still being used for its original purpose – flying.

19
LUDHAM

Ludham was Norfolk's most easterly airfield situated about 13 miles to the north-east of Norwich and close to Hickling Broad. It came into existence in October 1941 as the second grass satellite for Coltishall and in November received its first aircraft, Spitfire IIs of 152 squadron, which had spent several months at RAF Swanton Morley. The appearance of this renowned fighter aptly introduced wartime operational life to the small airfield. For virtually all of its existence Ludham would be known for the Spitfire squadrons that arrived and departed in quick succession; it was only for a brief period during the early summer of 1943 that any other type used the airfield.

In December the Spitfire Vbs of No 19 squadron arrived and stayed for about five months. It was a return to familiar territory for the squadron's pilots because during the Battle of Britain they had formed part of the famous Duxford Wing. It had also gained fame as being the first squadron in Fighter Command to receive the new Spitfire – K9789 – which arrived on 4th August 1938 at Duxford. The Spitfire V was probably one of the best known and popular marks (over 6,000 were built). It was powered by a Merlin 46 engine, which improved its speed to 375 mph and with the extra facility of drop fuel tanks increased its range. Cannon armed and able to carry two 250 pound bombs it was the first version to be used as a fighter/bomber and formed the backbone of Fighter Command during 1941/2. The squadron spent most of its time at Ludham giving fighter support to No 2 Group's bombing missions over Holland and northern France.

When it left in April 1942 to move to Yorkshire it was replaced by yet another Spitfire squadron – No 610 (County of Chester) – one of the more famous auxiliary squadrons of Fighter Command. It had a cosmopolitan collection of pilots – Canadians, Australians,

Spitfire 24: Ludham was known for its Spitfire squadrons.

Frenchmen, a New Zealander, Belgian, Rhodesian and Norwegian! Moreover it was commanded by one of Fighter Command's most illustrious pilots – Squadron Leader 'Johnnie' Johnson. He had joined the RAF Volunteer Reserve in 1939 as a sergeant pilot, had served with Douglas Bader at Coltishall in 1940 as a pilot officer and now two years later he had command of his own squadron. By the end of the war Johnson had risen to the rank of Group Captain, a highly decorated officer and the top scoring Allied fighter pilot of the war with 36 victories to his credit. He retired from the RAF in 1966 as an Air Vice-Marshal.

In August the squadron was detached to West Malling in Kent to take part in the disastrous raid on Dieppe: Johnson was outright in his condemnation, 'Tactically the Dieppe raid must be regarded as a complete failure, for none of its stated objectives were achieved in full measure...' When the squadron's Spitfires returned to Ludham they continued to mount a variety of 'Ramrods' and 'Circuses'. 'Ramrod' was the name given to bomber and fighter operations directed at a particular target, whereas a 'Circus' was a daylight bomber and fighter raid with the intention of bringing enemy fighters into action. They also helped out the Beaufighters from Coltishall in chasing enemy intruders along the East Coast.

Certainly it was a shock to the squadron when instead of being posted back to No 11 Group (Biggin Hill, Kenley or North Weald) they were sent to Castletown in the far north of Scotland – most of the pilots had no idea where it was! As soon as they had gone they were replaced by yet more Spitfires, this time belonging to No 167 squadron, of which one Flight was composed solely of Dutch pilots, so retaining the international flavour of the airfield. These airmen were some of the few who had managed to escape from their homeland when it was overrun in 1940. Their Spitfires, too, were largely employed as fighter escorts and they stayed at Ludham for eight months, making them almost permanent residents by the standards of Fighter Command. When it did leave for Hornchurch in May 1943 it was reformed as an all Dutch squadron.

Suddenly... surprise... surprise... a new aircraft landed at Ludham – the Hawker Typhoon 1b (see Matlaske). This squadron, No 195, had only been formed at Duxford in the previous November. It had spent a long time working up to operational readiness and its pilots suffered many minor accidents during training but within a few weeks of its arrival at Ludham the pilots claimed their first victory – a Me109 shot down over the English Channel. The squadron was detailed to operate what were called 'fighter nights' – sorties involving day fighters making night patrols above a certain height with strict orders to shoot at any aircraft with more than one engine! Seemingly a haphazard method of operation and they proved not to be very successful although Fighter Command had been using the tactic since November 1940. A further complication for the squadron was that the Typhoon was not really suited to such tasks, just another case of not recognising the right role and true worth of this remarkable aircraft.

Fairey Swordfish.

By July the Typhoons had moved to Matlaske and Ludham was closed to flying. It was due for redevelopment for what was expected to be its next role as an Eighth Air Force airfield, and three concrete runways and additional accommodation huts were built. The work took almost twelve months to complete but no Americans came to the airfield. The Royal Navy took over the facilities in August 1944 and named it 'HMS Flycatcher' as the headquarters of a Naval air force.

The RAF did not return to Ludham until January 1945, when Spitfire LF16s of No 603 'City of Edinburgh' squadron flew in from Coltishall, having spent most of the war in the Middle East as a Coastal Command strike force No 229 and been reformed as a fighter squadron at Coltishall. This Spitfire mark was specifically designed to improve the aircraft's performance especially at high altitudes. The new Spitfires proved to be quite successful at tackling V1 rocket sites and they were the first RAF aircraft to claim a victory over the new German jet fighter – Me262. No 603 operated with great success from Ludham, attacking V2 rocket sites, escorting Beaufighters on shipping attacks and escorting heavy bomber missions. During March 1945 it operated daily missions to targets in the advance of the Allied armies and on 16th its aircraft dropped 56,000 pounds of bombs – no mean achievement for what was basically a fighter squadron! For just three months it was joined at Ludham by another Spitfire squadron – No 602 the 'City of Glasgow'. However, towards the middle of April the land battle in Europe had passed out of the range of the Spitfires from Ludham and the airfield's wartime operations came to a close, with the final Spitfire mission being mounted on 1st May 1945. By the end of the year the airfield was closed down and has now been completely submerged under farm land.

20
MARHAM

Mighty does not seem a too extravagant adjective to describe Marham's time as a wartime airfield. From the very first hesitant flurries of action in 1939, through the dark days of 1940 and 1941 to the gathering strength of Bomber Command during 1942 and finally to the stirring derring-dos of its Mosquito squadrons of 1943/4, Marham always seemed to be in the forefront of the bomber offensive. Marham's Wellingtons, Stirlings and more especially Mosquitos all made a vital contribution to Bomber Command. And yet all this was achieved despite the fact that the airfield closed for business over a year before the end of the war by which time Marham's reputation had been truly made.

Marham can trace its origins back to the days of the First World War when Narborough, just about one and half miles north-east of the present airfield, had been established as a night flying landing field in August 1915 and in the following year it became an important training station for the Royal Flying Corps. Thus Marham can claim to be the oldest airfield in Norfolk still in operational use and last year celebrated 75 years as a RAF station. For most of the inter-war years the airfield lay idle and held in reserve, but with the expansion of the RAF in the mid-1930s considerable work was undertaken and on 1st April 1937 a splendid large station was opened as yet another airfield for No 3 Group of Bomber Command, effectively deciding Marham's future would lie with heavy bombers.

On 5th May 1937 No 38 squadron moved in with its ungainly Fairey Hendons. This squadron could be considered as very 'local' as it had first been formed at nearby Thetford in 1916 and had been commanded by a certain Captain A.T. Harris, who later became famous as 'Bomber' Harris, the Commander-in-Chief of Bomber

Command. Just one month later Handley Page Harrows of No 115, a newly formed squadron, landed and Marham was provided with its full complement of aircraft. Both of these aircraft were almost obsolescent and indeed looked as if they belonged to a different era! Before the outbreak of the war two squadrons would be re-equipped by the RAF's latest bomber – the Vickers Wellington.

On 6th October 1939 No 115 squadron mounted its first mission, a search for German vessels that were active along the Norwegian coast. The other squadron became operational five weeks later when six of its aircraft were sent out on a reconnaissance patrol of the North Sea. The first taste of any real action came on 6th December when aircraft from both squadrons were sent to bomb shipping targets off Heligoland. Like all Wellington squadrons during the so-called 'Phoney War' the crews were engaged on long hours of night flying just to shower thousands of propaganda leaflets over the enemy or do the odd spot of 'gardening' – the laying of mines along the German coasts. In the early days of April 1940 just after Denmark and Norway had been invaded, six Wellingtons from 115 attacked Sola airfield near Stavanger at what was really a suicidal height of 1,000 feet. Very fortunately only one aircraft was shot down although another was badly damaged but the pilot, Flight Sergeant Powell brought the aircraft back to Marham despite being wounded and for this gallant action he was awarded the DFM, the first of many honours to be gained by the squadron's crews.

The last week of 1942 proved to be a very auspicious week for Marham, as it was for another 52 airfields situated throughout eastern England and the Midlands. By Tuesday 26th it was quite clear to all on the station that something 'big' was being planned by Bomber Command. All weekend passes were cancelled, crews on leave were sent immediate recall telegrams and the ground crews told that every

A Wellington of 38 Squadron: Marham 1937-1940.

available aircraft was to be prepared for a special operation. 'Maximum effort' had been called for by every bomber station and that even included training stations. At Marham the Station Commander, Group Captain 'Square' McKee, a rather trenchant New Zealander interpreted this as 'maximum and a bit more'. Sixteen aircraft from each squadron was considered the normal operational figure, though this total was not very often achieved because of servicing problems and shortages of replacement items. However Group Captain McKee demanded that every aircraft at Marham, including the reserves (usually two or three per squadron), would be prepared for the coming operation, and McKee was a man who usually got his own way! By the end of the week Marham had 19 Stirlings and 18 Wellingtons ready to go – a quite amazing achievement.

As the days and weeks passed the rumours and counter-rumours became rife around the station, indeed the intense activity was likened to 'something out of a Hollywood film'! Most of the crews expected to be detailed for a large daylight operation on Berlin and as the weather conditions postponed the operation, bets were taken on what would be the target. After much speculation, early on Saturday morning the 30th May came the message from Group headquarters that a big operation would go ahead that night.

The briefing was at six o'clock in the evening, the doors of the room were locked and guarded and then very dramatically the paper covering the map of northern Germany was drawn aside to reveal the target – Cologne. There was considerable relief when the crews realised that it was not going to be a daylight mission and furthermore not to the 'Big B'. When they were informed that they were going to just one city with more than a thousand aircraft, the reaction was quite amazing, cheering broke out and had to be silenced for Air Marshal Harris's message to be read out, 'The force of which you form a part tonight is at least twice the size and has more than four times the carrying capacity of the largest air force ever before concentrated on one objective. You have the opportunity, therefore, to strike a blow at the enemy which will resound, not only throughout Germany, but throughout the world...Press home your attack to your precise objective with the utmost determination and resolution in the foreknowledge that if you succeed, the most shattering and devastating blow will have been delivered against the very vitals of the enemy. Let him have it – right on the chin.'

Air Vice-Marshal Jack Baldwin, the AOC of No 3 Group, had

decided to go on the operation but without the permission of his chief – 'Bomber' Harris. He accompanied Wing Commander Paul Holder DFC, in the lead aircraft of 218 squadron. The first aircraft left Marham at 10.30 pm and joined the immense bomber stream that was forming over East Anglia, it was said that the sky was full of bombers. One of the pilots recalled, '. . . it was an inspiring sight, everywhere you looked you could see aircraft, in some strange way it gave me a feeling of security to be part of such a force.' Of the 1,047 aircraft that were despatched some 868 managed to bomb the target causing indescribable damage, indeed days later the fires were still burning. Of the 41 aircraft lost, the majority came from the Wellington squadrons, which had formed the bulk of the attacking force. The first aircraft arrived back at Marham at 3.30 am and it would be an hour or so before they were certain that the two squadrons had each lost one aircraft. Marham's squadrons were also involved in the two other '1,000' raids to Essen and Bremen in June, which were not quite so successful.

However, Marham's days as a heavy bomber station were rapidly coming to a close. In July the Stirlings departed to Downham Market, its satellite airfield which would become a station in its own right. Then on 24th September No 115's Wellingtons left for Mildenhall in Suffolk. The airfield was transferred to No 2 Group and entered into its most famous period of wartime operations.

Within days of the change of Groups squadrons No 139 and 105 moved in from Horsham St Faith. The latter was already equipped with Mosquitos but 139 had to wait another month before it exchanged its sadly outmoded Blenheim IVs. Wing Commander 'Hughie' Edwards VC, DFC, had returned to command his old squadron with which he had won his VC whilst operating from Swanton Morley. Since then Edwards, along with other famous RAF pilots, had been on a VIP tour of the United States to promote Britain's war effort and the 'Lend-Lease' programme.

On 25th September 1942 a special target had been selected for 105 squadron – a low-level daylight attack on the Gestapo headquarters at Oslo in Norway. It was known that Quisling, the Norwegian collaborator, was holding a special Nazi rally in the city on that day and it was felt that it would be a great fillip to the Norwegian Resistance if a daring attack was made to mark the occasion. Four Mosquitos led by Squadron Leader D.A.G. Parry were detailed to pinpoint bomb 'a large building with a high dome' – as the building was described. On the low-level approach one Mosquito was shot down but the other three flew across the city at roof-top height, completely taking the ground defences by surprise. It was later said that the Norwegians cheered as the three Mosquitos roared across the city. The aircraft dropped their delayed fused bombs and managed to return to Marham without further loss. It was the first low-level Mosquito attack of the war and paved the way for the other famous low-level raids of 1943/44.

In October 1942 the British press were allowed, for the first time, to see and hear about the new wooden 'wonder' aircraft, hitherto the aircraft had been a closely guarded secret and even the mere mention of the name 'Mosquito' was strictly forbidden! There was universal praise in the press for the aircraft. The *Daily Mail* called it 'the grandson of the Comet [de Havilland's racing aircraft] and a prodigal son of the Albatross [four-engined wooden airliner], and another writer said, '... it is aptly named as it will sting the Nazis time and time again, proving far worse than its namesake and far more dangerous...' Despite all the secrecy, only in September Goering had praised the Mosquito and said, 'I wish someone had brought out a wooden aircraft for me'!

During the next few months both Marham squadrons were very active and by the end of November they had mounted no less than 282 sorties for the loss of 22 aircraft, a high operational loss (8%), at least compared with the Command's average of 5% but invariably the Mosquito raids were conducted by day, at low-level and, at that time, the aircraft was unarmed and relied purely on their amazing speed to escape the enemy fighters. Their main targets had been engine sheds, river and canal traffic, small industrial works and oil storage depots. The two squadrons had clearly demonstrated to all the sceptics in Bomber Command that it was possible to fly low-level in daylight without too heavy losses. 'Freeman's Folly' was beginning to prove its true worth.

One of the most famous Mosquito operations was the raid on the Burmeister and Wain factory in Denmark, which was making valuable U-boat components. Nine Mosquitos led by Wing Commander Edwards took off from Marham on 27th January 1943, they had already spent two hard weeks of training for this mission. The target was successfully bombed but two aircraft were shot down on the run-in. Then three days later came the most publicised Mosquito raid so far – a daylight bombing raid on Berlin. Intelligence sources had revealed that on 30th January, which was the tenth anniversary of Hitler's seizure of power, Goering was scheduled to

De Havilland Mosquito Is of No 105 Squadron, Marham.

address a mass meeting in Berlin at 11 am. Three aircraft from 105 squadron led by Squadron Leader R. Reynolds were timed to arrive over Berlin at precisely the right hour, which they did and bombed a railway junction to the north of Berlin. As a follow-up to Goering's speech, Goebbels had intended to speak at another Nazi rally at 4 pm. Three Mosquitos of 139 squadron led by Squadron Leader D. Dorling again arrived over Berlin at the exact time, and bombed an area just about half a mile from the city centre. Unfortunately the Squadron Leader failed to return from this mission. The two audacious raids were well publicised in the press and on the BBC news and they caught the British public's imagination, greatly helping to raise morale. The attacks were probably immortalised by Sergeant Fletcher's remarks to a reporter, 'We came out of a cloud and, God bless my soul, there was Berlin!' Squadron Leader Dorling received the DSO and all other members of the Mosquitos taking part were awarded DFCs or DFMs depending on their ranks.

The two squadrons went from strength to strength mounting spectacular and very effective daylight bombing raids. Wing Commander Edwards had been promoted and left 105 squadron to be succeeded by Wing Commander Longfield who lost his life shortly afterwards on a raid to Rennes airfield. On 27th May 1943 Marham launched one of the most spectacular daylight missions – to the Schlott Glass works and the Zeiss optical instruments plant at Jena, some 45 miles from Leipzig, which was the deepest penetration operation by Mosquitos so far. Fourteen aircraft led by Wing Commander Reynolds DSO, DFC left Marham. Despite encountering severe flak over the targets and very heavy fighter opposition on the way back, eleven Mosquitos returned safely but two of these were written off whilst attempting to land. Although a very costly operation, it proved to be most effective causing serious damage to the works.

The impressive results achieved by the two squadrons had not gone unnoticed by the chiefs of Bomber Command and it was now considered that the Mosquitos had a far different role to play in the Bomber offensive – as target markers for the main bomber force. Already one Mosquito squadron had been equipped with 'Oboe' and now No 105 was ear-marked to become the second 'Oboe' squadron in Bomber Command.

'Oboe', short for 'Observer bombing over enemy', was devised to replace the GEE navigational aid whose signals had proved to be easy for the enemy to jam. Oboe was a variation of a device used most effectively by the Luftwaffe in their night raids of 1940/1. The aircraft flew at the end of a radar beam laid by a ground radar station. The bombs or markers were released at the exact point of intersection with another beam from a second ground radar station. There was no scope for visual error, and 'Oboe' proved to be an excellent blind bombing device. The Pathfinder Force that had developed the techniques of marking targets had almost become a corps d'elite manned by crews of high navigational skills and had been formed into a new Group – No 8 – in January 1943.

On 4th July, No 139 squadron moved to RAF Wyton to allow the other 'Oboe' squadron – 109 – to move in. After considerable training the crews of 105 were ready to mount its first 'Oboe' mission. The change had not been universally welcomed by the crews as they felt that they had lost some of their individuality, and although their low-level attacks had been very dangerous they had also been highly exciting with very positive results to be seen for all the dangers and risks involved in such missions. However, 105 Mosquitos went out on 25th July to mark the Krupps factory complex for a force of over 750 bombers. But one of the drawbacks of 'Oboe' was its relatively short operational range, no more than 275 miles and as the bombers were now striking far into Germany, the two Mosquito squadrons turned their attention to attacking specialised and priority targets in and around the Ruhr. Under 'Oboe' guidance the two squadrons obtained some amazing night bombing results and all at a very low loss of aircraft (0.4%).

At the end of 1943 and into the early months of 1944 the squadrons were engaged in marking V1 rocket sites and making attacks on the German night fighter airfields in Holland and western Germany. There was a switch back to daylight operations in March when railway and other communication centres became the priority in advance of the Allied invasion. However, Marham had been selected for development into a very heavy bomber station. In March 1944 No 105 squadron took a sad farewell of Marham and it moved to Bourn, followed a week later by No 109, which departed for Little Staughton in Huntingdonshire. The airfield did not reopen again until February 1946 when the Central Bomber Establishment settled in.

Marham had seen many famous Mosquito pilots fly from the airfield. Other than 'Hughie' Edwards probably the most famous was Wing Commander John Wooldridge DSO, DFC, DFM who was the squadron commander of No 105 from March 1943 until he was promoted to Group Captain in July. Wooldridge became renowned for his courage and daring in leading many of the low-level operations mounted from Marham. He wrote a fine account of these operations called *Low Attack*, which is now considered a classic of war literature. Also at Marham during the same time was Flight Lieutenant Ralston, DSO, DFC, DFM, who completed 83 missions during the war and the citation to the award of a bar to his DSO read, 'his unswerving devotion to duty and heroic endeavours have set a standard beyond praise'. Squadron Leader 'Bill' Blessing DSO DFC was yet another one of those brilliant and brave pilots that flew with Marham's Mosquito squadrons. He received his DSO for the operation on the Zeiss optical factory. Unfortunately he was killed in July 1944 when 'marking' Caen for a heavy bomber attack. Marham should be justly proud of such brave airmen.

21
MATLASKE

Matlaske is a village neatly tucked away in a most pleasant and secluded corner of north-east Norfolk and today seemingly a most unlikely spot to house a small but yet very busy wartime airfield. It is difficult to realise that Hurricanes, Spitfires, Typhoons, Tempests, Whirlwinds and Mustangs – a veritable panoply of all the famous fighter aircraft of the war – once roared over this gentle countryside. The airfield owed its existence to the development of Coltishall, some twelve miles or so to the south-east, as a major Fighter Command station, and the grassed airfield was rushed forward during the summer of 1940 to become Coltishall's first satellite.

By October 1940 two relatively short, grass runways (1,600 yards and 1,300 yards) had been prepared and in retrospect this work may have been completed a little too quickly because the airfield frequently suffered from quite severe drainage problems, particularly during the cold and wet winters that seemed to be a feature of the wartime years. The living quarters were not fully completed by the time the first aircraft arrived during the latter days of the month, so the nearby Itteringham Hall was requisitioned to house both the air and ground crews. It was described as 'a charming converted millhouse which arched over a clear chalk-stream stocked with brown trout' – it sounds quite idyllic and a far cry from some of the accommodation at other Norfolk airfields!

Perhaps it was the bomb attack on Coltishall on 27th October that hastened the decision to use Matlaske, because some Spitfires from No 72 squadron almost immediately appeared. Not to be outdone, just two days later the Luftwaffe struck again when five enemy aircraft strafed Matlaske causing slight damage to the parked aircraft and a number of casualties.

Matlaske and its parent station operated more like one single integrated unit than most other satellite airfields and combined patrols and operations were mounted from both airfields. Just before Matlaske received slightly more permanent residents the airfield was under attack once again on 12th May 1941 by Luftwaffe aircraft using incendiaries, though only minor damage was sustained. Three days later No 222 squadron brought its Spitfire IIs to the airfield.

This squadron was probably best known for having been formed on the same day as the RAF – 1st April 1918. Like most Spitfire squadrons it had suffered heavily during the Battle of Britain and had been 'retired' to Coltishall late in the previous year. It was quite normal for Fighter Command to move its squadrons out of the 'front line' – the defence of London and the south east – for a period to relax and regroup. Whilst it operated from Matlaske it spent much of its time providing escorts for the North Sea fishing fleets and the patrols became known as 'Kippers'. When the squadron left, its place was taken by yet another famous fighter squadron – No 601 (City of London) – which had been selected to trial a new American fighter, the Bell Aircobra. The first two flights of this new fighter had ended in forced landings and there were several further accidents during training and conversion, but despite this the squadron was moved to Manston to see how the aircraft fared in operations; these turned out to be not very successful and the aircraft was never brought into general service with the RAF.

In November 1941 another strange new fighter appeared at the airfield – the Westland Whirlwind – belonging to No 137 squadron lately based at Coltishall, the first of only two squadrons to be equipped with the aircraft. It was a single seat twin-engined fighter, of which only 112 were produced mainly because there were continual niggling problems with the engines, making the maintenance of the aircraft most difficult. Furthermore it had a very high landing speed, which resulted in quite a few accidents until the pilots became used to it. But it was very fast at low altitudes with a far superior range than most fighters then in service and in theory should have provided a useful addition to Fighter Command. Perhaps it was best suited to the role of fighter/bomber but yet it tended to be used mainly on escort duties because of its long range. Shortly before the squadron arrived at Matlaske, it had lost its Commanding Officer in a collision with another aircraft whilst on sea patrol. This hardly endeared the aircraft to the pilots and it was never really trusted by them.

Hawker Typhoons first arrived at Matlaske in August 1942.

On 12th February 1942, the Whirlwinds became part of perhaps the RAF's most inglorious operations of the whole war, the vain attempt to prevent the 'Channel Dash' of German warships from Brest through the English Channel to safer German ports. The flotilla of vessels – the *Scharnhorst, Gneisenau* and *Prinz Eugen* were first sighted in the late morning. Four aircraft of 137 squadron were ordered off to escort some British destroyers that were steaming to intercept the heavily defended German battleships. The four Whirlwinds sighted the flotilla just off the Belgian coast and as they dived to investigate they were attacked by the covering escort of Me109s. Almost immediately two Whirlwinds were shot down, the other two managed to make their escape. Another two Whirlwinds that took off from Matlaske just half an hour later never returned, their fate can only be imagined. Four out of six aircraft lost in action was too heavy a loss. During the day 242 sorties were launched by Bomber, Fighter and Coastal Commands and that is without the Naval action, but because of poor visibility and quite atrocious weather most of the aircraft never located the enemy vessels and those that did bombed most ineffectively. A posthumous VC was won by a Swordfish pilot of the Fleet Air Arm for a very determined and brave attack on the vessels. The flotilla escaped relatively unharmed despite all the efforts of the RAF and the Royal Navy. The sheer effrontery of the 'Channel Dash' made a mockery of the three RAF Commands and most of the national press were loud in their ridicule – or at least as far as censorship would allow, even *The Times* thought the action 'mortifying'!

The Whirlwinds returned to their mundane patrols of the east coast and the eastern approaches to the Channel – the 'bread and butter' of their time at Matlaske. The squadron was not particularly successful, or at least not until May 27th when they claimed their first victim – a Ju88 and several others followed smartly once they had broken their duck. In late July, they were removed from operations whilst bomb racks were fitted and soon they had left for Kent to be closer to the action over northern France.

Like most Fighter Command stations during the war, squadrons arrived and departed with great regularity sometimes with hardly enough time to get settled before they moved elsewhere. The next squadron to arrive in August 1942 was No 56 with their Hawker Typhoon 1bs. This fighter and ground attack aircraft had come into service during September 1941. At first its performance was somewhat disappointing. There were considerable problems encountered with the engines – a new Napier Sabre IIA – and the aircraft had a suspect rear fuselage as certain stress fractures occurred near the tail section. But it was then the fastest fighter in service with the RAF with a top speed just in excess of 400 mph and it almost matched the performance of the new German fighter, the Fw190. This latest addition to the Luftwaffe's fighter force had been causing Fighter Command some deep concern as it constantly out-performed the existing Spitfires and Hurricanes. Unfortunately the Typhoon bore a certain resemblance to the Fw190 and so yellow bands were

Westland Whirlwind: 137 Squadron was one of only two to be equipped with these aircraft.

painted across the top of its wings and black and white bands under them as an extra aid to recognition for 'friendly' aircraft.

The squadron had one of the famous 'Few' from Battle of Britain days – Squadron Leader 'Cocky' Dundas, who managed to survive the war, ending up as Group Captain. Despite almost continual problems with their aircraft the squadron's pilots still managed to make regular shipping patrols as well as both day and night 'Rhubarbs' (the odd name given to individual squadron sorties over enemy territory). The RAF persevered with the aircraft and it gained a fine reputation as a ground attack fighter, becoming quite lethal against tanks and trains, using its rocket projectiles to devastating effect.

The various fighter squadrons had also shared the airfield with detachments of No 278 squadron of Fighter Command, which operated solely on air/sea rescue work for a distance of at least 40 miles from the coast. During September 1942 Matlaske was offered to the USAAF as a base for one of its Fighter Groups, though in fact the Eighth Air Force never availed itself of the offer.

In August 1943 the airfield was closed to all flying whilst its future expansion was considered. It was then not until September 1944 that the airfield welcomed back some operational aircraft – Mustang IIIs of No 150 Wing of the Second Tactical Air Force. The pilots spent most of their time acting as escorts for the waves of bombers attacking Holland and the Ruhr by day. Nevertheless they were only fleeting visitors because by October three different squadrons arrived – Nos 229, 453 and 602 – all equipped with Spitfire IXs with the Merlin 45 engine and designed to compete on equal terms with the Fw190. This mark of Spitfire was able to carry two 250 or one 500 pound bombs and the three squadrons became very involved in dive-bombing strikes and more especially attacking V2 rocket sites. Because the airfield became seriously water-logged during the winter of 1944/5 all the aircraft had to be dispersed to other Norfolk airfields.

It was the Spitfires of 453 squadron that last used the airfield for operational sorties, flying their final mission in April 1945. After the squadron had left for Lympne at the end of April the airfield became quite deserted and was quickly given up by the RAF in the October of that year, and it was one of the earliest wartime airfields to be handed back to farming. The old control tower still stands as a forlorn reminder of this rather forgotten little wartime airfield and it can be seen just east of the village off the road to Holt.

22

METHWOLD

Twixt forest and fen would aptly describe the village of Methwold and its airfield, situated as they are at the eastern extremity of the great spread of Thetford Forest and yet on the edge of Norfolk's fenland. The elegant, slender spire of the village church was often a most welcoming sight for returning aircrews.

The airfield itself owes its existence to the nearby RAF Feltwell, which is about three miles due south as the crow flies and as already shown the airfield was extremely important in Bomber Command's plans for its early war operations. Therefore, it was decided quite early – well before the outbreak of hostilities – that Methwold would be developed as a satellite for Feltwell. Within months of No 37 squadron being fully mobilised in August of that fateful year some of its precious Wellingtons were dispersed to this rather rudimentary grass airfield, nestling close to the comforting protection of the forest.

Although few operations were mounted from the airfield, it played host to a variety of Feltwell's squadrons, most notably No 57, and it was from Methwold that some of its aircraft left to bomb Berlin on 23rd March 1941. In August 1942 both Feltwell and Methwold moved out of Group 3 of Bomber Command and into Group 2, which had always signified the light and medium bomber squadrons, or the 'Death or Glory Boys' as they were so often described. The horrendous casualties they suffered during 1940/1 ensured that their exploits and bravery would never be forgotten, and they quickly passed into the folklore of the Service.

The first squadron to appear at Methwold was No 21 bringing with them their new and, as yet, untried Lockheed Venturas. These twin-engined patrol-bombers were intended as a replacement for the Bristol Blenheim and were produced by the American firm solely for

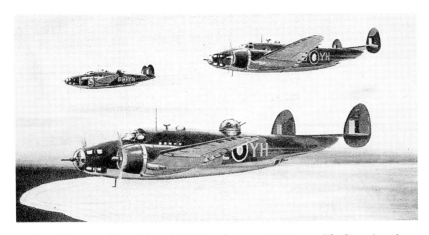

Lockheed Ventura: Nos 464 and 487 Squadrons gained fame with these American-built aircraft.

the RAF. The original contract for 675 aircraft had been placed back in the summer of 1940 but the planned delivery was delayed almost a year. The Ventura looked very similar to the Hudson, another Lockheed aircraft, which was then operating with great success in Coastal Command; in fact its design owed much to this reliable and useful aircraft. However, the Ventura had many strong critics in Bomber Command and the general view was that it could do nothing more than the Hudson but used far more fuel. Because of their rather porcine shaped fuselages they were dubbed 'The Flying Pig' or just plain 'Pig'. Even the operating crews' early misgivings were fully justified because the aircraft proved to be not very successful on daylight bombing missions and by September 1943 it had flown its last mission for Bomber Command and was transferred to Coastal Command.

It took several months for the Venturas to become operational and their first daylight raid was in November 1942. During the following month they were involved in a variety of 'Circuses' in conjunction with Spitfires from Coltishall. Bad weather during most of January and early February rather curtailed the operational programme. Then in April, No 487, a RNZAF squadron from Feltwell, settled in at Methwold and with them came Squadron Leader Leonard Trent DFC as flight commander. Trent, a New Zealander, had already proved to be a charismatic leader and was marked out for high promotion in the Service; in fact he had turned down a Staff College course to stay on operations. He had a fine and wide operational experience going back to the early battles over France in 1940. More recently he had been engaged in the famous raid on the Philips works at Eindhoven in the previous December.

On 2nd May Venturas of 464, an Australian squadron based at Feltwell, had attacked the Royal Dutch Steel works at Ijmuiden with not a great deal of success. Group headquarters decided to repeat the attack the following day using six Boston IIIs from 107 squadron to attack the steel works whilst twelve Venturas from 487 squadron made a diversionary attack on the Amsterdam power station. It was stressed that the operation would greatly hearten the Dutch Resistance workers, who were fostering industrial strife in the works. The whole mission would be strongly supported by nine squadrons of Spitfires and Mustangs from Coltishall. In theory the operation seemed most sound, a quick, unexpected follow-up raid with such a large fighter escort should have ensured a successful outcome. The two squadron leaders tossed a coin for the honour of leading the attack and Trent won.

The bombers planned to climb to 12,000 feet before making their final bomb run and when they were about ten minutes' flying time from Amsterdam they were attacked by a force of about 70 fighters. The Fw190s engaged the Spitfires and Mustangs whilst the Me109s laid into the Venturas. Three were quickly shot down, followed shortly by another two and a couple of minutes later another three went down in flames. So this left only Trent's aircraft and another two coming in on to the target. Even then when Trent was concentrating on his bombing line he accounted for one Me109 but just minutes later another Ventura plunged into the ground. After bombing the target Trent realised that his was the sole remaining aircraft. Suddenly there was a loud explosion in the aircraft and it went into an uncontrollable spin. Trent ordered his crew to bale out and just minutes later the aircraft blew up forcibly ejecting Trent into space at a height of some 7,000 feet. He landed by parachute on the outskirts of Amsterdam and was quickly captured. Shortly afterwards he was reunited with his navigator, who was the only other survivor of his crew.

Trent was sent to Stalag Luft III and immediately became involved in the Escape Committee. On 23rd March 1944 he took part in what has become known as 'The Great Escape' but he was captured just outside the perimeter wire – fortunately for him as subsequently 50 of the 76 escapees were murdered on the express orders of Hitler. It was not until 1945 when Trent and his navigator returned to England that the full details of the disastrous raid became known. Trent was awarded the Victoria Cross for 'his determined leadership and devotion to duty'. Long after the war had ended he returned to Norfolk, in March 1956, to become the commander of No 214 squadron at Marham just ten miles north of Methwold.

In such a relatively small and compact Service community, which probably never numbered more than 1,000 at any given time, to lose 55 aircrew on one single mission was a disaster of some magnitude especially as the crews were not aware of the full facts and the unfortunate reasons for such a calamitous raid. A note was written in the Operational Diary, '... A *very* black day in the squadron history ... a better set of boys could not be met in 30 years, everybody is feeling dazed by the news ...' Perhaps it was with a great feeling of relief that soon the squadron was moved away from Methwold when the airfield was transferred back to 3 Group.

It was the decision to greatly extend and improve Lakenheath, an airfield just across the county boundary in Suffolk, that brought back some flying activity to Methwold. In May 1944 No 149 squadron moved in with their Stirling IIIs just before the squadron was due to be converted to Lancasters. The 149th had a very fine record and tradition, indeed one of its pilots – Flight Sergeant Middleton – had been posthumously awarded the Victoria Cross for a raid on Turin in November 1942. The Stirlings had by now become rather upstaged by the Lancasters and Halifaxes, and their aircrews, who were totally loyal to their aircraft, felt that the Stirlings still should be employed on their rightful task – bombing Germany. Instead the squadron had lately been used for mine-laying and dropping supplies to the French Resistance. But it did fall to this squadron and Methwold to launch the last operational mission undertaken by Stirlings. On 8th September 1944 they attacked Le Havre and this was just one of a series of attacks on the Channel ports where some German garrisons were still stoutly resisting capture. The squadron was re-equipped with Lancaster IIIs and they proved to be the last operational aircraft to fly from Methwold.

Most of the airfield, like so many others in Norfolk, has long since disappeared as the land has gone back to farming. But an odd hangar and the few scattered remains of a ruined hut and messroom can still be seen among the trees. The airfield is found by taking the B1106 road north out of Brandon.

23
NORTH CREAKE

If Fersfield was Norfolk's most secretive airfield then North Creake can lay claim to be the county's most unobtrusive one; not only now when most of it has disappeared under the plough but even during its short operational existence. It was first developed in early 1941 as a decoy field for nearby Docking and was just one of the many 'sham' airfields to be found around the Norfolk countryside in those early war years. Their purpose was to confound the enemy and thus hopefully to draw air attacks away from the live operational airfields. This necessitated the construction of dummy hangars, living quarters and even mock aircraft to make the site look realistic from aerial photographs. These 'Q sites', as they were known, were also provided with flare path lighting which further helped to heighten the illusion. Then towards the end of 1942 it was felt that the threat from air attacks had sufficiently receded, and many of the decoy airfields were closed down.

In the case of North Creake it was developed into a full airfield for Bomber Command. Thus, during 1942, Taylor Woodrow built a typical bomber airfield with three concrete runways, two T1 and one Blister hangars and adequate accommodation for about 1,700 personnel – about the requisite number to man and service two operational squadrons. The airfield opened for business on 23rd November 1943 and for a brief period it was placed within No 3 Group acting as a satellite for Foulsham. Just two weeks later, on 7th December, it was transferred along with its parent station into the newly formed No 100 Group.

The airfield still awaited the arrival of its first aircraft whilst a long debate ensued in the Air Ministry as to whether North Creake should be further developed into a very heavy bomber station with even

Handley Page Halifax: 171 Squadron flew Mk 3 versions of these redoubtable bombers which became greatly involved in No 100 Group's operations.

longer runways and greater servicing facilities. The current thinking in Bomber Command was that there would be a need for a heavier Lancaster and possibly a new very heavy bomber, as yet only in the planning stage and known by the name 'Windsor'. Eventually, for whatever reasons, it was decided to greatly expand Lakenheath in Suffolk.

In April 1944 North Creake was granted full station status and on the first day of the following month No 199 squadron, then based at Lakenheath, arrived at the airfield but without any of its aircraft. Its Stirling Mark IIIs had been taken off bombing operations to be fitted with 'Mandrel screens' – one of the main tasks allocated to the squadron within 100 Group. 'Mandrel' was an electronic device that had been developed to transmit signals that effectively jammed the German 'Freya' radar. It had first been used operationally in December 1942 but since then had undergone considerable modification and was now quite a sophisticated system. The intention of the 'Mandrel' squadrons was to be present in the main bomber stream, either in the front to form an adequate screen or at other times mingling in the centre of the main force.

In early June, after a most intensive training programme, 199 squadron was ready for operations perfectly timed for D-Day. Sixteen aircraft (working in pairs) were involved on the night of 4/5th June setting up a Mandrel screen to give cover to the advancing invasion fleet. The squadron used what was known as the 'racecourse pattern', which had been devised at North Creake. It involved two aircraft flying around a compact circuit (hence the name) of ten minutes' duration to achieve the maximum intensity of jamming signals. The aircraft operated this pattern at a maximum altitude and this operation called for a very high degree of piloting and navigation.

During July the squadron made over 30 sorties, almost half of them in support of the main bomber force operations, in which they lost just one aircraft. Their other missions were 'spoof' operations conducted normally about 80 miles or so off the German coast in an attempt to fool the enemy radar about the direction of bomber raids. Some of the aircraft were also detached to a Special Window Force, the purpose of which was to divert enemy fighters away from the main attacking force by trying to create the illusion of a fake bomber stream. Their main weapon was 'window' dropping at a very high rate, some ten packets per minute, which would simulate the impression of a large attacking force. Often they would return to the same route or area night after night and then suddenly change. Bluff, counter-bluff and more bluff! Perhaps one of their more successful operations was in August 1944 which was mounted on Kiel, when the German fighters' controllers ignored their radar signals in the firm belief that it was just another spoof raid, mainly because the squadron had been active in the same area on the previous three nights.

On 7th September North Creake received a second squadron – No 171 – which was brought into the Group to assist on Mandrel duties. This squadron had been equipped with Handley Page Halifax IIIs but they were not available until November as they had to be fitted with all the necessary equipment. Subsequently 199 squadron were also equipped with Halifaxes but they were the last RAF squadron to fly the Stirlings operationally.

During the closing months of the war both squadrons were involved in several purely bombing missions in addition to their Mandrel and window dropping patrols, the last of which were mounted on 2nd May 1945. Although the work of these two squadrons lacked the glamour of bombing operations, the missions demanded a very high standard of flying and navigation and were essential to the success of Bomber Command during the latter stages of the war. In late July 1945 both squadrons were disbanded within two days of each other and the airfield was passed over to a maintenance unit and used to store scrap Mosquitos. The airfield was finally closed in September 1947.

24
NORTH PICKENHAM

On 27th May 1944 at a formal ceremonial parade, a RAF officer handed over the safe keeping of North Pickenham airfield to Colonel Eugene Snaveley, the Commanding Officer of the 492nd Bomb Group. This occasion marked the transfer of the 77th and final installation to the Eighth Air Force in the United Kingdom and the arrival of the last B-24 Bomb Group to serve in Norfolk. Not only was it the last but it also proved to be the unluckiest Bomb Group in the whole of the Eighth Air Force.

Over a month before the formal ceremony the Group's aircraft had arrived at North Pickenham in some quite atrocious weather – heavy driving rain, which made landing conditions quite treacherous but surprisingly there were no fatal accidents. The Group was placed in the 14th Combat Wing along with the 392nd at Wendling and the very experienced 44th at Shipdham; its Commanding Officer was well versed in European operations as he had previously served with the 44th Group. The Group's first mission was launched on 11th May when several railway marshalling yards in northern France were attacked. It was a reasonable first operation although on the return flight one aircraft was forced to crash-land at Bury St Edmunds and another in Sussex because of shortage of fuel.

Eight days later the Group found out just what the air war was about on an operation to Brunswick – as has already been noted this area was famed throughout the RAF and the Eighth Air Force for the expertise and tenacity of its fighter groups. When the formations of B-24s were attacked by a strong force of enemy fighters, they were virtually overwhelmed despite the escort of three squadrons of fighters. Four of the Group's aircraft were destroyed almost immediately, and another one, though severely damaged, continued on to the target but exploded just before the crew were able to release their bombs. On leaving Brunswick another three aircraft fell victim to fresh fighter onslaught, which was marked by its severity. One of the Group's B-24s named *Lucky Lass* collided with a Me109, which removed a large part of its starboard wing, but despite having only two engines the pilot still managed to bring the aircraft back home – it had been appropriately named! For this amazing piece of flying a young and very inexperienced pilot – Second Lieutenant Bridges – received a richly deserved Distinguished Flying Cross. Such a high loss on a single mission resulted in the Group's crews being stood down from the following day's operations.

The Group's fortunes then seemed to improve because by the middle of June it had managed to mount 21 missions with few material losses – apart from the disastrous Brunswick raid. But unfortunately this happy state of affairs was soon to change and in a most dramatic way. On 19th June one of its squadrons, No 858, was transferred to Cheddington to replace a squadron that had been engaged on dropping propaganda leaflets. None of the personnel left North Pickenham, they were just distributed through the other three squadrons.

On the following day (20th) the Eighth Air Force launched their biggest operation of the war. A large force of 1,402 aircraft attacked twelve large oil refineries in different parts of Germany and besides the heavy bombers over 700 fighters formed a most formidable escort. This was a massive air armada demonstrating the strength of the Eighth – well meriting its name the 'Mighty'. It now exceeded the Bomber Command in terms of aircraft and men. The Second Division, because of the greater operational range of its aircraft, were allocated to targets deep in central Germany – Pollitz and Osterburg. Two of the Fighter Groups were delayed, leaving just one Group of P-51 Mustangs to cover the whole of the Division's Groups, a quite impossible task, especially as the formation had become somewhat drawn out. The Group, along with the 44th from Shipdham, was in the 14th Combat Wing, which had fallen behind the strict time schedule that was necessary for such a major operation. With virtually no fighter protection the Luftwaffe fighters struck with deadly accuracy and at the end of the mission the Second Division had lost 34 B-24s of which 14 had come from the 492nd and another five landed in Sweden. The only aircraft from the Group to return to North Pickenham was one that aborted because of engine trouble.

The whole question of aircraft landing in neutral Sweden was quite a concern to the Eighth Air Force chiefs. Most of the crews that landed at Bulltofta, an airfield at the southernmost tip of Sweden, were genuine, their aircraft were badly damaged with little chance of surviving the North Sea crossing, let alone making it back to base. But there were some instances of undamaged aircraft landing so that their crews could seek sanctuary in neutral Sweden – a perfect way to get out of combat as all the crews were interned and the aircraft sequestered by the Swedish Government. In the early days the crews were under orders to fire their aircraft should they land in neutral territory. The Swedish Government was not prepared to do anything which might impinge on their neutrality and bring about some retaliatory action from Germany. After one mission to Berlin 18 aircraft landed in Sweden – quite an 'American colony' had been established there and even a special American air-attache was appointed to look after the American airmen's interests. These crews still received their full pay and were kept in fairly comfortable accommodation, all at the expense of the American government. Towards the end of the year a party of American ground personnel were allowed into the country to repair the damaged aircraft. Ultimately an

An aerial view of North Pickenham airfield. (Via K Thomas)

853rd Bomb Squadron on a mission to Germany, January 1945, with a B-24 taken by flak and going down. (Via K Thomas)

agreement was reached whereby the aircraft and crews were released on the proviso that neither the crews or aircraft would again be used in any operations over Europe.

After the Brunswick and Pollitz missions the Group must have wondered if things could get worse. It was difficult to think this possible but on 7th July disaster struck the 492nd once again. The Group was detailed for another large operation to Mersburg in southern Germany, where the Junkers aircraft factories were the targets. It was a deep penetration raid of over eight hours flying, which would be testing enough. But tactics were changed for this operation; the B-17s of the First Division were planned to join the B-24s some 100 miles west of Berlin rather than over the North Sea, which was the normal practice. However, for various reasons the B-17 formations were delayed and the Luftwaffe, which had gathered in considerable force, attacked the B-24s. And once again the 14th Combat Wing bore the brunt of the onslaught. In rapid succession twelve of the Group's aircraft were shot down, almost half of the Division's total losses. Such heavy casualties could not be concealed from other Groups in the Division and although many reasons were put forward to explain such appalling losses – poor formation flying, inexperienced crews and even the very distinctive natural metal colouring of the Group's aircraft which was thought to attract the enemy fighters! In reality it appeared that several unfortunate happenings had left the Group's aircraft in the wrong place at the wrong time. But there was no doubt that the severe losses experienced by the Group had an impact on the whole of the Second Division.

After mounting just another four missions in August, in which the Group lost another four aircraft, the 492nd was taken off operations and effectively disbanded. Its mission of 7th August was its 64th and final one. In barely three months 57 aircraft had been lost and over 540 airmen were missing in action. It was decided to redesignate the 'Special Operations' Group – the so-called 'Carpetbaggers' who dropped supplies to the French Resistance as well as landing Allied secret agents – as the 492nd Group. Most of the disbanded Group's aircraft and crews were distributed throughout the Second Division. It was also decided that the 491st, known as 'The Ringmasters', then operating from Metfield in Suffolk, should fill the vacant place in the 14th Combat Wing and move into North Pickenham. They arrived on 15th August 1944 and this Group had a vastly different record to the late lamented 492nd; in the previous three months of operations they had lost only ten aircraft.

During mid-September the 491st along with other Groups in the 14th and 20th Wings were greatly involved in flying low-level practice runs for about two days. Of course the crews were not aware of why they needed such training. However, the Allied airborne landings at Arnhem, Eindhoven and Nijmegen on 17th September probably supplied them with the answer. The Group's aircraft would be part of a 252 strong B-24 force dropping supplies to the airborne forces. Each aircraft was loaded with 20 containers on the evening of the 17th and on the following afternoon the force took off. The aircraft were to arrive over the dropping zones and then descend to 300 feet for the actual drop at a speed of about 150 mph. It was fully accepted that this was a delicate and dangerous operation calling for coolness and nerve. Although two Groups of fighters were present to try to draw and suppress the enemy's ground fire, the B-24s encountered very fierce and heavy opposition. In total seven aircraft were shot down, including one from the 491st. Well over half the aircraft taking part were damaged to some extent and two aircraft from the Group were forced to use Woodbridge, the special emergency landing field known to all aircrews as a 'Prangdrome'! Another three aircraft had to make emergency landings at Watton, Hawkinge and Brussels airfields because they were so badly damaged. It proved to be a quite costly exercise especially as some of the packages missed the dropping zones and were never recovered by the Allied troops.

On 26th November the Group faced its sternest test of the war. They formed just part of a large force of B-24s attacking oil refineries at Misburg, which was sited to the east of Hanover. Thirty-one aircraft left North Pickenham but shortly into the flight three aircraft had to abort with engine trouble. When the bomber stream was above Dümmer Lake with still some 80 miles to go to the target, their strength, route and speed were carefully noted by three enemy aircraft that were shadowing them. Within the next 20 miles or so a strong Luftwaffe fighter force attacked the escorting P-51 Mustangs but carefully avoided the bombers, who carried on to the target but without any fighter escort. Just as the B-24s were making their approach they were set upon by an enemy fighter force thought to be over 100 strong. The Group, which was flying well in the rear of the formation seemed to attract the most attention and within minutes 15 aircraft were destroyed and the remaining twelve were

Dropping supplies to ground troops, Wesel, March 1945. (Via K Thomas)

only saved by the sudden appearance of a couple of squadrons of P-51 Mustangs. With coolness and great discipline the tattered remnants of the Group's three squadrons managed to regroup into just one formation and went on to bomb the target. Only eleven out of the original 28 aircraft returned to North Pickenham. For their determination and courage shown on this mission the Group was awarded a Distinguished Unit Citation.

Despite such a shattering blow life still had to go on, and the following day 16 new B-24s arrived at the airfield. Two days later the Group's crews were back in business bombing Altenbeken to the north-east of the Ruhr, all the aircraft returning safely to North Pickenham. This was just another mission bringing the crews closer to the magical 35 to complete their tour. But it requires great courage to sally forth into the skies so soon after seeing so many of one's comrades plunge to their deaths. And yet all Bomb Group crews had to do just that day after day after day, they and their colleagues in Bomber Command fought a very special kind of war that demanded great resolution and unusual bravery.

Like virtually every Bomb Group in Norfolk war for the 491st came to a close on 25th April 1945. In just eleven months this Group had flown 187 missions and by the end of June all the aircraft and men had departed 'Stateside'. Some American Air Force units returned briefly to the airfield in the 1950s and today parts of the runways can still be discerned as can the rather distinctive water tower. It is not one of the easiest airfields to locate but can be found by taking the B1077 road to South Pickenham and taking a right-hand turning which will lead to a small commemorative stone to the memory of the men of the two Bomb Groups that served at North Pickenham.

25

OLD BUCKENHAM

'A few years ago I had the chance to visit Old Buckenham again. A train ride and a taxi ride landed me at our old base. The base was gone. The memories remained. I stood where the runways used to be and I cried a little because I could see so clearly so many close friends who didn't get home again. If I should get another chance to return to Old Buck I will gladly do so though I know full well that I will cry again and I will see my crew again and I will see our plane.' Just one veteran of the 453rd Bomb Group expressing his deep feelings of sorrow on his return to Norfolk. He really speaks for thousands of his fellow wartime comrades, who have made similar painful and emotional journeys back to those airfields, to remember that time when life seemed so unreal, so short and yet so precious.

Without doubt the Group's most famous veteran is James Stewart, the celebrated film star, who from March 1944 was the Group's Operations Officer. He too made a nostalgic return in May 1983 and formally opened the extension to the village's community hall, which now contains a display of memorabilia relating to the Group's time at the airfield. It is possible though that Walter Matthau, another Hollywood star, might just debate the point about the most famous 'old boy'? He also served at Old Buckenham under his real name Walter Matasschauskayasky – it is not surprising that he was not very well known at the time!

What remains of the old airfield – most of the main runway, some of the perimeter track and the odd hut – lies to the north-east of the village, which is attractively grouped around the great Church Green. Though much of the airfield has been returned to farming, part of the original runway is still used by light aircraft.

The first detachments of the ground personnel arrived at Old

453rd Bomb Group's B-24s flew 255 missions from Old Buckenham, losing 58 aircraft in the process. (USAF)

Buckenham just a couple of days before Christmas 1943 but the B-24H Liberators did not fly in until the first week of January. The Group had been placed in the Second Bomb Wing and its headquarters was just up the A11 road at Kettringham Hall. The 453rd was the last Group to arrive to complete the Wing, the other members were stationed at nearby Hethel and Tibenham.

It was not until 5th February that they were ready for action and their first operation was to be Tours in central France where there was an important Focke-Wulf assembly and repair plant. Despite it being a fairly stiff mission for an opener, the Group's inexperienced crews fared well and managed to complete their first mission without loss. Perhaps a good omen for their future operations, and as it turned out the Group had one of the lowest loss rates of aircraft in the whole of the Second Air Division. One of its squadrons – No 733 – managed to complete 82 missions without losing a single aircraft, a truly amazing record considering some of the heavy losses sustained by other B-24 Groups. The Group's pilots had obviously taken to heart the Eighth Air Force's adage 'The tighter you fly, the lighter you fall'. Formation discipline was the watchword of all squadron and Group commanders, they had learned by bitter experience that close formation needed to be maintained at all times to ensure that the squadron or Group was not put under undue risk.

On 24th February a large and combined operation had been planned by the Eighth. First Division Groups were being sent to Schweinfurt, the Third to the Baltic ports and the Second were allocated targets deep in central Germany with the main target being Gotha and its complex of Me110 factories. The Group's aircraft were placed in the leading formation and largely because of encountering different wind speeds than had been forecast, the leading groups soon found themselves well ahead of schedule and thus rather isolated from the main bomber stream, which was following far back in their wake. When the lead formation still had over an hour to go to the target it was attacked by a large enemy fighter force – a brutal onslaught which continued without respite almost until Gotha. Although the Second Division suffered very heavily on this mission – 33 aircraft were destroyed (almost 14% loss) – the Group managed to extricate themselves without losing a single aircraft. Considering the duration and ferocity of the air battle this was an unbelievable feat. Indeed the 453rd was one of the few Bomb Groups in the whole of the Eighth who managed to avoid heavy losses on one single mission. On this particular Gotha mission 16 aircraft came down in Switzerland, the highest figure for one operation. So these 16 aircraft were effectively lost as were the 160 crew members. This operation was just another part of the so-called 'Big Week' of the Eighth Air Force when over 3,300 sorties were flown. Certainly it was a very costly week of operations but it did cause quite an appreciable amount of damage to the German fighter production, which later was estimated to have been reduced by almost 50%. The American airmen were engaged in waging a war of bloody attrition against the German fighters, not only by their continuous heavy bombardment of aircraft factories and airfields but in the air also where the gunners and fighter groups were taking a very steady and costly toll of the Luftwaffe's fighter resources.

On 18th March the Group was detailed to take part in a long and deep penetration raid to Friedrichshafen, situated on the banks of Lake Constance close to the border with Switzerland. Although the weather conditions over the target area were expected to be nigh on perfect for visual bombing, when the attacking force arrived they found that the Germans had set up a very effective smoke screen largely coming from barges anchored on the lake. To add to the crews' discomfort and difficulties the B-24 Groups found themselves coming under very concentrated and accurate flak as well as encountering quite sustained fighter attacks. Although most of the force managed to bomb the targets, the results were later found to be rather disappointing. Once again, although the Second Division lost 28 aircraft, only one aircraft from the Group was shot down but this was their lead aircraft with their Commanding Officer on board – Colonel Joseph Miller. Then on the return flight one badly damaged aircraft crash-landed at Goudhurst killing four of its crew.

Purely on the law of averages the Group's admirable record could not last for ever and their heaviest loss on a single mission came on 8th April on a mission to Brunswick, where once again the B-24s met and suffered most intense fighter opposition. The Luftwaffe fighters stationed around Brunswick were noted for their determination and expertise and were called 'The Battling Blue-Nosed Bastards of Brunswick'. This time the 453rd lost seven aircraft. But almost as if to right the balance of this unusually unhappy mission, the Group went through the next three months of operations with the occasional loss of one aircraft or two at the most. Indeed the Group despatched 24 aircraft on the Eighth's major raid to Berlin on 21st June and succeeded in coming out of this cauldron of flak and fire completely unscathed – again a remarkable achievement.

During the latter days of November the Group was deeply engaged in the numerous attacks made on railway viaducts, marshalling yards and various oil installations in Western Germany. In three days of operations they lost just one aircraft and that crashed at Kenninghall shortly after take-off, unfortunately killing all the crew. One 453rd pilot later recalled his time at Old Buckenham, '... we were known as the meanest Group in the Division, we hated giving the enemy one of our ships, and that's the way we liked it. Some of our buddies in the Wing envied the record of Old Buck ... it made us real proud.'

The early winter months of 1944/5 were bad as far as the weather was concerned and not conducive to mounting air operations. Frequently heavy blankets of fog closed airfields and even if the aircraft did manage to get airborne they were often recalled and then found great difficulty in locating their bases. Quite naturally accidents increased, especially when the freeze set in and Norfolk suffered from several weeks of snow. The accident rate in the Eighth was always quite high, one in six of the aircraft it lost was due to accidental causes and many of these occurred when the large number of aircraft were forming up over Norfolk. Human error played as much a part as adverse weather conditions; the Group commanders tried to minimise these losses by emphasising greater care and discipline on assembly. Once again the 453rd Group seemed, as far as the figures are concerned, to be more successful in this respect than most Groups.

The appalling weather did not help either the mood or morale of the Group at the end of 1944. Most had confidently expected the war to have ended by Christmas and then suddenly only days before the German Armies launched a strong counter-offensive in the Ardennes, which seemed to threaten the progress of the Allied advance. The Group had already been over 'The Bulge' on a couple of missions to support the beleaguered Allied forces but not, they felt, with much success. So on 29th December they were more than a little despondent as they gathered for their early morning briefing. This time it was disclosed that the Second Division had been detailed to bomb the Rhine bridges in an attempt to prevent the enemy bringing forward troop reinforcements and urgent supplies. Hitherto the Rhine bridges had been kept scrupulously off-target as they needed

Some damaged bridges en route to Wesel. Like most Bomb Groups the 453rd were involved in support of the Ardennes campaign and the Wesel crossing. (Via K Thomas)

to be kept intact for the Allied armies' advance into Germany. The crews now assumed that matters must be serious if the bridges were to be destroyed. The Group's specific target was the Ludendorff bridge at Remargen, which was later to become famous for the battle to secure it.

The weather was quite appalling, very cold with heavy driving rain; and there was concern that the heavily loaded B-24s would have difficulty in taking off in the conditions. The weather forecast was for heavy cloud cover all the way to the target, so the bombing would have to be completed by radar, and a bridge is a relatively small target to hit at 21,000 feet; even in perfect conditions it would be difficult – given the poor conditions it now seemed an impossible task. The aircraft encountered no problems on the way out and just as they were over the target area a sudden and unexpected break in the clouds revealed the bridge. The Group's aircraft released their bombs just as the clouds closed in again, but most of the crews knew instinctively that they had missed the target. The return home was uneventful and fortunately not one aircraft was lost. Although there would be many more attempts to destroy the bridge it did survive relatively undamaged and, of course, ultimately provided the Allied forces with their first entry into Germany.

During February and March quite a few of the operations over Germany were successful, often over 900 aircraft were sent out and all returned safely. Perhaps the Group's finest hour came on 15th March when the First and Second Divisions mounted a large operation against the Zossen Army Headquarters just outside Berlin. Not only did the Group lead the Second Division but they had the honour of leading the whole of the Eighth Air Force on that day; perhaps this was in recognition of the Group's admirable record. The operation proved to be the Eighth Air Force's last major raid on 'Big B'; it was over 670 strong and included Groups from all three Divisions. The operation was a demonstration of the might of American air power and only one aircraft was lost in the action, although a couple more crash-landed in Poland but fortunately all the crews escaped with their lives.

Less than one month later the Group flew its last mission on 12th April, which proved to be its 259th. It was then taken off operations with talk of it being transferred to serve in the Pacific. In the event this move did not materialise and by 9th May most of the personnel had left Old Buckenham, one of the first Bomb Groups to leave Norfolk. The 453rd departed quietly and with little fuss, rather as they had conducted their war – calmly, efficiently and very effectively.

26

OULTON

Several Norfolk country houses were used by both the RAF and the USAAF during the Second World War but no station could compete with RAF Oulton, where Blickling Hall, a lovely red brick 17th century house was used by the personnel from the nearby airfield. In fact it was said that the Station Commander had the use of a bedroom once used by Anne Boleyn! This country house has, since 1940, been in the possession of the National Trust and is now open to the public from the end of March to October.

The grass airfield first opened on 31st July 1940 as a satellite for Horsham St Faith and within a week the parent station despatched a squadron of Blenheims (No 114) to the airfield to mount operations – day attacks on the Channel ports, enemy airfields at night, anti-shipping strikes and oil installations in northern France – quite the normal routine for any No 2 Group squadron. During October it was decided that one aircraft from each squadron could operate individually against a target providing the cloud cover was suitable. These sorties became known as 'Rangers', which later became so much a feature of the Mosquito squadrons.

When 114 squadron was transferred to Coastal Command duties in March 1941, it was replaced the following month by another squadron of Blenheims (No 18) which went into action mainly against shipping targets, but soon returned to Horsham St Faith. But nevertheless a squadron of Lockheed Hudsons continued the airfield's maritime activities before it disappeared to the Far East. Oulton seemed to be used as a very handy airfield to take the odd squadron for a month or so until a more permanent home could be found for them.

A perfect example of this was the arrival, in July 1942, of a Coastal

Blickling Hall: this very fine mansion was used by RAF Oulton during the war.

Command squadron of Bristol Beaufighters. This squadron – No 236 – had only recently been fitted with under-wing carriers for two 250 pound bombs and it was busy conducting trials using the aircraft as a torpedo/bomber against selected shipping targets. So satisfactory were the trials that the squadron was transferred to North Coates to form part of the first Beaufighter Strike Wing – a concept that proved so successful for Coastal Command.

Largely because of the creation of a Pathfinder Force there was a general realignment of airfields and squadrons within both Nos 2 and 3 Groups, with the result that Oulton now became a satellite of RAF Swanton Morley, a move which foreshadowed the arrival of the famous No 88 squadron and its Douglas Boston IIIs. Within days of their arrival at Oulton they were engaged in operations over Northern France and more especially to the port of Le Havre, where the large German vessel *Neumark* attracted their attention on four separate raids. It is also interesting to note that on several nights the squadron's Bostons were flying over Belgium and Holland dropping propaganda leaflets, which gave the news of the Allied victory at El Alamein.

The operation that gained the squadron some of its fame, as it did indeed to other No 2 Group squadrons, was the daylight attack on the Philips Radio and Valve works at Eindhoven on December 6th. This was planned as a 'Ramrod' mission on a massive scale. The Eindhoven raid was the biggest operation yet mounted by No 2 Group and was code-named 'Oyster'. Eight squadrons were detailed to take part, a mixture of Venturas, Bostons and Mosquitos. The Bostons of 88 squadron were to be the first to attack and would be led by Wing Commander Pelly-Fry, who when he heard of the proposed plan of attack vouchsafed the opinion that a loss rate in the region of 30% could be anticipated.

When the Bostons took off from Oulton on that Sunday morning, the weather was cloudy with just the hint of light rain. The aircraft were armed with 250 pound bombs with eleven-second delay fuses and the crews were under orders to attack at the lowest possible level. Despite all the planning and training for this operation, the approach to the target was rather ragged and the return home was even more so. Nevertheless 60 tons of bombs were dropped and the evidence showed that the mission had been conducted most successfully. Unfortunately the cost was high – 15 aircraft lost (16%), five Bostons, nine Venturas and one Mosquito with another 53 damaged. Wing Commander Pelly-Fry received the DSO for his leadership of the raid and a further two DSOs, eight DFCs and two DFMs were awarded to the crews of various squadrons.

On 1st April a Ventura squadron (No 21) arrived from Methwold, this squadron had also been engaged on the Eindhoven operation. Within days the squadron was making daylight raids on shipping targets in Brest and Cherbourg, where a large German vessel *Solglint* seemed to be the attraction, with the Venturas making at least three separate raids within one week. Their 'favourite' target during their four and a half month stay at Oulton appeared to be the Benzole plant at Zeebrugge in Belgium with four individual strikes. On 22nd June twelve Venturas took off for a daylight raid of Abbeville airfield. Wing Commander R. King, who led the operation had with him Group Captain Spendlove, who was the station commander at Swanton Morley. It was not unusual for station commanders to go on the odd operational sortie, it gave them valuable experience of what their crews had to face. Over the target the wing commander's aircraft received a direct hit and crashed in flames killing all the crew including the group captain.

The squadron's last mission from Oulton was on 16th August to Tricqueville airfield. On this occasion the Venturas had the luxury of the escort of two squadrons of Spitfires and the attack was so successful that the fires were said to be visible from a distance of at least 100 miles. The squadron then disappeared to Hartford Bridge – better known now as Blackbushe – because the airfield had been transferred to No 3 Group. Also Oulton was earmarked for further development as a heavy bomber station for the new Group – No 100. Hence from September 1943 it was closed to flying to allow for a major refit and runway improvements.

Oulton returned to the fold in May 1944 and received a squadron from RAF Sculthorpe, which itself had recently closed for major redevelopment. On 16th May the rather sinister black B-17 Flying Fortresses of No 214 squadron landed along with a detachment of the Eighth Air Force – No 803 squadron – which was also engaged in various radio-counter measures. The B-17s mainly operated on 'Jostle' sorties, which was equipment designed to produce a high powered and continuous signal to jam the enemy's radio transmissions on a variety of wavebands. During the late summer of 1944 a variant was produced known as 'Big Ben Jostle' – aimed at jamming the radio control of V2 rockets ('Big Ben' was the RAF's code name for the rockets). All of the aircraft were full of electronic equipment aimed to confound the German defences. All of these devices had strange and seemingly inappropriate names – 'Mandrel', 'Carpet', 'Piperack', and 'Dina II'. 'Mandrel' jammed enemy radar such as 'Freya', whereas 'Carpet' was specifically designed to interfere with the German Wurtzberg radar. 'Piperack' was American produced equipment which had been developed to jam the enemy's radar on certain wavebands, and only to complicate matters it was also called 'Dina II'.

The Americans went out on their first daylight mission on 3rd June and their first night operation was made a couple of days later in support of the D-Day operations. It was then considered that the B-24 Liberators were better suited to the work and also more able to accommodate all the intricate jamming apparatus. So by the time the squadron (although it was now designated the 36th Group) moved to a new base they were left with only two B-17s, the rest of the aircraft were B-24s.

As the Americans left Oulton in late August they were immediately replaced by a second 'Jostle' squadron – No 223 – which was also equipped with B-24 Liberators. It had originally operated in the Middle East and had latterly become No 300 squadron of the South African Air Force serving in Italy. It was reformed and renumbered at Oulton and most of its first aircrews came from Coastal Command training units. The Command, of course, had been operating Liberators for several years. Very many of the crews had been trained in the United States and had really expected to find themselves 'water watching' rather than in Bomber Command and operating its secret electronic offensive.

The early missions of this squadron were directed against V2 rocket sites by daylight but in late October the Command's experts concluded that the airborne jamming of V2 rockets was not really effective and such operations were abandoned – much to the relief of the aircrews! Both of the Oulton squadrons were engaged on a mixture of 'window spoof raids' (so called because of their intention to confuse the enemy defences as to the real target of the main bomber stream) and straightforward target missions with the main bomber streams. The squadrons' destinations read like a roll-call of Bomber Command's favourite targets – Hamburg, Essen, Coblenz, Mannheim, Duisberg, Augsburg, Chemnitz, Dresden and Leipzig.

When returning from a mission on 3/4th March one B-24 was attacked within sight of Oulton and just a few minutes later a B-17 from 214 squadron was shot down and crashed near the Station sick quarters killing most of the crew – only two gunners escaped. Oulton was just one of over 25 RAF airfields which were attacked by a large force of 100 enemy fighters. The Luftwaffe code-named the

A B-17 Flying Fortress of No 214 Squadron at RAF Oulton 1944. (No 100 Group/RAF Oulton Memorial Association)

operation 'Gisella' and it resulted in the loss of 20 RAF aircraft, and it seems strange that this tactic had not been used before or indeed was repeated.

In the early days of April No 223 squadron were converted to B-17 Fortresses. The reason for this change of aircraft at such a late stage of the war appears to have been because of the servicing problems of the B-24s and the slowness of the aircraft compared with the Lancasters and Halifaxes that formed the main bomber stream. The first B-17 mission was launched by the squadron on 19th April but by now it was clear that the final operational days were very close. Both squadrons responded to the maximum effort which was required for the night of 2/3rd May on a mission to Kiel – 15 B-17s and five B-24s left Oulton for the last time in the heat of battle. During their nine months of operations from Oulton No 223 squadron had only suffered five losses of aircraft whereas the other squadron had sustained almost three times that number. For the rest of the month, like many other bomber squadrons, both were engaged in mounting many flights over the Ruhr to show ground crews the colossal damage that had been inflicted on Germany. No 223 squadron was disbanded at Oulton, whereas No 214 was sent out to the Middle East. By August the airfield was dormant, although it later became a storage airfield for Mosquitos before closing in late 1947.

On Sunday 15th May 1994, a memorial stone, situated at the crossroads in the village of Oulton, was formally dedicated by the Bishop of Lynn. It remembers all those airmen, both RAF and American, that served at RAF Oulton as well as those who lost their lives. Also a Book of Remembrance has been placed in St Andrew's church at Blickling. These fine memorials had been organised and arranged by No 100 Group/RAF Oulton Memorial Association. They are uncommon as so few RAF memorials exist in Norfolk.

27
RACKHEATH

One of the last B-24 Bomb Groups to arrive in Norfolk was the 467th, which was stationed at Rackheath, about five miles north-east of Norwich. It was rather late on the European scene – its first aircraft flew into the airfield on 12th March 1944, but the Group quickly made its mark and developed into one of the most efficient and effective units in the whole of the Eighth Air Force. The excellent performance of the Group, named the 'Rackheath Aggies', owes much to the inspired leadership of its Commanding Officer, Colonel Albert J. Shower, who was the only officer to remain in command of a Bomb Group throughout all its service in England.

Shower was only 34 years old when he was given command of the Group in October 1943, one of the youngest commanders in the Eighth Air Force. He had already gained battle experience in the south-west Pacific and proved to be a stern disciplinarian and very hard task-master. Whenever the operational programme allowed, he ordered Saturday morning parades, and training missions became a regular feature of the Group's activities. On one training flight a pilot had the misfortune to crash his aircraft and was immediately downgraded to co-pilot, compelled to prove his worth on operations before Colonel Shower agreed to him being reinstated to pilot. No mere 'paddlefoot', as the ground officers were called, Colonel Shower led his men by example, in fact within two weeks of the Group's first operation Shower had been awarded a Distinguished Flying Cross for leading his aircraft on a raid to Leipham.

Rackheath became quite a remarkable base. Colonel Shower, despite the strict regime he maintained, fully recognised that recreational facilities were important for the men's morale. Regular

Main briefing for 467th Bomb Group. (D Hastings)

dances and film shows were held in the Red Cross Club and the base even had its own band called 'The Airliners'. Regular tennis matches were arranged at the courts on the nearby estate of Sir Edward Stacey. Considering that Rackheath was one of the nearest American airfields to Norwich, it is really quite surprising that so much entertainment should be made available at the airfield.

The Group had been placed in the 96th Combat Bomb Wing, along with another two newcomers, the 458th at Horsham St Faith and 466th at Attlebridge. It is perhaps a mark of Shower's achievement as a commander that the Group was ready for operations in less than a month of its arrival. Even on this first mission Shower was adamant that all crew members carried their escape kit, which normally carried photographs for false identity cards, minute compasses, maps and even a pair of GI shoes, which were tied to the men's waists in case there was a lot of walking to be done!

Thirty aircraft left Rackheath, on 10th April 1944, for an aircraft assembly plant in Bourges in central France. The Group was fortunate on this occasion, hardly any flak was encountered and there was good visibility over the target area, which resulted in 26 aircraft bombing the target. All returned safely and photographic evidence later showed that considerable damage had been wrought – quite an impressive start. The following day the Group's aircraft were over Germany, which again proved to be a successful mission. Their first setback came on 20th April, their eighth mission in ten days. This was a 'No Ball' target at Sirncourt in France, none of the Group's crews was able to locate the target so they all returned to Rackheath with their bombs. No Bomb Group was happy with such a situation especially in view of the inherent dangers in landing fully loaded aircraft. On this occasion there were no accidents but one wonders what Colonel Shower had to say about it?

On 22nd April, like other American airfields around Norwich, Rackheath suffered a severe air attack. One aircraft crashed near Barsham killing seven of the crew and another aircraft was destroyed on the ground whilst the airfield was being bombed. Considering that the Group had survived intact from the operation over Hamm marshalling yards it was a very unfortunate incident. The month of May was one of the most successful weeks of operations. The Group mounted five missions without a single aircraft being lost in action. On the 11th, they were on an operation to Mulhouse railway yards in southern France near the Swiss/German border. One aircraft was shot down when they encountered very heavy flak near to the target area and a second aircraft was so badly damaged that it was compelled to land in Switzerland. Despite this one slight setback, the Group's reputation for its bombing accuracy was growing fast, certainly within the Second Division.

This reputation was only enhanced by a quite superlative operation on 11th June. Along with the 466th at Attlebridge, the Group were detailed to destroy an important bridge at Blois St Denis, which was providing a vital link in the German supply lines to the battlefront in Normandy. This was the first time that low-level bombing tactics would be used by heavy bombers from England. The operation led by Colonel Shower proved to be an outstanding success, the bridge was utterly destroyed. On the following day the Group's aircraft were active over the beach-heads in Normandy and one of the aircraft, which had become badly damaged, landed on an emergency airstrip in Normandy – the first four-engined bomber to use the strip. For all their operations over northern France, the Commanding Officer of the Eighth Air Force, Lieutenant-General 'Jimmy' Doolittle cited the 96th Bomb Wing for 'Its extraordinary heroism and

Selecting operations and crew, 467th Bomb Group. (D Hastings)

outstanding performance'. By 15th August the 467th had completed their 100th mission in a record time of 140 days, in which time they had lost 27 aircraft with 97 crewmen killed or wounded and another 182 listed as missing.

From 19th September the Group flew no combat missions as they set up a forward base at the recently captured airfield at Clastres in northern France. Just one month earlier the Group's aircraft had been bombing the same airfield when it was in German hands and now the airmen helped the French civilians to fill in the bomb craters on the runways that they had created! The Group was based there to supply much needed fuel for General Patton's tanks and armoured vehicles. The petrol was brought in from Rackheath in five gallon cans and two trips were made daily with five crew and two passengers. As night-flying was not allowed it meant that the crews had a stop-over on French soil. Many of the crews managed to make a quick trip to Paris, which had only recently been liberated, and they returned to Rackheath with rather exaggerated stories of 'wine, women and song'! In just a fortnight of these 'Trucking' operations the Group managed to move over 650,000 gallons of fuel.

The German Ardennes offensive in late December 1944 demanded a maximum effort from all Bomb Groups in the Eighth Air Force. The instruction from Headquarters was very clear, 'Bomb the Luftwaffe airfields in the Ardennes and eliminate fighter support for Von Runsteadt's tanks'. On Christmas Eve over 2,040 bombers and 850 fighters took part in what proved to be the biggest air operation ever mounted by the Eighth during the war, every Bomb Group in the Eighth was engaged. Clear skies brought perfect bombing conditions but ground fog and ice on the runways did cause some accidents on take-off. There was a total loss of 22 aircraft – both bombers and fighters – but over 90 enemy fighters were destroyed. This massive air armada was a testimonial to the awesome power of the Eighth Air Force with over 5,000 tons of bombs dropped.

From this operation until the New Year the Group's aircraft flew every single day. But on 29th December the 467th experienced their most difficult day. The targets for this day's operations were various communication centres in western Germany. The weather around the Norfolk airfields was quite unfavourable for flying. There was a thick ground fog as the pilots attempted to take off purely by instruments and the visibility was so bad that most of them had great difficulty in locating the end of the runways. Two aircraft crashed at the airfield killing 15 crew and another two were damaged on take-off, one was abandoned over the coast whilst the other crashed on its approach to Attlebridge. The Group also suffered the only casualty due to enemy action – the worst operational day for many months.

By the middle of January 1945 the harsh winter weather was easing slightly, enabling the Eighth to mount yet another major operation against oil refineries and installations in western Germany. On this day (14th) the Group's aircraft were directed to attack a steel plant at Hallendorf. One of the aircraft engaged on this mission was *Witchcraft*. Each Bomb Group seemed to have at least one 'lucky' aircraft that had managed to survive fairly intact after an endless number of missions and the *Witch* had flown no less than 100 missions without once being compelled to abort. During its operational life it had suffered some 300 flak holes but not one of its crew members had ever been wounded. By the end of the war the aircraft had completed 130 successful missions.

B-24 of 467th Bomb Group taking off. (D Hastings)

Within a fortnight of the Group's last mission, its crews made Eighth Air Force history when they were detailed to bomb some German batteries at the Pointe de Grave on the Gironde estuary, which were still stubbornly holding out against sustained ground attacks. Twenty-four aircraft bombed the garrison and every single bomb fell within 1,000 feet of the target or MPI (Mean Point of Impact) and over half landed within 500 feet – an accuracy not previously attained by any Bomb Group. Again like most other Bomb Groups their last and 212th mission was completed on 25th April. However, before the crews returned to the United States the 467th had one final and important operation to complete – they were selected to lead the Victory fly-past on 13th May over the Eighth Air Force's headquarters at High Wycombe. A proud moment for Colonel Shower.

By the middle of the following month most of the aircraft had gone from Rackheath. The old control tower still stands and there is a fine memorial to the Group in the village of Rackheath, unveiled by Colonel Shower in 1990 when he was aged 80 years. What is left of the airfield can be found by taking the A1151 road out of Norwich and after about five miles take a minor road to the right which is marked 'Rackheath'. The entrance to the old airfield is now an industrial site.

28

SCULTHORPE

Sculthorpe is perhaps one of the easiest of Norfolk airfields to locate because of its massive development by the USAF in the early 1950s. It now sprawls over a large area about five miles west of Fakenham just off the A148 and certainly cannot be missed even by the most casual passing motorist. Great feats of imagination are needed to visualise how the airfield would have appeared in January 1943 when it first opened as a mere satellite station for West Raynham in No 2 Group of Bomber Command.

Built during 1942 the first 'aircraft' to occupy the airfield were Airspeed Horsa gliders, stored there until the first operational squadron arrived in May 1943. This was No 342 of the Free French Air Force, better known as the 'Lorraine' squadron. They brought with them their Douglas Boston IIIs, on which they had trained at West Raynham, and while at the parent station they had been granted full RAF squadron status. The most famous member of the squadron was undoubtedly M. Mendes-France, who later became Prime Minister of France during the mid 1950s. The Bostons were, as their name suggested, an American light bomber, which the RAF had modified for daylight intruder raids. It had been first introduced into squadrons in July 1941. The Boston was a most effective bomber, ideal for low-level strikes. One of its main features was its considerable speed – just in excess of 300 mph – a startling advance in performance on the Bristol Blenheim that it replaced. But it lacked the all-round excellence of the Mosquito and suffered in comparison with it – indeed what aircraft did not? However, the Bostons gave very good service to No 2 Group and when their operational days were over in Europe they served with distinction in the Middle East.

The squadron sent out just three Bostons on their first operational sortie on 12th June to attack a power station in Rouen over their own homeland. As most of their subsequent operations were against targets in northern France, one wonders how they felt about that? In mid-July they left for Great Massingham and for the next six months or so Sculthorpe became known for its Mosquito squadrons.

On 1st June No 2 Group of Bomber Command virtually lost its identity as it was transferred into Fighter Command and absorbed into the newly created Second Tactical Air Force, formed to prepare the way into France for the Allied armies and then to provide close support for the armies, a task that No 2 Group had been trying to do since the early days of 1940. The new Tactical Air Force comprised large wings of different types of aircraft all of which were considered the most suitable for a ground support role. No 140 Wing of this new Force was to be based at Sculthorpe and the officer selected to lead this Wing was Group Captain P. Pickard, DSO, DFC, who in July was appointed Station Commander at Sculthorpe. Pickard or 'Pick' was then only 29 years old and remarkably young for such a senior post. He was last noted as a Flight Lieutenant at East Wretham, when he had already gained a certain fame for his appearance in the propaganda film *Target for Tonight* as 'Squadron Leader Dickson'. Pickard's lasting claim to fame came with his leadership of the most amazing raid on Amiens prison in February 1944 in which sadly he lost his life. Pickard had collected around him a whole galaxy of highly talented and much decorated pilots, all of whom were well experienced in the art and techniques of low-level bombing.

It was solely due to Basil Embry, the outstanding Commander-in-Chief of No 2 Group that the Group's squadrons were re-equipped with Mosquitos. Having flown them operationally he was a dedicated admirer of the 'Wooden Wonder', but nevertheless it needed all his powers of persuasion and utter determination to ensure that Mosquitos were selected in preference to a new light dive-bomber called the Vultee Vengeance. After putting it through a most rigorous test flight, Embry considered this aircraft vastly inferior in performance to the Mosquito, and likened it to an updated Fairey Battle, totally unsuited to the plans he had for his squadrons! How his view finally prevailed and how ultimately he obtained eight squadrons of Mosquitos for his Group is now part of RAF history.

On 29th July the first two squadrons arrived at Sculthorpe – Nos 464 (RAAF) and 487 (RNZAF) both of which had been formed at Feltwell in the early days of the war. The squadrons brought their Lockheed Venturas to Sculthorpe but the crews were already aware

"... these beautiful, graceful, little grey machines..." the three squadrons of Mosquitos became known as the Sculthorpe Wing.

that they would soon convert to Mosquitos as and when aircraft became available. The excitement of the crews at the thought of flying these new and amazing aircraft clearly shows through the official forms and reports. One pilot with 487 squadron wrote, 'Two Mossies should have arrived today ... Perhaps tomorrow [20th August] ... Here they come ... Just two today ... bags of excitement ... All everybody talks about here is Mosquitos ... these beautiful, graceful, little grey machines ...' Perhaps no other RAF aircraft, the Spitfire included, elicited so much interest and enthusiasm with crews.

The third squadron to complete what became known as the Sculthorpe Wing arrived in early September. It was No 21, which really could be considered a 'local' outfit as it had been previously stationed at Bircham Newton, Bodney, Methwold and Oulton. On 27th September it was reported, '... there are over seventy Mosquitos here now, which is a most impressive sight.' Major Hereward de Havilland, the younger brother of the aircraft's designer, often made visits to RAF stations flying Mosquitos but perhaps Sculthorpe was his favourite call because '... Pickard, the Station Commander, has a large country house as a Mess and so far I have always had partridges for lunch, and a hare to bring home with me ...'! Pickard had been completely disenchanted with the officers' mess at Sculthorpe and had managed to find a 'suitable' country house – the White House – which was a fine Georgian mansion, and he and his aircrews moved in.

By the beginning of October the Wing was at last at operational readiness and on the following day 24 Mosquitos from 464 and 487 squadrons led by Pickard set out to attack two power stations north of St Nazaire. On this mission Air Vice-Marshal Embry was flying in the rear of the formation, acting as 'Tail End Charlie'. It was almost unheard of for an officer of his rank to actually take part in such an operation but that was the nature of Basil Embry, who appeared on the Operations record as 'Wing Commander Smith'! The aircraft had to refuel at Exeter and the operation was a complete success, not a single aircraft was lost and both targets were bombed very effectively. However, Pickard's aircraft was damaged by enemy flak and he was forced to land at Predannock in Cornwall on just one engine.

The second Mosquito operation took place on the 9th but was an utter failure. The target was an aircraft plant in Metz and after crossing the English coast the Wing encountered very heavy low cloud. A couple of miles over the Channel the aircraft were forced off course to avoid a large British convoy that was flying barrage balloons. From that point nothing seemed to go right for the mission. The Mosquitos were carrying instantaneous fused bombs, which when released at low-level could cause severe explosions and probably this fact accounted for two of the aircraft just disintegrating. Another two were lost to heavy flak, all these sad losses were for nothing as the target was not even hit because of the very cloudy conditions. One of the pilots who failed to return was Wing Commander 'Dickie' England and by an ironic twist of fate the following day came the news to the station that he had been awarded the DSO for a mission in the previous August. As Embry commented, 'His loss is a severe blow... he was a great leader who commanded universal respect and admiration.'

Following this costly operation Pickard concentrated his crews on low-level attack techniques, unfortunately three aircraft crashed on these training flights but mercifully without any loss of life. All three squadrons were involved in a series of missions over northern France attacking power stations, bridges, engine sheds and rail marshalling yards. The discovery of the V1 rocket sites later on in the year resulted in the squadrons being diverted to these targets. On 22nd December 29 aircraft found a site at St Agathe near Dieppe and suffered heavy damage from sustained and accurate flak. The following day a large force of Mosquitos made a brave determined low-level attack on two sites near Pomerral. On 31st December the squadrons' final operation from Sculthorpe was to Le Ploy in northern France and the crews flew back not to Sculthorpe but to their new airfield – Hunsdon in Hertfordshire. It was from this airfield that they would set out on their most famous mission – the attack on Amiens prison – 'Operation Jerico'. As a postscript it is interesting to note that later photographic evidence concluded that it would take at least 100 Mosquitos to destroy just one V1 rocket site, the reason the task was mainly given over to the heavies of Bomber Command and the Eighth Air Force.

After the disappearance of the Mosquito Wing the airfield was passed over to No 100 Group and it must have seemed a quiet and desolate place without all the bustle of the Mosquito squadrons. Then on 17th January 1944 along came the heavy and ponderous (by comparison) B-17 Fortresses of 214 squadron. This had previously been a bomber squadron at Downham Market, and it also went under the name 'Federated Malay States' having been 'adopted' by the Malaysian Federation in September 1941. On the same day there arrived under the command of Captain G. Paris a detachment of American personnel who were to help train the air and ground crews of the squadron on their new aircraft. This small detachment unit was later designated the 803rd Bombardment Squadron(P) and were the precursors of the massive American 'invasion' of Sculthorpe in September 1949.

Douglas Boston IIIs: operated from several Norfolk airfields.

The reason the Fortresses were chosen for Radio Counter Measures operations within the new Group is not very clear; certainly their operational use in the RAF had been anything but successful. Of course there was plenty of space for all the electronic equipment that needed to be installed but perhaps their high altitude ceiling might have had some bearing on the decision.

Wing Commander D. McGlinn, the squadron commander, became a little frustrated in the lack of aircraft – only 14 had been received by the end of February – and most of these were sent away for the lengthy procedure of equipping them with all the gadgets. Just four aircraft remained at Sculthorpe for crew training purposes. About this time the Eighth Air Force was suffering quite heavy losses and they had the first call on any spare B-17s.

It was not until mid-April that the squadron was ready for operations and it quickly made up for lost time, for in just over a fortnight it had mounted 35 missions (usually comprising five aircraft at a time) and one crew had claimed a Me109 destroyed. The squadron's main method of operation was to accompany the main bomber streams but flying well above them and using their special transmitters to interfere with the enemy's radar. In particular the aircraft used 'Jostle', a device to jam particular radio transmissions. But almost as soon as the squadron had become settled into its routine it was decided to close Sculthorpe and the squadron left for Oulton in May 1944.

Sculthorpe was planned to be one of the three airfields capable of taking the very heavy bombers of the next decade. Ultimately the airfield covered over 750 acres and had a new very long runway some 3,000 yards long and 100 yards wide, which was double the normal width. This was such a major project that Sculthorpe's days as a wartime airfield were over. It did not finally reopen for flying until December 1948 and about three months later the first Boeing B-29s arrived heralding a long association with the Strategic Air Command of the United States Air Force.

29
SEETHING

On 3rd November 1943 the B-24Hs of the 448th Bomb Group took off from the final training base at Sioux City, Iowa for Herrington Field in Kansas. The crews had completed six weeks of intensive final training and were now considered ready for war. With the final processing complete the crews did not know their ultimate destination until they had been airborne for one hour, only then were they allowed to open their sealed orders. The news that they had been allocated to the Eighth Air Force in England and an airfield called Seething would have been greeted with some relief by the majority of the crews. Most of the young American airmen desperately wanted to be part of the Eighth's fight against the 'real' enemy – Germany. They were imbued with a strong sense of purpose and determination and were confident of their superiority, which had been largely fostered by all the publicity in the American press about the American Army Air Force's successes in Europe. As yet the American public were not fully aware of the terrible costs in men and aircraft that the Eighth Air Force was suffering over Germany.

Two different ferry routes to Great Britain were used by the Eighth's Bomb Groups – the northern and the southern. The former took the crews up to Gander in Newfoundland and then either directly to Prestwick in Scotland or sometimes via Iceland. The other route was much longer and far more time-consuming, taking the crews from Trinidad to Brazil before crossing the Atlantic to Dakar or Marrakesh in north Africa. The final leg was flown due north to Cornwall avoiding the Spanish and French air spaces for obvious reasons. The Northern route was only used during the summer months, so the 448th came over via the southern route, which was quite a strenuous test for the young and inexperienced pilots and navigators and often resulted in some unfortunate accidents. The 448th lost two aircraft on the long flight, one crashing in the Atlas mountains and the Group also lost a third aircraft which crashed in flames on arrival in Cornwall.

One young pilot recalled his first sight of England, '... as we approached we were given an unusual greeting... out of nowhere I spotted two beautiful Spitfires on each wing, which escorted us to the nearest airstrip [the normal procedure] ... This was my first introduction to the fine English hospitality ... This place was now 'home' to us ... Every day we flew the expression 'home' was used on our intercom in our ship ...'

The first aircraft touched down at Seething in the last days of November; the ground crews had only just arrived themselves. The young Americans found Seething to be, '... one pub, one small store, a church and maybe six houses not very large but very picturesque ... Numerous farms were scattered around the 'field' ... they were typically English – right out of the history books many of the buildings still used thatched roofs and stone walls ...' The airfield had been specially constructed for the USAAF's use and most of the twelve different living and mess sites were well to the south of the airfield itself close to the tiny village of Thwaite St Mary. Like many airfields in Norfolk, Seething suffered drainage problems and often during the two winters that they spent there the Americans fought a long battle with the mud!

Within three weeks of their arrival at Seething the crews and their aircraft were ready to launch their first operation, an excellent performance as most Bomb Groups took at least a month to work up to operational readiness. The crews were not given a gentle introduction to the war, they were thrown into the deep end – Germany! On 22nd December they were detailed for a mission to Osnabruck, where the large railway complex had been a 'special' target of Bomber Command since 1941. This particular area was long known to be heavily defended but on this day the flak was not really the problem, rather the number of enemy fighters that suddenly materialised. 'They appeared in a great abundance... At this point all seemed unreal and I guess I was doing things purely automatically and practically as I had been taught...' recalled one of the Group's airgunners. Colonel James Thompson, the Group's Commanding Officer, who led the mission, must have been pleased with the way his inexperienced crews had coped with their first taste of action because although two aircraft were lost, other more battle-hardened

B-24 D You cawn't miss it, the assembly ship of 448th Bomb Group. (Via Mrs P Everson)

Groups suffered heavier losses.

Just four days into the New Year the Group was detailed for an operation to Kiel, another heavily fortified target. A ragged assembly caused almost half of the aircraft to abort and return to Seething, but the Group's remaining aircraft carried on doggedly despite the fact that they were now vulnerable to enemy fighters. Over Kiel Major Squires, a squadron leader, received a direct hit and his aircraft hurtled to the ground minus its tail. A horde of Fw190s attacked the bombers from beneath and in minutes three more aircraft were shot down although most of the crews managed to escape by parachute. It was a brutal day for the Group, emphasising the harsh reality of daylight bombing over Germany.

The weather conditions during most of January were certainly not conducive to operational flying, but the Eighth Air Force now had a new Commander – Lieutenant General 'Jimmie' Doolittle, who was itching to mount a massive air offensive against the German aircraft industry. His simple philosophy was that the air war had to be won at all costs. But not until the third week in February did the weather become sufficiently settled for the Eighth to launch an all-out bombing offensive. What later became known as 'The Big Week' commenced on Sunday 20th February. During the next six days the 448th, along with all other Groups in the Second Division, was in action over Brunswick, Magdeberg, Holland, Gotha and Furth.

This major offensive was a traumatic time for all the crews that took part. Purely in terms of aircraft lost the Group survived the savage week of operations relatively lightly but what it did to the nerves of the young men who daily risked their lives was another matter. Indeed to go to the dreaded Gotha and its Me110 factories and only lose one aircraft was no mean achievement. And then to find on the next day the target was Furth near Nuremberg – a deep penetration mission of maybe nine hours of flying. Such missions were dreaded by all crews and most considered that they should count as double for their individual totals. Nevertheless they managed to survive with just one aircraft lost in action and another that crash-landed at Chipping Ongar because of a fuel shortage. After one of the missions in the week one of the Group's aircraft, *Bag o Bolts*, arrived back at Seething with 400 flak holes – an amazing example of the durability of the B-24.

There was no let-up in March; the Eighth Air Force flew nearly 12,000 sorties in which 350 aircraft and over 3,300 airmen were missing in action. On the 6th the Group were sent to Berlin, on what proved to be the Eighth's heaviest loss of the war on a single raid. Considering this fact the 448th managed again to escape lightly, as it did on the 22nd when it returned to the 'Big B' and all its aircraft came home to Seething safely. To survive two visits to perhaps the heaviest defended area in all Germany says much for the discipline of their formation flying. Berlin had proved to be the downfall of many Bomb Groups.

April turned out to be a rather disastrous month for the Seething Group. On the 1st its aircraft were sent to Ludwigshafen, near Mannheim. The weather conditions over northern Europe were atrocious with heavy thick cloud cover up to 21,000 feet. The 448th along with two other Groups strayed away from the main formation and this slight error was harshly punished by the Luftwaffe's fighters. In their first attack the Group's lead aircraft was shot down and with it their Commanding Officer – Colonel James Thompson – unfortunately his parachute failed to open. Without a leader the rest of the Group were lucky to survive with just a few casualties.

Three weeks later, on the 22nd, the Group were sent to bomb the Hamm marshalling yards – a target so beloved by Bomber Command that their aircrews called them 'ham and eggs raids'! Although the operation was planned for an early morning start, as indeed were most of the Eighth's operations, the raid was delayed until the afternoon because of unfavourable weather conditions. By the time the

Nose art – Daisy Mae *of the 712th Bomb Squadron. (Via Mrs P Everson)*

crews left Seething they had already been awake for twelve hours, having been called at 2 am! Despite heavy flak the Group lost only one aircraft over the target but on the return flight several of the crews noticed that there was an unusual amount of fighter activity along the French coast. As the returning aircraft neared Southwold it was quite dark although the sky was clear. The complicated exercise of landing several hundred aircraft, many damaged, on to different airfields all in a small area, was difficult enough in daylight let alone at night.

By about 9.30 pm the aircraft had started on their landing patterns and at that precise time the Luftwaffe struck. The enemy aircraft had followed the bomber streams back and had come in low to avoid the radar beams. As one pilot recalled, 'they were waiting like vultures for us to come in . . . we were being shot at like sitting ducks . . . it was like if all hell had broke loose . . . there were ships everywhere . . . some going down in flames . . . It doesn't bear thinking about . . .' One aircraft was shot down over the sea and another at Kessingland with yet another falling in flames near Worlingham. Even on its final approach into Seething one aircraft was shot up and crash-landed on to the runway in flames and later two aircraft collided at the end of the runway; unfortunately both crews were killed. The whole airfield was lit up, attracting the enemy fighters, who strafed it from all sides. The fires were not finally put out until 3.30 am the following morning. The Second Division had lost seven aircraft on the mission and another 14 over Norfolk. It was a calamitous evening for many airfields in Norfolk, none more so than Seething.

Some German targets were considered worse than others and on two successive days in May (28th and 29th) the Group was required to mount missions to two places high on their 'danger list' – Merseburg and Tutow. The first was a synthetic oil refinery considered to be the second largest in Europe and it literally bristled with heavy flak batteries. When the crews were within 200 miles of the target they could see the pall of smoke rising almost to 12,000 feet and over Merseburg the flames reached nearly 2,000 feet. As one pilot recalled, 'it was like flying into hell's kitchen . . .' Tutow was an important Junkers 88 assembly plant situated close to the Baltic coast. It had become a favourite target for the Eighth and the aircraft ran the gauntlet of strong fighter opposition for most of the trip, with the possibility of ditching in the North Sea on their return – the survival rate for American aircrews being rescued was not that high. On both these missions the Group escaped very lightly and a high percentage of the crews very effectively bombed the targets. Two operations conducted in a highly professional manner and a credit to the Group.

Although most of the American bases put on parties for the local

713th Bomb Squadron's ground crews at Seething. (Via Mrs P Everson)

children, the men at Seething went one step further. Major Newton McLaughlin, the Special Services Officer, along with the chaplain and the surgeon became very involved with the Jenny Lind Crippled Children's hospital in Norwich. With the agreement of the Commanding Officer, Colonel Charles Westover, the men 'adopted' the children. Not only did they share their rations with them but collected money to provide Christmas presents which were handed out at the big party they arranged at Christmas. As one crew member said, 'it was a splendid way to cement relationships between the Yanks and the English'.

Shortly into the New Year the Group became involved in what was known as 'Operation Thunderclap', which was an attempt to attack and seriously damage vital supply and communication targets in eastern Germany as support for the advancing Russian armies. On 15th January the target was Dresden and its synthetic oil plants. The aircraft had to take on the full 2,700 gallons of fuel for the long flight. The crews were operating at more than 22,000 feet and found the temperature to be as low as $-38°F$! Considering the length and duration of the operation the overall losses were slight, just 20 aircraft in total, and the Group lost one aircraft – *Roses Rivets*, which was forced to land at Lille in France, although the crew finally returned to Seething via the French Resistance. This raid on Dresden predated the famous or infamous RAF operation of 13/14th February, which was quickly followed by a daylight operation by the Eighth, both of which wrought such horrendous damage.

During the last months of the war the 448th was involved in all the prominent operations mounted by the Eighth Air Force. On 4th April the Group's crews once again visited Kiel and on this day they found that the Luftwaffe still had sufficient fuel and aircraft to cause problems. The Group lost three aircraft, victims to the Me262 jet fighters. Losses were hard to bear at any time but when they came so close to the end of hostilities they seemed even more tragic.

Three weeks later the Group's aircraft went out on its last mission, its 262nd. During its time at Seething it had lost 101 aircraft in action – a higher than average figure – which shows the immense contribution and sacrifice the Group's crews made to the Mighty Eighth's offensive. This has been splendidly remembered in the memorial museum housed in the renovated control tower. It is open on the first Sunday in each month from May to October. There is a memorial to the 448th in Seething parish church and another two on the airfield itself, which may be reached via the B1332 road from Bungay and is about ten miles south-east of Norwich.

30
SHIPDHAM

'The Flying Eightballs' or to use their official title, the 44th Bombardment Group, was one of the most famous Groups of the Eighth Air Force and the first to arrive in Norfolk. It operated with great distinction from Shipdham from October 1942 until the end of the war. The Group had been first formed, or activated (as the Americans described it) in late 1941 and was the first to be fully equipped with B-24s or Liberators; it was for that reason that the Group became very involved in the massive B-24 training programme that had been set up in the United States. So useful were they in this role that the Group's planned early departure to England was postponed. Several new Bomb Groups were formed from their existing personnel, including the 93rd which would operate from Hardwick airfield in Norfolk.

Shipdham was a three runway airfield, which had been quickly constructed for the RAF at the cost of over £1 million and was almost completed by midsummer 1942 when it was handed over to the USAAF. In September Marauders of the 319th Medium Bomb Group arrived for a very short stay as they were destined for North Africa and when they departed for Horsham St Faith they were quickly replaced by the advance parties of the 44th.

They found the airfield as just 'a sea of mud not a blade of grass to be seen'. The living quarters were very basic – small single storey barracks well dispersed away from the airfield. Shortly after their arrival the men were required to attend various lectures and briefings on English social customs and it would be at least five weeks before they were allowed out to sample the delights of Norwich. This was in the very early days of the American presence in Norfolk, it would not be until later in the next year that the build-up of the Eighth Air

B-24 of 44th Bomb Group. Glory Bee *leaves RAF Valley for the USA. (IWM)*

Force would greatly accelerate.

Although the Group was under strength, one of its squadrons had remained in the United States on training duties and would not arrive until March 1943, it mounted its first mission on 7th November to Cap de la Hague on the Cherbourg peninsula but the operation experienced several problems. These were heightened by the Group's first raid on St Nazaire, rightly known as 'Flak City'. The aircraft had to come in over the sea at a height of 500 feet to avoid the enemy radar and then climb to some 18,000 feet to bomb. At this altitude most of the crews experienced frost-bite, many wore their flying suits for a long time before take-off and their body moisture turned to ice. Ultimately electrically heated flying suits proved to be the solution to the problem. But throughout the duration of the war all crews of B-24s operated under intensely cold conditions.

The Group's first raid on Germany took place on 27th January 1943 and it was, like all Eighth Air Force operations, made up of formations of aircraft from squadrons from many Groups. On this day the B-17 Fortresses were to bomb U-boat construction yards at Vegesack, whilst the 44th Group's B-24s were to make a diversionary attack on Wilhelmshaven. Poor weather conditions over the target area prevented very effective bombing and strong fighter opposition was encountered. It didn't help matters that the gun and turret mechanisms froze and the crews' oxygen masks had to be regularly rubbed with salt to prevent ice forming. Moreover the Group felt that they were being used as bait, whilst the B-17s managed to escape relatively unscathed and on their return received all the publicity. They were dubbed by the B-24's crews as the 'Glory Boys'.

There was a marked antipathy between the crews flying the two different heavy bombers which would continue throughout the war. Each side fervently extolled the virtues of their aircraft. The B-17 crews were justly proud of their sleek and elegant aircraft, which they considered vastly superior to the bulky and rather ugly Liberator. Indeed they were quite derogatory, referring to it as 'The crate that ours came in'! It was certainly felt that the B-24 was far more accident prone although this belief was not really borne out by the statistics; on average a B-17 was expected to survive ten missions whereas the B-24 one more. There was no doubt that the Liberator was more difficult to fly in close formation especially at high altitudes and some flying accidents were caused on this account. Furthermore the B-17 was considered more robust and able to survive greater damage, though many B-24s managed to arrive back home with quite frightening damage, but perhaps this was more due to the exceptional skills of the pilots than the design of the aircraft. Without doubt the B-17 was a better appointed and more comfortable aircraft to fly compared with the rather cramped and very draughty B-24. There was really no right answer to the debate and both aircraft served the Eighth Air Force very well indeed.

Apart from these prejudices, there were differences in performance which did cause some operational problems with both aircraft flying in large formations. The B-24 was faster – about 20 mph or so – and it had a greater range as well as being able to bomb from a higher altitude – at least in the early days. Although both aircraft had the same armament there were minor differences in positioning, which resulted in varying fields of fire. The B-24s had a larger bomb capacity, usually 8,000 pounds compared with the B-17's 6,000 pounds, both far behind the RAF's Lancasters, which normally carried 14,000 pounds and even higher with modifications. One rather interesting fact to come to light after the war, was that the Luftwaffe pilots were convinced that the B-24s were more vulnerable and easier to set on fire. Therefore, when given the choice, they would direct their attentions first to the B-24s, and this might account for some of the heavy losses experienced by B-24 Bomb Groups compared with their B-17 comrades. In fact the B-17 crews often maintained that the best 'escorts' they ever had were the B-24s!

On 14th May 1943 they were detailed for a mission to Kiel along with squadrons from three other Bomb Groups. Because of severe weather conditions the mission was aborted about an hour or so after the Groups had formed but unfortunately the message did not get through to 44th Group and they ploughed on, now completely on their own. The 17 aircraft did manage to bomb despite heavy cloud over the target area but they came under intense enemy flak and were opposed by a heavy fighter force. The Group's gunners claimed 21 fighters destroyed with another 13 probables. However, the Group lost five aircraft over Germany with another ten quite badly damaged, one further aircraft was abandoned quite close to the Norfolk coast but the crew managed to bale out and were rescued near Sheringham. For this mission the Group was awarded a Distinguished Unit Citation – the first of two that the crews gained during the war.

After this savage mauling the Group was taken off operations along with another two Groups in Norfolk. Most of the B-17 crews thought that the B-24s were being permanently withdrawn from action

706th Squadron badge of the Flying Eightballs *– a wall mural at Shipdham.*

because of their heavy losses, but nothing was further from the truth, the two Group's crews were put on low-level flying practice and were seen roaring over the Norfolk countryside just a couple of hundred feet above the ground and in very close formation – quite a frightening and daunting experience for crews and local people alike! The crews, of course, were not aware of the reason for this training and were just thankful for some blessed relief from operations.

Then on 24th June all personnel at Shipdham were mustered for a special parade, the occasion was an official visit by Anthony Eden, the Foreign Secretary. The official view was that such visits were thought to help the morale of the aircrews and perhaps more importantly they influenced the British Government as to the value of the Eighth's missions that were at that time being conducted at such heavy costs. It was also at a time when Winston Churchill was beginning to express some disappointment at the slow rate of build-up of the USAAF in England, a matter that would be fully aired at the Allied Leaders' famous Conference held in Casablanca in January 1944.

Just three days later the Group was ordered to Portreath in Cornwall and from there 41 of its aircraft flew to Libya to join the 15th Air Force. During July they were involved in ten operations over Sicily and Italy, including Rome, which was bombed for the first time on the 19th. Further low-level formation flying was carried out over the desert, all in preparation for the 'Big One' – the raid on the Ploesti oilfields in Rumania on 1st August 1943. As this heroic mission has been already fully described elsewhere it is just sufficient to say that the 44th received their second Distinguished Unit Citation for their part in this epic operation and that Colonel Leon Johnson, the Group's Commanding Officer, who had led the 44th, was awarded the Medal of Honor.

Thirteen days later the Groups were sent on an operation to bomb Wiener Neustadt in Austria, which was a centre of Me109 production. This was another gruelling mission, almost at the very extent of the B-24s' range. Fortunately the enemy opposition was light and major damage was inflicted on two of the works. The twelve hour mission took a toll on both crews and aircraft, which meant that the return to England was further delayed. The three Norfolk Groups were asked to support the final Allied advance in Sicily. Three missions were flown in which the 44th lost eight aircraft, and there were even further losses on another mission undertaken to Foggia on 16th August when another four aircraft were destroyed. The Group had suffered quite grievously for its spell in the sun.

Their return to Norfolk proved to be of rather short duration and by mid-September they were back in North Africa but this time in Tunis, where once again they became active over Italy. But within just three weeks they had exchanged the sand and heat of Tunisia for the mud and cold of Norfolk and back again to missions over Germany.

Like many other Norfolk airfields Shipdham was often used as a blessed haven of relief by heavily damaged returning aircraft or those short of fuel. But on the night of 3rd November 1943 the Americans played welcome hosts to a most distinguished pilot and his crew. A heavily damaged Lancaster of 61 squadron based at Syerston near Newark, was staggering back from a raid on Dusseldorf, when the pilot Flight Lieutenant William Reid spotted some searchlights. Reid, who was suffering severe injuries, knew that the aircraft would not make it back to base so he circled the airfield and flashed his landing lights as a warning to the ground crews of his damaged aircraft. The effort involved in circling the aircraft had resulted in reopening Reid's serious head wounds, which greatly impaired his vision. Nevertheless he still managed to bring the Lancaster down on to the runway but immediately the undercarriage collapsed. The aircraft careered along for about 60 yards before finally coming to a halt. One of the crew was already dead and one died later in the Shipdham medical centre. Reid was later awarded the Victoria Cross for this raid on Dusseldorf and the citation read, '... tenacity and devotion to duty beyond praise'. He later joined 617 (The Dambusters) squadron and was shot down in July 1944 but survived as a prisoner-of-war.

Perhaps the Group's most inglorious hour came on the 1st April 1944. The Eighth Air Force had been planning a major operation to a variety of targets in southern Germany for the previous week but unsuitable weather conditions had delayed the mission. However, on the 1st it was decided to go but the thick cloud over many of the airfields resulted in several Groups having to abort. The 44th and 392nd (from Wendling) managed to take off but because of the heavy cloud formations (even at 21,000 feet) over southern Germany some minor navigational errors were made which caused the aircraft to stray off course. However, both Groups were convinced that they had located their target – Ludwigshafen (near Mannheim) and duly released their bombs. Tragically they had actually bombed the Swiss town of Schaffhausen, just ten miles from the German border and about 120 miles from their primary target town. It was a serious error that Goebbels, the German Propaganda Minister, was very quick to exploit in a vain attempt to divert the Germans' attention from the heavy bombardment they were suffering day and night at the hands of the RAF and the Eighth Air Force. There was an intense amount of American diplomatic activity at the highest level, which finally resulted in over one million dollars being paid in compensation. It had proved to be a most expensive operation.

Undaunted the 44th continued their operations over Germany, returning to Kiel, which had proved so costly on previous occasions, but this time the mission was much more successful. Their pattern of operations followed closely that of most of the other Bomb Groups – support for the Normandy landings, supplies to the Allied armies and the airborne invasion of Holland. At the end of hostilities they had undertaken 343 missions, one of the highest totals in the whole of the Eighth Air Force and certainly the most of a B24 Group. Against this they had suffered a considerable loss of aircraft and men – 153 aircraft missing in action but they had claimed well over 300 enemy aircraft destroyed. They were the longest serving B-24 Bomb Group in England – a fine and distinguished record.

One of the ground crews well remembers the scene on 8th May 1945, '... the entire air base was in a happy mood, awaiting a trip home. In a short time the order came, Air-crew personnel *only* were allowed to fly home in the Liberators with just 40 pounds of luggage. Needless to say those of us left behind had a wistful look on our faces as we watched B-24s take off into the blue yonder... After the final inspection, four United States and four RAF men stood to attention at the flagpole. One lone bugler played whilst the American flag was lowered for the last time and the British flag raised for the first time. This seemed to me a very quiet unpretentious ceremony to end the three years of occupation by 44th Bomb Group at Shipdham...'

For a short period during 1946-7 the airfield was used as a transit camp for German prisoners-of-war from Florida en route back to Germany. Then the airfield stayed idle for a number of years until it was sold off in 1963. In 1970 it reopened for flying and parts of the runways have been refurbished, with Arrow Air Services using it for charter and taxi flying. A memorial to the 'Flying Eightballs' can be seen close to the Arrow offices and there is another memorial stone in the village church. Shipdham can be found on the A1075 road to East Dereham and there is a sign in the village pointing to 'Shipdham Airfield'.

31
SNETTERTON HEATH

Many people would readily recognise Snetterton as intrinsically involved with motor racing, and certainly since the early 1950s Snetterton has attracted untold numbers of motor racing enthusiasts but not many of these spectators would have realised that the motor circuit is situated on an American airfield from the days of World War II. For just over two years it was the home of one of the most illustrious Bomb Groups in the whole of the Eighth Air Force – the 96th. This Group's battle honours make the most impressive reading – Regensburg, Schweinfurt, Poznan, Kiel, Hamm, Merseburg, and Berlin... the list seems endless. But sad to say the Group paid a very heavy toll, it gained the unenviable record of suffering the second highest total of casualties in the whole of the Eighth Air Force.

The 96th first arrived in England in April 1943 and settled in at Grafton Underwood near Kettering in Northamptonshire. Within a month they moved on to Andrew's Field in Essex, which was the first American airfield in England to be built by American engineers. The Group's B-17s had been allocated to the Third Bombardment Division and was the first Group to form the 4th Combat Bomb Wing. From this Essex base the 96th gained its introduction into war over Europe. Like all new Bomb Groups the young flyers of the 96th arrived in England with an overweening confidence in the might of the American Army Air Force, largely bolstered by articles in the American press, which had rather exaggerated the Eighth's success in England and had not been particularly honest over the casualty figures. The Group's early operations were to airfields in northern France such as St Omer and Courtrai, which were then considered easy targets for the new Groups to cut their teeth on. Six months later new Bomb Groups were not allowed the luxury of such 'milk runs', because of increasing pressure on the Eighth Air Force they had the misfortune of being sent out on full operations. On the Group's very first mission its aircraft were late in forming up and so missed the operation but they still managed to lose one aircraft, a self-inflicted wound caused by one of the aircraft's own machine guns. The accuracy of the novices' bombing was never expected to be good so these missions were thought as nothing more than nuisance raids, very good for training purposes but little else.

The Group's crews were soon to be blooded over Germany when on 15th May they were sent to Emden. Although on this occasion they returned back to base intact, they were now well aware of what the European air war was all about. At the end of the month they, along with other Groups in the Fourth Bomb Wing, were detailed to bomb marshalling yards at Rennes in north-west France. The Luftwaffe fighters carefully bided their time, waiting for the escort fighters to reach the limit of their operational range and return for home before they struck at the bomber formations. Although the fighter attacks were of short duration they were nevertheless very telling and could have become costly for the bombers but for the timely intervention of ten squadrons of RAF Spitfires that had been sent out to rescue the American bombers. The British cavalry flying to the rescue?

The Group's personnel found themselves once again on the move but this time it was to their permanent home at Snetterton Heath, which they occupied for the rest of the war. The airfield had originally been intended for the RAF but later the Air Ministry offered it to the USAAF. The first American Group to use it was No 386 Medium Bomb Group, who with their B-26 Marauders stayed for just a week before leaving for Boxted in north Essex. The heavies of the 96th arrived on 11th June and set off two days later to Kiel.

This operation was later described by the USAAF as 'the greatest single air battle of the war'. It is not too clear why they considered it so important and certainly other later operations were strategically far more significant. Earlier in the month the Eighth had mounted a large operation on the same target, but using solely B-24s the raid had proved to be rather costly and not very successful. The second mission was planned for the 13th and the plan was to attack in two waves within several minutes of each other, in the hope that this new and different tactic would effectively confuse the enemy's radar and split the fighter force. As soon as the two formations of B-17s arrived over the German coast they were met by the largest formations of enemy fighters yet seen by the Eighth and they launched a series of most fierce and determined attacks. One of the first aircraft to be shot down contained Brigadier General Nathan Forrest, a senior Headquarters officer, who became the first American general to be killed on active service in Europe. Most of the Groups taking part in the operation suffered quite heavy losses, although the 96th escaped relatively lightly. To rub salt into the wounds, from photographic evidence, it was later disclosed that the bombing had generally been of a very poor standard. As the depleted formations returned back to East Anglia they were attacked by twelve Ju88s about 30 miles off the Norfolk coast. The tired and mentally exhausted crews were completely taken by surprise and several aircraft were quickly shot down; indeed it was later discovered that some of the gunners had already dismantled their guns and were busy cleaning them when the enemy struck!

Almost as if to emphasise the fact that the Group was still a mere novice in this war game, the *Memphis Belle*, the first B-17 and crew to complete a tour of operations left for the United States on 9th June 1943. Besides the inordinate amount of publicity the aircraft and its crew received on their arrival in the United States and more so when the aircraft went on tour of many American cities, the aircraft's fame became ensured by William Wyler's classic war film of the same name. And its celebrity and glory has recently been resuscitated by the very successful remake of the 1940s film.

One of the features of the Eighth Air Force and its aircraft that has been firmly fixed in the public's mind is not only the various names given to the aircraft but the way these names were illustrated on the noses of the aircraft. This 'nose art' has rightly become quite famous. Obviously the notable examples were those of scantily clothed ladies in a variety of poses. Many of the paintings were of a very high standard and their quality depended on the artistic talent available at each base. Some of the best examples of 'nose art' have passed into the folklore of the Eighth Air Force. Of course many of Bomber Command's aircraft were named and there are examples of RAF 'nose art' but those paintings tended to be more decorous.

Because of the Group's close proximity to the Third Division's headquarters at Elveden Hall, which was a few miles south of Thetford, the Group often found itself acting as a convenient transport flight for senior officers. On the 17th August 1943 the Group not only was given the honour of leading the Division to Regensburg but it also had General Curtis Le May, the Division's

Commanding Officer, as co-pilot in one of its aircraft. The previous evening's briefing told the crews that they were going on a major and important operation – a double-headed attack deep into southern Germany. The two targets – Regensburg and Schweinfurt – were destined to be writ large in the history of the Eighth Air Force. Rather jokingly the crews were told to pack an overnight bag, it was then that they knew for certain this mission was going to be very different. As the details were unfolded – an important target – expected to be strongly defended – a flight over the Alps – right down the length of Italy to an airfield in North Africa! Most of the crews felt that they would be exceedingly lucky to survive (see Thorpe Abbotts).

Considering the terrible losses sustained by some of the other Bomb Groups involved in this quite remarkable and outstanding operation and the Group's vulnerable position in the lead formation, it was almost unbelievable that all of the 21 aircraft despatched by 96th Group on such a traumatic eleven hour mission managed to survive intact, although many were heavily damaged. The Group had more serviceable aircraft than any other Group to bomb Bordeaux on the journey back to England from North Africa. All the Groups involved in the 'Regensburg Shuttle' were awarded Distinguished Unit Citations. But the Group, and their near neighbours 100 Group at Thorpe Abbotts, brought back a more tangible reminder of their short spell in Africa – a donkey – which was named 'Lady Moe' and needless to say became their mascot.

Shortly after their return to England, the Group was involved in a mission to Stuttgart, which turned out to be a most expensive debacle. Some 330 aircraft were despatched on 6th September and mainly because of the weather conditions – very heavy clouds up to a high altitude – the target objectives were not located. The weather conditions also caused the tight bomber formations to become rather ragged and broken, giving the Luftwaffe fighters some easy targets with a resultant high loss rate, over 13% of the aircraft were shot down. To add to the mayhem many of the B-17s from the First Division ran short of fuel, a serious miscalculation by the operation's planners. Twenty aircraft were forced to ditch or crash-land for lack of fuel as soon as they reached English shores. When the casualty figures were finally totalled it was found that besides 45 missing in action over 120 aircraft were seriously damaged with almost 500 men either killed or seriously wounded – a very black day indeed for the Eighth Air Force. Fortunately 96 Group escaped with only 14 aircraft damaged and just one crew member injured.

However, the fortunes of war dictated that no Bomb Group operating at this time could expect or indeed hope to escape for too long before the balance was redressed and sometimes most dramatically. The second disastrous mission to Schweinfurt in October 1943 brought this fact home to 96th Group. Selected once again to lead the Division's formation, the Group lost seven aircraft and another twelve heavily damaged – virtually half of the Division's total casualties. Now with losses running at about 20% on most major operations, the whole concept of unescorted daylight bombing came under heavy criticism and the policy was very close to being abandoned. The Eighth Air Force's chiefs held their nerve, but until adequate long-range fighter protection was available, the long suffering Groups would continue to sustain heavy operational wastages of both aircraft and crews, many of whom were well experienced and thus most valuable.

During the first four months of 1944, the 96th had the very unenviable record of having the highest loss rate incurred by any Group in the whole of the Eighth. It was not uncommon for new crews to arrive, have just time to unpack, then be posted 'missing in action' within a day or so. The empty beds in the huts with the neatly packed boxes of belongings and the empty chairs in the messes had a deeply distressing and debilitating effect on the remaining crews. This forlorn atmosphere prevailed more heavily at Snetterton Heath than at any other American airfield because from April 1944 until D-Day the Group lost 100 aircraft and, of course, almost 1,000 aircrew. This was a staggering figure especially when one considers that some Bomb Groups did not lose this number of aircraft and crews throughout the whole of their service in Europe. It is not surprising to learn that at times Snetterton 'seemed to be like living in a transit camp, unknown faces suddenly arrived and just as quickly they disappeared . . . sometimes we didn't even get to know the guys' names before they were gone for ever. Most crews felt that their next mission would be their last . . . it was a depressing time . . .'

Perhaps the Group's proudest hour came in April 1944 when Snetterton Heath was visited by three generals and all their various entourages – Spaatz, Doolittle and Le May. Ostensibly they had come to help the Group celebrate its 100th mission but I suspect that they also went along to explain and give the reasons for another 'Shuttle' mission, only on this occasion the Eighth was to fly to Russia and return via Hungary, Italy and France – almost a European Grand Tour! This kind of operation was well in favour with the

The delightful chapel in St Andrew's church, Quidenham, in memory of the airmen of 96th Bomb Group.

Eighth's hierarchy and it also had the added political bonus of showing the Allies' commitment to their Russian allies by striking at strategic targets in eastern Germany and Poland.

Almost as a preliminary to the Russian operation, the Group was sent out on the 9th April to attack aircraft factories at Poznan, which was just over the German border in Poland and so far had been immune from the Eighth's bombers. Because of the unfavourable weather – very heavy clouds over most of Northern Europe – one of the Wings was recalled but three Bomb Groups, with the 96th in the lead, did not receive the message and they continued on to the target. They successfully bombed the primary targets – most accurately and very precisely as it was later proved. Then as the aircraft were on the return flight home they were requested to divert and give some added protection to a bomber formation that was attacking another target at Marienburg. The whole operation was one of the most successful undertaken by the Eighth and due largely to the determination and leadership of the 96th; quite rightly the Group received a thoroughly deserved second Distinguished Unit Citation. Just two days later another mission to Poznan was ordered. This time the target was completely obscured by heavy clouds so the Groups went for the secondary target – Rostock. Here they encountered very heavy fighter opposition – Me410s, Ju88s and some Fw190s and after a short but very harsh air battle 25 of the Division's B-17s had been destroyed with the 96th losing ten of its crews.

Like all other Bomb Groups in the Third Division the 96th departed with 21 aircraft for targets in eastern Germany and Poland and from thence on to Russia to land at Poltava airfield, where the Luftwaffe struck with devastating and damaging effect. The few tattered remnants of the Group returned via Italy, where nevertheless it still managed one mission over Rumania. Then when they were on their return flight they bombed a marshalling yard in France before arriving back in Norfolk with just three aircraft left out of 21 of the original force sent out to Russia. Just three months later, in September, the Group went back on another Russian shuttle, this time they bombed oil plants and installations at Chemnitz on the flight out.

The Group was actively involved in all the various operations that figured large in the Eighth's strategic bombing offensive – Berlin, Merseburg, Ardennes, Ruhrland, and Dresden. Its last operation in Europe was despatched on 21st April 1945, which made a grand total of 316. During all these many and varied operations they lost 189 aircraft, the second highest in the whole of the Eighth Air Force and more than the 'Bloody Hundredth' at nearby Thorpe Abbotts. There were plans for the Group to serve in Germany so it continued to operate many transport and training flights from Snetterton Heath long after most of the other Groups had left Norfolk. Finally it was decided that the 96th would indeed return to the United States and as Christmas was fast approaching the aircraft of the 96th began to leave and soon the airfield was left vacant.

Although there are several of the original wartime buildings still dotted around the race circuit, which uses part of the old airfield's perimeter track, it is along the narrow and winding country lanes to the east of the circuit that the best reminders of the 96th are to be found. In the delightful St Andrew's church at Quidenham there is a fine chapel dedicated to the memory of the men of the 96th who lost their lives. Dominating the chapel is a very attractive stained-glass window portraying an American flyer. This was the earliest memorial to any Eighth Air Force Bomb Group in Norfolk, it was dedicated in November 1944 and the cost of the chapel (£600) was borne by the then serving members of the Group.

32
SWANNINGTON

Swannington was the last RAF airfield in Norfolk to be opened during the Second World War. Its construction had begun in November 1942 but the work was seriously delayed and it was not ready for occupation until April 1944 when it was allocated to No 100 Group of Bomber Command. What really decided which squadrons would finally come to the new airfield was the disastrous raid on Nuremberg conducted by Bomber Command during the night of 30th/31st March 1944. Of the 795 aircraft taking part in this operation, 95 failed to return and another ten were damaged beyond repair – the heaviest loss ever sustained by the Command throughout the whole of the war. Largely as a result of this calamitous mission it was decided that No 100 Group desperately needed additional fighter support and two squadrons of Mosquito XIXs were rushed to the only available airfield – Swannington.

The first one to arrive on 1st May was No 85, then considered to be one of the crack night-fighter squadrons and which had recently been commanded by Wing Commander John Cunningham – the renowned night-fighter pilot. One week later No 157 squadron arrived from RAF Valley in Anglesey. Their duties in the Group would be many and varied as befitted the aircraft they flew. Patrols over enemy airfields and enemy fighter assembly points, pure bomber escort duties, intermingling with large bomber streams and low-level intruder raids. All the aircraft were equipped with AI radar (Air Interception) and were later supplied with 'Monica', a device designed to give warning of the approach of an interceptor from astern. The initials 'SD' denoting Special Duties were added to their titles. Coming from the more informal method of operations in Fighter Command, the squadrons' crews took some time to conform

The old control tower at Swannington.

to the more rigid environment of Bomber Command but they soon settled into the Group's routines.

The two squadrons were largely held in reserve for D-Day operations and on 5th/6th June 16 missions were flown from Swannington not only directly over the Normandy beaches but also over many enemy airfields in Holland. The 85th's first victory came on the 11th when Wing Commander Miller DFC destroyed a Me110 whilst returning from a bombing mission over Normandy. This was just the first of many as the two squadrons made their presence felt. However, by the middle of the month came the first threat of the V1 rockets and it was decided that the Mosquito squadrons would be best utilised on 'Divers' operations as they were called. After the aircraft were modified to increase their surface speed they left for West Malling in Kent, where they completed over 140 sorties against the V1s claiming at least 70 rockets destroyed.

When they had returned to Swannington they were quickly back into very successful operations destroying eight enemy aircraft in September for the loss of two Mosquitos. It was the high-altitude patrol work, the weaving in and out of the bomber streams that were so attractive to the crews. As one pilot of 85 squadron recalled, 'Flying high we had the added perk of witnessing night after night the most stupendous avalanche of fireworks that made the pre-war Crystal Palace and Blackpool rolled into one look like a damp squib.' The following two months were particularly fruitful with over 50 aircraft destroyed for the loss of only two missing. Christmas Eve 1944 was to be the highlight of 157's operations to date with four victories on the day for not a single loss.

During the last six weeks of the year the two squadrons shared Swannington with the Spitfire IXs of 229 squadron, who had moved out of Matlaske because of the waterlogged condition of the airfield. The Spitfires were mainly used on escort duties though occasionally they were bombed up to tackle V1 rocket sites in Holland. When they left at the end of the year, they were replaced by another Spitfire squadron – No 451 – who were almost solely engaged in providing withdrawal cover for Lancasters returning from operations over Germany and at times even escorting them on long-range missions.

The two other bomber support squadrons continued to operate throughout the last months of the war although with a diminishing number of victories to their credit, a sure sign that the Luftwaffe night-fighter force had virtually been destroyed and the squadrons were operating against a depleted enemy. Both squadrons flew their last missions on the night of 2nd/3rd of May providing high-level support for several attacks on Kiel, which proved to be Bomber Command's last offensive operation of the war.

After VE Day 85 squadron quickly left Swannington to return to Fighter Command, but 157 squadron stayed a little longer and was finally disbanded on 16th August. The airfield, like North Creake and Oulton, was passed over to a unit of Maintenance Command and all flying ceased in June 1947. It was to be another ten years before the airfield was sold and returned to farming. There are still signs of the old wartime airfield; the old control tower can be seen near an industrial estate and parts of the runway and perimeter track are still evident. The site is about one mile to the north of the village off the road to Brandiston.

33
SWANTON MORLEY

Swanton Morley has gained everlasting fame in the annals of RAF history for two notable 'firsts', both of which had a most significant and almost incalculable effect on the war in Europe. It was the airfield where the de Havilland Mosquito first entered service in an RAF squadron, this historic event occurred in November 1941. Then six months later the airfield played host to a small detachment of USAAF airmen, who on 26th June 1942 became the first American aircrews to enter operations in the European war. It is probably very appropriate that this famous wartime airfield now houses another wooden 'aircraft' – the Viking T1 gliders of No 611 Volunteer Gliding School.

The airfield came into being in September 1940 as a full station within No 2 Group of Bomber Command and by the end of October the Blenheims of 105 squadron took up residence, destined to become one of the most famous squadrons to operate from Norfolk during the Second World War. Its first few months of operations followed the general pattern of the Group's activities at a time when its squadrons were waging a steady, continuous but very costly bombing offensive against the enemy. During November it was engaged in airfield attacks and in the following month its attention was directed against targets in western Germany – Cologne, Bremen and Hamburg. The severe weather of January 1941 gave the squadron some respite from operations but when the conditions improved oil targets became a main priority. March saw another change of targets – enemy ports. Because of the serious losses of Allied shipping much of the Group's resources were directed towards the docks at Ostend, Rotterdam, Antwerp and Flushing.

During April the crews were ordered to undertake low-level training over East Anglia with some practice bombing raids over the

Wash. On some occasions they were making four sorties a day, all in preparation for their new task – anti-shipping strikes. The Blenheims lost their brown and green camouflage and black undersides and were repainted green with duck-blue undersides in the theory that they would blend with the colour of the sea. A typical anti-shipping raid was made on 15th April when six aircraft were detailed to attack an enemy convoy just off Borkum. The Blenheims attacked at dusk from a level of 50 feet through an intense barrage of flak put up by E-boats. Only two of the aircraft managed to bomb the vessels, most of the bombs fell on the town. All of the aircraft returned safely but not to Swanton Morley because fog had closed down the airfield and they were eventually forced to land at Steeple Morden in Cambridgeshire. This particular situation was the perennial concern of both the Group's planners and station commanders as so often the weather closed in on Norfolk airfields, causing considerable difficulties for the returning crews in aircraft that were often badly damaged or short of fuel.

The following month the squadron was out on another shipping strike to Stavanger. This operation resulted in the loss of Wing Commander Arnold Christian, the squadron commander, who was one of the most experienced Blenheim pilots in the whole of No 2 Group, and had been instrumental in bringing the squadron up to a very high standard. Such experienced pilots were impossible to replace and his sad death was a blow to the squadron. But there is always a silver lining to the darkest cloud, and this came in the shape of a very fine Australian airman – Wing Commander 'Hughie' Edwards DFC, who made a tremendous mark on the squadron.

The squadron's day of glory came on 4th July when Wing Commander Edwards led nine aircraft on a mission to Bremen, code-named 'Operation Wreckage'. The Blenheims came in at rooftop level over what was considered one of the heaviest defended areas of Germany. The aircraft were forced to fly below high tension cables and then zig-zag through the barrage balloons. Four aircraft were shot down but the other five managed successfully to bomb the docks, railway yards and some factories. Wing Commander Edwards received the Victoria Cross for his leadership of the raid and his citation read, '... although handicapped by a flying accident [he] has repeatedly displayed gallantry of the highest order in pressing home bombing attacks from very low heights against strongly defended objectives ... on reaching Bremen he was met with a hail of fire, all his aircraft being hit and four of them were destroyed. Nevertheless he made a most successful attack, and then with greatest skill and coolness withdrew the surviving aircraft without further loss. Throughout the execution of the operation, which he had planned personally with full knowledge of the risks involved, Wing Commander Edwards displayed the highest possible standard of gallantry and determination . . .'

Twelve days later the squadron was detailed for an almost replica of the Bremen raid – an attack on Rotterdam docks, already covered elsewhere. All the eleven aircraft despatched from Swanton Morley survived intact and returned safe and sound. By the end of the month the squadron was detached for three months to Malta and during its absence Blenheims of 88 squadron used the airfield as well as Spitfires from 152 squadron, who were engaged in escorting Coastal Command anti-shipping strikes.

Not very long after the squadron had returned from their spell in the sun, they were once again the centre of attention. On 15th November 1941 Geoffrey de Havilland brought the squadron its first Mosquito (W4064). He gave the excited crews a fine display of aerobatics as he put the aircraft through its paces. As one pilot commented 'Another great day in the history of 105 squadron. All crews watched with great enthusiasm the performance in the air. Even the Spitfire pilots of 152 squadron were impressed . . .' This was just the opening of an amazing chapter in the history of the RAF; for

De Havilland Mosquito: No 105 Squadron was the first to be equipped with these 'wonder' aircraft.

the next three years or so the Mosquito would prove to be the most exciting, versatile and successful aircraft of the Second World War. It was to be a very brief moment of glory for Swanton Morley because by 9th December the squadron moved to RAF Horsham St Faith. The squadron was replaced by No 226 squadron, which had only recently been re-equipped with Douglas Boston IIIs.

The Bostons were at first treated with some suspicion by the crews; as their landing speeds were far higher than the Blenheims it took the pilots some time to adjust. Also there were stories about high speed stalls but after weeks of practice at the 'shooting gallery' off Brancaster on the Norfolk coast, the crews' confidence slowly grew. The squadron's first real taste of action came on 26th February 1942 when four Bostons attacked shipping off the Dutch coast and despite heavy and accurate flak all four returned safely, though one had to crash-land at Coltishall. Then on 8th March the squadron, along with No 88 squadron, were detailed for a raid on Matford armaments works at Poissy near Paris and the Comines power station. For the first mission 14 aircraft would use Thorney Island in Sussex as a forward base because of the range involved. Wing Commander Butler of 226 squadron led the mission and although the target was successfully bombed his aircraft crashed whilst he was trying to land his damaged aircraft in France. The plane hit a tree and exploded in flames. The Comines mission was an equally successful bombing raid with no aircraft lost. The Bostons were beginning to prove most effective at these daring low-level bombing strikes.

On 24th June 1942 nine four-men crews from the 15th Bomb Squadron of the Eighth Air Force arrived at Swanton Morley to receive training in RAF flight procedures and low-level bombing attacks. Five days later one of the Bostons sent out by 226 squadron to attack the Hazebrouck marshalling yards was crewed by Americans with Captain Kegelmann as pilot – the first time an American crew had flown operationally in the European war. Obviously, the Fourth of July – Independence Day – was considered a perfect opportunity to launch another combined Anglo/American operation. This time six American crews were involved in an operation with No 226 crews and the targets selected were four Luftwaffe airfields in the Low Countries. The aircraft set out in four flights of three aircraft, each flight had an experienced RAF pilot in the lead and each was given a separate airfield to attack. From this mission three aircraft failed to return – two American and one British. Captain Kegelmann's aircraft was severely damaged but he

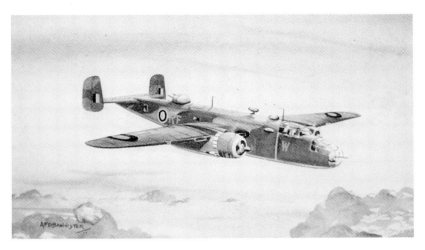

North American Mitchell: three squadrons operated from Swanton Morley.

still managed to bring it back to Swanton Morley on just one engine. For this act he was awarded the Distinguished Service Cross, which was the second highest American bravery decoration. Several other American missions were undertaken in conjunction with 226 until the Americans received their own Bostons in August.

Until 226 squadron left Swanton Morley in February 1944 it took a very active part in nearly all of the Group's large operations including the famous raid on Rotterdam in December 1942. In May 1943, the squadron was taken off operations whilst it re-equipped with North American Mitchells; their last mission with Bostons was on 1st July. After retraining the squadron was involved in the offensive against the V1 rocket sites or 'Operation Crossbow'.

The very first assault of these sites began on 5th November when a large formation of Bostons and Mitchells were directed against a huge site at Mimoyecques to the south-west of Calais. The crews involved in the operation were not informed of the precise nature of the target, only that it was of utmost importance and comprised 'large enemy excavations and installations'. However, as they roared over the target area they encountered such heavy and sustained flak that they quickly realised they were attacking a target of some significance. During the next week the crews bombed this specific target on no less than three occasions, and it became known as 'The Valley of Death' from the *Charge of the Light Brigade*. Right up until they left Swanton Morley the crews gained a rare reputation for their attacks on these sites and by January they were credited with four separate sites destroyed. From November 1943 to May 1944 over 4,700 sorties were mounted by the RAF and the Eighth Air Force against the V1 rocket sites, which proved to be one of the largest bombing offensives of the war.

Swanton Morley had long been considered as No 2 Group's practice camp with various flights arriving regularly to avail themselves of the Bombing and Gunnery Flight (No 1482) which had a mixture of Bostons, Mitchells and Venturas. There was also a Blind Approach Training Flight (No 1508) at the airfield, with Airspeed Oxfords, which had on several occasions been used for air/sea rescue flights – a rare operational role for these innocuous aircraft. During the spring of 1944 the station was very busy preparing aircrews of the Second Tactical Air Force for their future operations in support of the Allied armies in Normandy.

Swanton Morley later became a computer and maintenance centre for the RAF but the station closed in 1995. There have been several reports that an Anglo/American company is interested in purchasing the airfield and they have plans to establish a wartime theme park. It is said that the war years and aviation will figure large in the exhibition but the displays will cover other aspects of the period – watch this space!

34

THORPE ABBOTTS

'So if a guy tells you he flew with the 100th, be nice to him, he deserves it' – a sentiment that would surely be echoed by most, if not all, Eighth Air Force veterans. Without doubt the 100th Bomb Group became a living legend in the USAAF and in the process earned the sobriquet 'The Bloody Hundredth' because of its appallingly crippling losses of aircraft and men during certain periods of their time in England. As one survivor of the Group later admitted, 'When we lost, we lost big... We lost with panache.' The Group became known throughout the Eighth Air Force as 'the jinx outfit'! It fought a long and bitterly contested campaign and suffered grievously – 177 aircraft missing in action and 732 airmen killed – such statistics need no embellishment to show the immense sacrifice of all the young men of the 100th Bomb Group.

First activated in June 1942 it was originally intended to be a B-24 group but by November had received its first B-17s and set about training. In early June 1943 the Group had arrived in England and on the 9th the first of its aircraft began to land at Thorpe Abbotts airfield set deep in the south of the county and just a couple of miles east of Diss. It became the first B-17 Group to serve in Norfolk and was placed first in the Third Bomb Division and No 4 Combat Wing, then three months later in the 13th Wing, and to those of a superstitious mind perhaps this was the start of the Group's ill-fortune?

The first arrivals found their new home to be 'a cluster of huts right in the middle of some farm buildings with cows going through the squadron yard.' The airfield, originally planned as a satellite for Horham, had been built on two farms, one of which was owned by Sir Rupert Mann, whom the Americans thought was 'the epitome of an English squire'! All the living quarters were well-dispersed around

Working on aircraft of 100th Bomb Group. (100th Bomb Group Museum)

the farms and a fair distance from the runways, so the first essential task was to obtain a bicycle, and the going rate for these valuable items of equipment, at the time, was £4. Within a week the Group was joined by another B-17 Group (96th) based at nearby Snetterton Heath and quite quickly a strong but friendly rivalry arose between the two Groups, which was to last throughout the war.

The 100th spent the next three weeks on training flights and familiarising themselves with the Norfolk countryside from the air. Like all other new Bomb Groups it was sent on practice missions and the crews did not endear themselves to the Division's chiefs when two aircraft were lost to enemy fighters on one of these. An official visit from General Le May, the Divisional Commander, in July revealed the Group as somewhat disorganised and quite undisciplined. So were the first seeds of doubts sown at Elveden House (the headquarters of the Third Division) that the 100th was going to become a 'problem' Group? Indeed by the end of July it had received its third Commander – Colonel Neil Harding – an officer who was destined to lead the 100th through some of its most 'bloody' missions.

Its first major mission was launched in late July and the target was Trondheim in Norway – a 1,900 mile round trip. One of the problems that the Eighth Air Force was to encounter throughout the war, was the assembly of the large formations of aircraft coming from so many East Anglian airfields especially in cloudy and overcast conditions. On this occasion a new technique was introduced, the use of splasher beacons, which were British medium frequency radio stations situated at intervals throughout East Anglia. The various Groups were instructed to assemble around a certain splasher signal and it proved to be a very successful method. This long mission to Norway was most effective, very little flak was encountered and hardly any enemy fighters. The primary targets were bombed and it was later disclosed – via the Norwegian underground – that one U-boat had been sunk, a destroyer badly damaged and most of the shore installations set on fire.

Possibly the Group's fame or infamy all started with the Regensburg raid of August 1943. The object of the operation was an attempt to neutralise the Luftwaffe fighter opposition and the main target was the Me109 factories, which were then supplying almost 50% of the German fighter production. At the same time another large force would attack Schweinfurt, a large ball-bearing complex. But on previous deep penetration operations the Eighth Air Force's formations had suffered heavily on their return flights because by then the Luftwaffe had time to organise their fighter squadrons and were able to take a serious toll of the bombers. So, in this instance, it was decided that the Regensburg force would fly directly south after bombing the target and land at USAAF airfields in North Africa. The date of the operation (17th) was specially selected as being the anniversary of the Eighth Air Force's first independent operation in Europe.

The 147 strong force was led by General Le May, the Divisional Commander, in an aircraft from the 96th Bomb Group at Snetterton Heath. The 100th was detailed to be at the tail of the formation, which quite pleased them as until then the Luftwaffe's fighters had mainly concentrated their attacks on the leading Groups. There were seven Bomb Groups involved, each providing 21 aircraft. Flying with one of them was Lieutenant Colonel Bernie Lay, a senior headquarters officer, who was acting as an official observer as well as gaining experience as he was to take command of a new Bomb Group.

The aircraft had left Thorpe Abbotts at 7.30 am and just after 10 am they had crossed the Dutch coast, encountering their first flak about

15 minutes later. The first premonition of the impending disaster came when only one Group of P-47 Thunderbolts appeared, and as the bomber armada was now stretched over five miles, the Luftwaffe realised the rear formation was unescorted and in a very exposed position. Taking full advantage they attacked swiftly and in great strength – the time was just 10.20 am. The ensuing action was so brutal that Lay wrote, '... the sight was fantastic and surpassed fiction ... emergency hatches, exit doors, prematurely opened parachutes, bodies and assorted fragments of B-17s and Hun fighters breezed past ... After we had been under constant attack for a solid hour, it appeared certain that the 100th Group was faced with annihilation. Seven of our group had been shot down, the sky was still mottled with rising fighters and it was only 11.20 hours with the target-time still 35 minutes away. I doubt if any man in the Group visualised the possibility of our getting much further without 100 per cent loss. I knew that I had long since mentally accepted the fact of death and that it was simply a question of the next second or the next minute...'

Despite the almost continual fighter onslaught the Group's eleven remaining aircraft still managed to bomb the target although by then Regensburg was completely obscured by smoke and fires. On the

'Any mail today?' (100th Bomb Group Museum)

way south two aircraft crash-landed, one in Switzerland (the first American aircraft to seek sanctuary in that country) and the other in Italy. The very tattered remnants of the Group finally landed in North Africa at 6.15 pm after eleven hours of 'sheer and utter hell'. Lay said, 'We all felt the reaction of men who had not expected to see another sunset'. He also considered that just 'one stint to Regensburg took more out of an airman than twenty normal missions.' Le May cabled England to report that he 'considered the objective had been totally destroyed.' Certainly subsequent intelligence proved that substantial damage had been inflicted. The newspapers greeted the operation as 'the most ambitious and cleverly conceived mission' but the cost had been very high, a total of 34 aircraft lost and over 50 damaged. Some of the aircrews commented that many of the German fighters were fitted with air-to-air rockets, which had not previously been encountered by the Eighth's bombers. Every Group that took part in this mission was awarded a Distinguished Unit Citation and probably none was ever more deserved.

No sooner had the Group returned to England and so called 'normal' operations than it was to suffer even greater losses. In September they lost seven aircraft in just two missions and in the following month the position became graver. During just one week of operations the Group lost 21 aircraft. On the 8th seven were destroyed over Bremen and an eighth aircraft, which was badly damaged, was forced to crash land at RAF Ludham. At that time the airfield was unoccupied as the runways were considered too short even for fighters. The aircraft called *Just a-Snappin* landed safely but managed to hit the one tree on the whole airfield. Captain Harry Crosby, the navigator, recalled, 'we are stopped. No one gets out. We just sit... Silence. At first. Then, as always, in the English countryside, we hear the birds.' Crosby, who survived 37 missions with the 100th (including Regensburg) has written an excellent account of his war experiences in *A Wing and a Prayer*. Just two days later, despite the losses over Bremen, the Group sent 13 aircraft to Munster and on this very black day for the 100th just one aircraft made it back to Thorpe Abbotts.

During January and February 1944 the USAAF had been totally engaged in an all-out assault against aircraft factories – including a week long offensive in late February, which was called 'Operation Argument' although it later became known as 'The Big Week'. It was now felt that the Eighth was ready, willing and able to attack the ultimate of German targets – Berlin or 'Big B'. The RAF had struck their opening blows in the Battle of Berlin in the previous November and largely because of these heavy raids, the flak batteries around the city were greatly strengthened and the fighter protection vastly increased. Previously St Nazaire had been the benchmark for the weight of German flak, but now the position had changed with Berlin becoming the heaviest defended area in the whole of Germany.

The first American operation was planned for 3rd March but this had to be aborted because of the very high cloud cover. On the following day, though the conditions had not greatly improved, the operation was given the green light, only for the formations to be recalled when they had almost reached the German coast. Three squadrons did not receive the recall message – two were from 95th Group and one from 100th Group. The three squadrons ploughed on and did manage to bomb the targets although they were almost five miles high because of the cloud cover. One gunner from the 100th claimed and was awarded a Me109 shot down – the first victory for a B-17 over Berlin. On return to England both Groups were delighted to be the first B-17s to bomb the 'Big B', and this was especially so at Thorpe Abbotts where only one crew had been lost.

Two days later the Eighth returned to Berlin, this time with a big force – 730 strong (both B-17s and B-24s) and well escorted by 706 fighters including two RAF squadrons of Mustangs. The main object of this operation was the Erkner ball-bearing plant some 16 miles south-east of Berlin. In just one disastrous 30 minute onslaught by enemy fighters No 100 Group along with 95 Group lost 23 aircraft. The first big Berlin raid was the Eighth's most costly operation of the whole war – 80 aircraft destroyed and over 100 severely damaged. Of this total the 100th sustained 15 losses, once again the highest of any Bomb Group taking part. Their reputation as 'the jinx outfit' gained even more credence throughout the Eighth. Besides the severe operational losses the Group were prone to a high degree of accidental losses, on one occasion seven aircraft crashed into each other at the end of the runway after returning from a mission.

Amazingly just 36 hours later the Group were again detailed for the third Berlin raid and on this occasion they would be leading the Wing. I suspect this was a deliberate attempt to try to bolster the Group's sagging morale. But because of a navigational error by the lead squadron, the 100th found themselves leading the whole Eighth Air Force on to Berlin. This time the weather conditions were perfect, there was little fighter opposition and the bombing accuracy was of a very high standard, at least 75 direct hits were made on the target.

The Group returned to Thorpe Abbotts having lost only one aircraft and that was due to engine trouble. For the Group's participation in the three Berlin raids it received its second Distinguished Unit Citation. Perhaps at long last their fortunes were turning?

In June they took part in the shuttle to Russia though this time Dame Fortune smiled on them because their aircraft were based at an airfield that did not suffer the Luftwaffe raids, which caused so much damage to other Groups. Still their operational losses remained high, 23 aircraft were lost on three individual missions. On a raid to Merseburg, the notoriously well-defended oil plant, eleven of their aircraft were accounted for in just ten minutes. On the final day of the year on a mission to Hamburg twelve aircraft failed to return – half the Third Division's total. Their reputation would now never die.

The 100th flew its last major mission, also its 300th, on 11th April 1945. They found themselves back over southern Germany attacking targets to the north of Munich, very close to Regensburg – perhaps a fitting climax to their glorious but very bitter operations over Germany. In the first week of May they, like many other Groups, were active in 'Operation Chow Hound' – the supply of food to the starving people of Holland. Special routes and dropping points had been agreed and provided the aircraft did not stray outside these limits the Germans had agreed to allow free passage. All of the crews found these were the most pleasant and rewarding missions they had undertaken. Later in May, after the war in Europe came to an end, the Group were engaged on the so-called 'Revival' flights. With just a five man crew their aircraft landed on old Luftwaffe airfields to pick up and bring back over 40 prisoners-of-war on each trip, and even managed to meet some old friends whom they thought they would never see again.

The old control tower at Thorpe Abbotts has been splendidly restored and now houses a fine and fitting museum in memory of the 100th Bomb Group. It is open at weekends throughout the year and additionally on Wednesdays from May to September. Although the airfield is tucked away in the countryside, the museum is well signposted from the main A143.

35
TIBENHAM

Virtually every Bomb Group in the Eighth Air Force suffered heavy losses on a single mission at some time or other during their operations over Europe. Mostly these tragic aberrations could be explained by sheer bad luck, a moment when conditions, circumstances and the odd human error all conspired to exact a terrible toll on aircraft and men. But no Bomb Group ever suffered more grievously than did the 445th on 27th September 1944, when in just about a half an hour their losses were so catastrophic that the Group, as such, almost ceased to exist. A tragedy on such a scale naturally left deep and lasting scars on the surviving members of the Group, and when the dire news quickly spread through the Wing and Division, morale slumped; the thought uppermost in most of the other aircrews' minds was that perhaps the next time it would be their turn.

The 445th had left the United States in October and the aircraft finally arrived at Tibenham in the early days of November 1943. The men found the airfield to be a bare and rather inhospitable place, a far cry from the comforts of their training base in Sioux City, Iowa. The airfield, which was situated just to the south-west of the village, was yet another example of one built especially for American use during that mad scurry of construction that took place in 1943.

With this Bomb Group came James Stewart, the well-known film star, who was the commander of 703 squadron. Stewart had volunteered for the Army but was considered too underweight, so he offered his services to the USAAF. It was reckoned that at that time Stewart had given up $3,000 a month to serve in the Armed Forces. He did, of course, have a highly successful career in the Eighth Air Force, being promoted to operations officer with the 453rd Group at

Old Buckenham in March 1944, and ending up with rank of colonel as Commander of the Second Wing before he returned to his life in Hollywood. Having a celebrity like James Stewart on the base did mean that the Group gained a fair amount of publicity.

The Group had been placed in the Second Bomb Wing and by 13th December the aircraft and crews had completed their 'local' training, which was effectively practice training flights over Norfolk to familiarise themselves with the locale and landmarks, assembly and landing procedures and more importantly to perfect their close formation flying. It was now felt that the crews were ready to move into operations. Their very first mission was not to be the usual gentle introduction into operational life with a fairly innocuous run over northern France but the Group's crews were going to be set a stern test of their discipline and character; the target was Germany and in particular Kiel, which was treated with great respect by all those Groups who had experience of this strongly fortified area. Only 15 crews were considered ready for such a stiff first test. From this mission not only did all the aircraft return safely but moreover all the crews managed to bomb, which was quite remarkable for a new and inexperienced Group.

By the time the Eighth's so called 'Big Week' of operations commenced in the third week of February, the Group's crews were beginning to feel like veterans as they had been as active as the weather conditions would allow and they had survived with relatively few losses. Their date with destiny came on 24th February 1944 when the Group was detailed for a large operation that was being mounted by the Second Division against Gotha. This place was thought by the Eighth's chiefs to be 'the most valuable single target in the enemy's twin-engine fighter complex', for it was the place where the dreaded Me110s were built in great numbers. Gotha meant a long trip over enemy territory, over 400 miles due east of Dover and, as the Eighth Air Force knew only too well, it was heavily fortified with large 110 and 85mm gun batteries. The Second Wing was deputed to lead the operation with the senior and very experienced Bomb Group – the 389th from Hethel – leading the whole formation of some 240 B-24s.

Twenty-eight aircraft left Tibenham shortly after nine in the morning, taking off at 30 second intervals. The assembly of eight Bomb Groups took some considerable time and three of the Group's aircraft aborted and returned to base. The leading formation soon became separated from the main bomber stream and when about 200 miles from the target, it was attacked by a very heavy concentration of enemy fighters. Within five minutes five of the Group's aircraft were shot down, quickly followed by another three. The enemy fighter onslaught was sustained right up to the target area and another three aircraft had been lost by the time the group were over Gotha. Then occurred one of those human weaknesses that can have such an effect on the success or failure of any mission. The lead bombadier of 389 Group tragically suffered oxygen failure and he collapsed over his bomb sight, triggering the release lever, and most of the aircraft from the Wing followed suit releasing their bombs well short of the target. When 445 Group realised that an error had been made they continued on to the primary target, but finding that they were bombing it on their own. The flak was as fierce as had been expected and it was quite amazing that only one aircraft was lost after the Group's aircraft had finished their bombing. The surviving twelve aircraft limped back to Tibenham sustaining varying degrees of damage. Most of the aircraft had landed by 4 pm and then the grim reckoning began. Thirteen aircraft had been destroyed, another nine

B-24s of 445th Bomb Group on a mission. (USAF)

heavily damaged and 122 crewmen lost, including the commanding officer of 702 squadron and the operations officer of 700 squadron. The Gotha operation had proved to be a very sad day for the Group, which was only ameliorated by the news that the Group had been awarded a Distinguished Unit Citation for this brave mission. Little did they realise that they would face an even more disastrous day in the near future.

On 22nd April the Group's Commanding Officer – Colonel Terill – led the Second Division's operation to the Hamm marshalling yards. This target was well known to both RAF and the Eighth's aircrews, so frequently had it been bombed. The long mission went well, only two of the Group's aircraft failed to return and the remaining aircraft returned to Tibenham long after blackout time. As they neared their home base they quickly realised that something was sadly amiss as they did not receive any landing clearances and furthermore the AA batteries were firing away and not too circumspect with their aim. The crews were not aware that several American airfields in Norfolk were under heavy enemy attack. Things were slightly more complicated at Tibenham because a badly damaged aircraft from nearby Old Buckenham had crash-landed blocking the main runway. For well over an hour the 22 aircraft were forced to circle the airfield with fast dwindling reserves of fuel until it was considered safe to land.

For most of the month of May the Group's aircraft were very active in attacking a variety of targets in France as a 'softening-up' before the Allied invasion; in fact they mounted 18 missions in just over one month with only slight losses. In the middle of July the Group's aircraft returned to Gotha, only this time they escaped without a single aircraft being lost. By September, along with other Bomb Groups, they made several trips to Holland to drop supplies and materials to the Allied airborne forces. These missions were fraught with danger and demonstrated how vulnerable the B-24s were to concentrated ground fire. The crews had found by experience that the best chance of survival was to fly as low as possible; this in itself was a frightening experience without having to contend with enemy ground fire. Although these operations were conducted with strong fighter escorts, several Groups lost aircraft on the missions and virtually every aircraft returned with some form of damage, it was a hectic time for the ground crews patching up the aircraft.

It was on the 27th of the month that the Group's most tragic operation was mounted. Thirty-seven aircraft were leading the formation on that day and the target was the Henshel engine works at Kassel in central Germany. The Group's lead aircraft were navigating by GEE and at the Initial Point the lead navigator made a serious miscalculation, which resulted in the Group's aircraft heading away in the direction of Gottingen, at least 30 miles to the north-east of the primary target. The Group's aircraft were now well to the east of the main bomber stream and because of the thick and heavy clouds that had been present for all the flight the crews were not aware of the error. Unfortunately those same clouds afforded excellent cover for the large formation of enemy fighters waiting to pounce on the isolated and very vulnerable B-24s.

These fighters, almost 100 strong, were part of the famed 'Stormgruppen', a special Bomber assault unit of heavily armoured and armed Fw190s. They attacked in tight formations of up to 40 strong with frontal attacks of ten fighters flying line abreast with the intention of breaking up the bomber formation at their first pass. Within minutes a heavy toll had been taken of 445's aircraft. As one survivor recalled, 'In one glance I saw four fighters and four of our bombers going down. It was indescribable. Hollywood couldn't think of anything to match the horror.' All told 25 B-24s were destroyed and it was only the timely intervention of P-51 Mustangs from the 361st Fighter Group that saved the Group from complete annihilation. On this mission the Fighter Group from Little Walden claimed 18 victories, the highest total for a single operation.

On their return flight to Tibenham, two damaged aircraft crash-landed in France and another one crashed at Old Buckenham. The loss of 28 aircraft (75%) was by far the highest casualty rate for any single mission of the war. Over 80 crewmen survived the debacle and were made prisoners of war; it was later discovered that they were forced to collect the charred remains of their comrades from the crashed aircraft. The news of the disaster quickly spread throughout the Division, who most firmly believed that '445 had been wiped out'. It was decided that all new crews arriving in Norfolk would be allocated to the 445th. On the following day in an act of incredible bravery the Group managed to get ten aircraft airborne for another mission to Kassel. The ten aircraft not only bombed the target successfully but did so without a single loss. Some blessed relief was given at the end of October when the Group was taken off operations for ten days whilst urgent attention was given to the concrete runways, which seemed to be breaking up. All crews were granted leave passes and just for a short while they could forget the traumas

Memorial to the men of 445th Bomb Group.

of the previous month but alas all too soon they were back.

On the 26th of November the Eighth Air Force launched a massive offensive against rail marshalling yards and oil installations in western Germany. The 445th Group was despatched to Misburg in an attempt to destroy one of the very few German oil refineries which was still in operation. On this day the Luftwaffe managed to summon up over 500 fighters, in fact the biggest enemy force the Second Division had ever encountered. Wave upon wave of enemy fighters attacked the 445th and their neighbouring Group 491st as they approached the target area. I am sure that many crews in the group had visions of another Gottingen. But on this day it was the 491st who suffered the heaviest casualties. The 445th were 'fortunate' to escape this savage air battle with the loss of five aircraft and a further one written off when it crash-landed at Tibenham. In this very costly operation the Eighth lost 42 aircraft and another 300 damaged, and against this the Luftwaffe lost 130 fighters – the bitter war of attrition waged on and on. . .

An uneventful mission to the Rhine valley was the Group's 200th mission and six days later, on 16th December, they decided to celebrate it in great style. As one veteran recalled, 'We had expected to be home by Christmas but now it didn't seem like it because on the day of the party we heard about the Ardennes, so we thought it best to enjoy ourselves!'

During the last six months of operations the Group gained a high reputation for the accuracy of their bombing, and for this reason they were frequently called upon to drop supplies to the French Resistance fighters and for their success in these operations the Group was awarded the Croix de Guerre. Like many other Groups the 445th set off on their last mission on 25th April, their 282nd. In all these operations they had lost 108 aircraft in action and another 25 in accidents. Within a week of VE Day the Group's aircraft started off on the long haul back to the United States and by July the RAF took over the airfield.

Most of the main runway and the perimeter track is still intact and is now used by the Norfolk Gliding Club, who have been at the old airfield since 1961, and the old control tower was used as a clubhouse until 1975. It had a reputation for being haunted, some members were convinced that they had seen a figure wearing Second World War flying gear wandering around the rooms at night! The Club built a new clubhouse and the control tower was demolished in 1978, but near to its site is a memorial to the Bomb Group. The old airfield is best approached by the A140 north of Scole on to the B1134 and then taking the second right-hand road marked to Aslacton until one sees a sign 'Private Airfield'.

36

WATTON

Some of Norfolk's wartime airfields will forever be linked with certain types of aircraft; Feltwell was known for its Wellingtons, at Marham it was Mosquitos, Downham Market had its Stirlings, and Watton became famous for its Blenheims. For the first two and a half years of the war the Blenheim squadrons from Watton and its satellite Bodney were involved in all the various operations mounted by No 2 Group of Bomber Command. The losses sustained during these missions were quite staggering. The determination and bravery of the Blenheim crews were quite outstanding and they gloriously wrote their names into the pages of the history of the RAF. The techniques that they developed in the early years of the war, at such a high cost, ultimately prepared the way for the daring escapades of the Mosquito squadrons some three years later.

Watton was just one of a handful of Norfolk airfields that were constructed in the immediate pre-war years, and John Laing and Son Ltd built an airfield capable of housing heavy bombers as Watton was destined to be placed in No 6 Group, then a training rather than operational Group. However, when it was opened on 4th February 1939 there had been a change of plans and it was allocated to No 2 Group, which meant Bristol Blenheims.

In the early days of March 1939 the airfield greeted its first squadrons of Blenheim 1s – Nos 21 and 34. Both squadrons could trace their origins back to the First World War and the latter had been the first to test and develop low-level flying over the trenches in Flanders. Like most early squadrons they had been disbanded after the war and were only reformed again at Bircham Newton during 1935. No 21 became known during the war as 'Norwich's own squadron'. During those innocent weeks of the last peacetime

Bristol Blenheims of No 82 Squadron at Watton, 1940. (RAF Watton)

summer the crews practised and trained with their Blenheims in preparation for a war, which now seemed so imminent and certain. They little knew that in May 1939 their Commander-in-Chief, Air Chief Marshal Sir Edgar Ludlow-Hewitt, had stated in a secret memo that, '. . . [his] Command [Bomber] could not within any predictable period attain the strength or efficiency to declare it ready for war. . .' Ready or not the Watton squadrons were engaged in action within weeks of war being declared.

In August No 34 squadron left for the Far East but was quickly replaced by No 82 with its most exceptional Commanding Officer, Wing Commander the Earl of Bandon. On 27th September the squadron entered the war when the Earl led three Blenheims on a photo-reconnaissance mission over north-west Germany seeking enemy airfields. The crews had to wait until the middle of December before they were again in operation, this time they were sent to a specific area of the North Sea, where they found some enemy minesweepers to bomb. The squadron's first notable success came in March 1940 when Squadron Leader Miles Dunlap surprised a German U-boat on the surface in the Schillig Roads, which he bombed and sunk. This was the very first RAF victory against a U-boat in the war. The Germans later salvaged the boat and it returned to active service only for it to be destroyed again but this time by a Naval vessel in November 1940.

The squadron's first real test coincided with the German offensive or 'Blitzkreig' against France and the Low Countries. On 17th May 1940 twelve aircraft from No 82 squadron were despatched to attack German armoured columns in France but en route they were set upon by a group of Me109s and within minutes eleven of the Blenheims were shot down, only the Earl of Bandon surviving the brutal onslaught to return to Watton with his heavily damaged Blenheim. Thirty-three airmen had gone, including Squadron Leader Dunlap, who became a prisoner of war. With virtually two thirds of the squadron lost it was seriously suggested by No 2 Group chiefs that the squadron should be disbanded. The Earl of Bandon had other ideas and was utterly determined that the aircraft of No 82 would fly again, and through his resolve within just two days, the squadron was again ready for operations. The Earl of Bandon had a most distinguished RAF career, in 1950 he returned to No 2 Group as its Commanding Officer.

With the fall of France the Blenheims' targets were changed. In the short term, at least, the invasion barges in the French Channel ports became the priority and then later on as the invasion threat receded enemy airfields and oil installations mainly in northern France received almost constant attention from the squadrons. The losses of aircraft and crews still remained desperately critical – there was a very steady but continual blood-letting of valuable airmen – though it was still maintained that 'even when crews were being lost faster than they could unpack, they did not once shrink from doing the job.' Sometimes it was said that crews' names were often not even entered in the operations records as they were not expected to last the week. There is the apocryphal story of 'Ten Minutes Jenkins', who came into the squadron, took off on his first mission and was shot down and killed all within ten minutes of crossing the Belgian border.

But disaster seemed to dog the squadron. On 13th August twelve aircraft took off for Aalborg airfield in northern Denmark. On paper it seemed a very ill-conceived mission – a long haul across the North Sea, no fighter support and a target almost at the very limit of the aircraft's range. One aircraft aborted shortly into the flight and returned to Watton (the pilot was later court-martialled). The remaining eleven arrived over the target area and five quickly fell to enemy flak. Then on the return flight the remaining six were shot down by a group of Me109s. It was the second time in almost four months that the squadron had been virtually annihilated.

Maybe as a result of this disastrous mission daylight operations by Blenheims were greatly reduced and increased emphasis was placed on night intruder raids. Then another calamity struck on 4th December when a mission was planned to Essen steelworks in what turned out to be most appalling weather, the kind feared by planners and crews alike – thick fog over the home airfields. In reality the mission should have been aborted but at least the crews were instructed that 'if fog continued to close in on their return they could bale out but only as a last resort' – a reassuring thought! And on their return the crews were faced with quite atrocious conditions. One aircraft crash-landed at Mildenhall, two more came to grief just over the Suffolk coast, a fourth crew baled out near King's Lynn and only one pilot managed to find Bodney with sufficient fuel to cruise around until dawn when he could effect a safe landing. On one winter's night some Ju88s followed the Blenheims home and shot six aircraft down as they were attempting to land at Watton. The Blenheim crews must have felt that all the odds were stacked against them – flak, fighters, bad weather and now not even safe when they were within sight of their home base!

Ill-luck still seemed to stalk the squadron's crews even when they

Pilots of No 21 Squadron at Watton 1939.

went away from Watton. In May 1941 the crews were detached for a short period to St Eval in Cornwall with the intention of joining the bomber offensive against the U-boat pens sited along the French Atlantic coast. Their first mission was a dawn attack on La Rochelle and most of the aircraft returned safely to St Eval airfield. During the evening, however, the airfield suffered a heavy dive-bomb attack by Junkers Stuka bombers, which left the squadron with just a handful of serviceable aircraft. Despite this setback two days later the remaining Blenheims were involved in another low-level attack on St Nazaire and on this raid the squadron lost their new commanding officer, who had only been in command for one week. The situation did not greatly improve when they returned to Watton, because on 29th May 1941 their new commanding officer led just three Blenheims on a shipping strike off Heligoland; none of the aircraft returned. This meant that the 82nd had its seventh commanding officer in a period of eleven months!

During August 1941 both 21 and 82 squadrons were detailed for major Group operations. The first of these was mounted on 12th August and was directed to Cologne and a large power station at Knapsack and a generating plant at Quadrath. A total of 18 aircraft from both squadrons joined the formation, which was ordered to fly at a height of 100 feet throughout the outward journey and although the Blenheims were given the luxury of a large fighter escort, 12 out of the 54 aircraft failed to return (22% loss). Just two weeks later (the 28th) came the Group's famous attack on Rotterdam docks, where success was achieved at the cost of six aircraft. Winston Churchill was shocked at the casualty losses of the Group squadrons on these missions and drafted a message on 30th August to be passed to all the crews who had taken part in the raids, 'The devotion of the attacks on Rotterdam and other objectives are beyond all praise. The Charge of the Light Brigade at Balaclava is eclipsed in brightness by these almost daily deeds of fame.' These words were well deserved and fully justified because during the month of August No 2 Group had lost 30% of its Blenheims in action and another 16% in various accidents and other operational losses. And yet it would still be another twelve months before the Blenheims flew their last operations of the war.

But Watton's Blenheims disappeared sometime before that date; No 82 squadron left in March 1942 for India and it spent the rest of the war in that country. No 21 squadron, which had served the previous four months in Malta, returned to Watton in the same month and quickly departed to Bodney. Watton now became the centre of an Advanced Training programme for pilots who had just completed their basic flying course. The Miles Master IIs used on the course stayed at the airfield until May 1943 when Watton was passed over to the USAAF.

The airfield now underwent a massive development programme. It was originally just grass surfaced but a long 2,000 yard concrete runway was completed and to the south of the airfield the Americans greatly developed the area around the village of Griston and named the station Neaton, where the 3rd Strategic Air Depot would work. The USAAF took over the airfield on 4th October 1943.

The depot's main task was the supply, maintenance and repair of the B-24s for the 14 Bomb Groups of the Second Bombardment Division, which was quite a formidable task considering that by D-Day the Division had over 1,000 aircraft ready for action. One of the most onerous duties undertaken by several teams from Watton was the location and salvage of all B-24s that had crash-landed throughout the country. Mobile field units went to the site of every crash to see whether the aircraft could be repaired on site, or if not, to salvage as many parts as possible. They then had to arrange for the return of the aircraft to Watton. Soon the sheds and large hangars resembled an aircraft factory. Each Bomb Group would telephone their needs for spare and replacement parts and a fleet of trucks would make two deliveries per day to the various Groups. It was a massive logistics exercise, which needed a highly organised system of control.

During the first weeks of February 1944 two squadrons of B-24s, painted all over in non-glare black, arrived at the airfield from Alconbury. They belonged to 36th and 406th Bomb squadrons, which were involved in 'Carpetbaggers' – a name which recalled the days of the American Civil War. These operations involved the dropping of supplies to the French Resistance and parachuting Allied agents into France. The B-24s had to be specially adapted for this work, the front ball turrets were removed and a cargo hatch installed, known as 'Joe Holes' – 'Joe' was the American nickname for agents. The squadrons also became involved in 'Operation Sonnie', which involved sending ground crews to Sweden to service the grounded B-24s and also to bring back American airmen who had been interned in the country. The aircraft stayed at Watton for about two months flying 213 sorties before moving to a more permanent base at Metfield in Suffolk. During their operations they flew over 2,800 missions, mostly deep into enemy territory. The squadrons had first worked with RAF units at Tempsford in Cambridgeshire, which by 1944 had great experience in such 'carpetbagging' operations.

When the rather sinister black B-24s left in April, they were replaced by 25th Bomb Group (Reconnaissance) which brought a mixture of B-17s and B-24s from St Eval in Cornwall. This was a weather squadron that had been operating over the North Atlantic collecting data. No sooner had they arrived at the airfield than the Group was supplied with Mosquito XVIs and began both weather and photographic missions over Germany. The Group's aircraft were often detailed to fly ahead of the large bomber formations to distribute 'chaff', the American equivalent to the RAF's 'window' metal strips. During all these various operations the Group lost 15 aircraft whilst mounting 3,000 sorties over enemy territory.

During April 1945, when it was obvious that victory was close at hand, there was a constant movement of supplies to the two United States Base Air depots at Wharton and Burtonwood, both in Lancashire, for onward transmission to either bases in Germany or back to the United States. By the middle of the summer nearly one third of the personnel had left and it was not until November that the last of the Americans had finally departed, although by that time the RAF had taken the airfield back.

Watton has played an important part in the post-war RAF and although it is still active as a base there is no flying from the airfield. At the time of writing some of the land is due to be sold off. The large American air depot has been converted to a prison but opposite to the RAF station's officers' mess is a memorial to the Blenheim squadrons that operated from Watton in the early years of the war. It is a propellor recovered from a Blenheim that had crashed at Aalborg in Denmark. Near the officers' mess is a splendid wartime museum, which graphically recalls the days of the Blenheim squadrons and RAF Watton during the war, with a room dedicated to the American presence at the airfield; the museum is open to the public every Wednesday and Sunday afternoons and it is certainly well worth a visit. By the side of the RAF memorial is a stone to the memory of all those who served at the Third Strategic Air Depot, USAAF.

37
WENDLING

The 392nd became the fourth B-24 Group to arrive in Norfolk. Its aircraft, the brand new B-24Hs with powered gun turrets, flew into Wendling during the early weeks of August 1943 and landed at an airfield that had been specially constructed for USAAF use. It was planned to house over 2,800 men, all of whom would live, eat, and sleep in Nissen or 'Quonset' huts – as the Americans called them – in ten different sites situated well to the east of the airfield towards the village of Beeston.

As with all American airfields a bicycle was essential not only to get around the well-spread out base but also, and perhaps more importantly, to get to the nearest public house either in the surrounding villages or further afield in East Dereham or Swaffham. These forays into the Norfolk countryside to sample the warm English beer became known as 'low-level missions' and often proved to be quite dangerous! One American service doctor suggested, no doubt with his tongue in his cheek, that bicycles became Hitler's secret weapon, at least when allied to British beer and the blackout! He recorded 310 broken arms all caused by cycling accidents after visits to pubs – quite a serious blow to the operational efficiency of a Group at any given time.

Before the Group's aircraft went out on their first operation they were painted with a large white disc or circle on the tail fins and one wing, which then carried the Group's identifying code letter – 'D' in the case of the 392nd. Previous to this none of the Second Division's aircraft carried any marks of recognition. The Group started its operations on 6th September 1943, a harmless diversionary run over the north German coast whilst 'the big boys ... those guys who knew the score ...' were attacking Stuttgart, which proved to be a rather costly fiasco. Three days later the Group went out on a 'proper' mission, they formed just a small part of a large 'Starkey' operation against Abbeville airfield in northern France. These operations were the brain-child of the combined Allied chiefs and their object was to try to deceive the enemy as to the Allied forces' invasion plans. It was later conceded that they proved to be almost a total waste of time, certainly in terms of their deception value.

Because the other three B-24 Groups in Norfolk had been detached for service in North Africa, the 392nd was left to soldier along on their own. Not of sufficient strength to join with the B-17 Groups on their missions, they found themselves on endless training flights with the odd diversionary exercise over the German coast thrown in for good measure. On one such mission they were successful in attracting the Luftwaffe away from the main bomber force. They were set upon by over 40 fighters and the ensuing short but very sharp fight resulted in four aircraft lost and several others quite heavily damaged. It was the Group's first initiation into the perils of air combat over Germany.

The return of their B-24 comrades in the first week of October meant that the crews were back to Germany with a vengeance. Their first mission, on the 8th, was to Vegesack to attack shipyards, which always tended to be heavily defended targets, and on the following day to the port of Gdynia in Poland. On the latter raid, heavy smoke screens had effectively obscured the main targets so the operation was inconclusive. The 21 aircraft returned to Wendling but most bore the scars of this long and tiring mission.

During November the Group undertook two missions to Norway. The first was mounted on the 16th and the whole operation was surrounded with the greatest secrecy, which added a little spice to the proceedings. At the briefing when it was revealed that the target would be Rjuken in Norway, there were many blank faces among the crews. However, when the intelligence officer added that it was believed to house a large heavy water plant, which was essential to Germany's manufacture of secret weapons, the crews became very enthusiastic despite the fact that it would be a difficult mission. Rjuken in the Telemark province of southern Norway was surrounded by mountains, which would need precise and very exact approach bombing runs as there were no margins for errors. It was also thought to be well defended with heavy flak batteries. Twenty aircraft took off in the early morning after some difficulty in assembling the formations in the dark. As they reached the target area the crews were greeted by a strong fighter force from bases in

B-24 Pregnant Pig *of 577 Bomb Squadron of 392nd Bomb Group which was lost on a mission to Germany, 3rd March 1944. (Via D Duffield)*

Denmark. Conditions were not favourable – scattered and broken cloud. But the bombardiers were using automatic flight control equipment which was linked to their Norden bomb-sights; this enabled them to control the movement of the aircraft whilst it was on the bombing run. It turned out to be a most successful operation, intelligence sources revealed that the damage caused to the plant delayed progress on rocket propulsion fuel for at least a couple of months. All the Group's aircraft returned safely and there was a great deal of satisfaction because of the very favourable result of the mission.

The second operation to Norway came two days later when a B-24 force attacked a Junkers Ju88 assembly plant just outside Oslo. The whole operation took over ten hours, and on the return flight, because the aircraft had to battle against 100 mph head winds, many aircraft ran low on fuel and some were forced to ditch in the North Sea while still a fair distance from the Norfolk coast.

Like most Bomb Groups the crews at Wendling became most involved in the 'No Ball' missions, attacks on the V1 rocket sites in northern France. At their briefings it was made very clear that these operations were of the utmost importance. The German High Command put great store in this weapon and the later A4 (V2) rocket, which they felt would have a deleterious effect on British morale. Not only were London and south-east England at grave risk but the invasion of Europe might even have to be delayed. All of the crews responded well, they felt that these types of operations were different to the normal missions and the urgency of the whole matter made them feel that they were at last doing something positive towards the war effort. The intelligence staff at Wendling managed to make a mock-up of a normal V1 site and what with photographs and maps the crews were probably better informed about these missions than any others during the war. By February 1944 the 392nd had flown its seventh 'No Ball' mission. By now, however, the Germans had moved in heavy rail-mounted AA guns and they were no longer the 'milk runs' of a month or so earlier. As a result the bombing altitude was increased from 12,000 feet to 20,000 feet which reduced the accuracy of the bombing. On one mission to the Pas de Calais in March the Second Division lost one aircraft, belonging to the 392nd, but over 40 aircraft were heavily damaged.

In late 1944 the Air Ministry called for a special study to be made of the efficacy of the whole 'No Ball' operation. H.E. Bates, the novelist, who was then working in the Air Ministry intelligence reported that the damage to the sites was quite minimal but the surrounding French countryside had been devastated with many French casualties, seemingly accepted with great equanimity by the French people, who had readily conceded that the bombing was an essential part of the horrors of war.

The famous raid on the fighter aircraft factories at Gotha on 24th February has already been noted in connection with the 453rd at Old Buckenham. On this mission the Wendling crews had a very tough and torrid time. They lost seven aircraft and another three badly damaged, which did manage to limp back to Wendling. The Group's gunners claimed eight enemy fighters destroyed. For the Group's courage and determination on this operation it was awarded a Distinguished Unit Citation.

In March, the Group was to suffer even more severely. On the 16th they were part of a large formation attacking targets in southern Germany and in particular Friedrichshafen. On this occasion their B-24s survived the long flight with relatively light losses. Two days later the operation was repeated and this time it was a different matter. Most airmen felt unhappy about returning to the same target so soon, it was almost as if they were tempting providence and in this instance their premonitions were justified. On the flight out two of the Group's aircraft collided over France and then over the target area they suffered 'the biggest mass of flak I was ever to see . . .' recalled one Group survivor. Then they were set upon by large formations of Fw190s and Me109s, and in a very short time twelve aircraft were shot down and two heavily damaged planes had to land in Switzerland. One aircraft *Doodle Bug* was very badly damaged and flying on just two engines; it was brought back to England only to crash-land at RAF Gravesend, but most of the crew survived. This mission was the single worst disaster in the Group's history and their losses on the day totalled half of all the Division's casualties; though their comrades in the 14th Wing – the 'unlucky' 44th at Shipdham – also lost eight aircraft.

On the first day of April the two Bomb Groups encountered trouble once again. This time it was on a mission to Ludwigshafen, when because of heavy cloud formations at high altitudes the two Groups strayed badly and tragically released their bombs in error over a town in Switzerland, which became the most expensive bombing exercise of the Second World War.

During July the Second Division directed much of their efforts towards the battlefields of northern France. Large numbers of aircraft were despatched to saturate bomb targets directly in front of the

Helen Malsed of the American Red Cross naming a base defence vehicle, August 1944. Lt Colonel L Johnson, CO is on the right. (D Duffield)

Allied armies. The first of these was at Caen, where the Germans had very strong defensive positions, and later to St Lô, where the American armies were held down. These missions brought their own kind of pressures for the aircrews, who were only too aware that the slightest errors in their bombing techniques could have catastrophic results on their own armies in the field. There were at least three instances of bombs falling on Allied positions during this campaign, the last being the most serious when over 100 US Army personnel were killed and nearly 400 injured.

There is a memorial in the central library at Cheshunt in Hertfordshire to Second Lieutenant John Ellis and his crew of 577 squadron from Wendling. Ellis's aircraft collided with a B-17 during assembly on 12th August 1944 and the pilot deliberately risked his own life and those of his crew by avoiding a heavily built-up area. Subsequently the aircraft came to grief on farmland near the A10 with a total loss of life. The memorial was financed by the local residents in recognition of the crew's ultimate sacrifice.

During September all the B-24 Groups in Norfolk were very active over Holland supplying the US airborne forces in the Nijmegen and Eindhoven areas. These operations were quite dangerous as they required the crews to fly in at a very low altitude, often at no more than roof-top height and in the face of severe ground fire. Each aircraft carried up to 20 bundles of supplies, which had to be dropped precisely in a very restricted area. On the 18th the Second Division lost seven aircraft on one such operation with many more quite severely damaged by the intensity of ground flak. The Group lost two aircraft on this mission and a third crash-landed at a Belgian airfield.

Even well into 1945 when most Bomb Groups managed to get away with very minimal losses and some mounted several operations without losing a single aircraft, the 392nd still lost crews. For instance in the famous raid in March 1945 against the Zossen Army Headquarters just outside Berlin, the Second Division despatched 372 aircraft and only one B-24 was shot down and that came from the Group. Another of the Group's aircraft ditched in the North Sea some 30 miles north-east of Great Yarmouth and six of the crew were rescued.

Neither of the two American heavy bombers was really designed to sustain a forced sea-landing or indeed to allow the crews a quick exit in such instances. Also their survival equipment tended to be rather inferior compared with the RAF dinghies, which could not be stored in the American planes. In the early months of the Eighth's air operations many American aircrew died at sea and most of the successful rescues were made either by RAF Air/Sea rescue teams or lifeboats. However, things did improve with the Eighth Air Force establishing their own Air/Sea finding network based at Saffron Walden and an emergency rescue squadron operating from Boxted also in Essex. This squadron made regular patrols during the whole period of an operation and many of the rescues were due to its pilots' patience and vigilance. Nevertheless few American aircrews felt confident that they would be rescued if they had the misfortune to come down in the sea.

Like most Bomb Groups the 392nd flew its last mission on 25th April 1945 to Hallein in Germany. A total of 285 missions were flown from Wendling with a loss of 127 aircraft missing in action and another 57 due to operational causes, which was higher than average. By the end of May all of the aircraft and ground personnel had gone and the airfield returned to farming. Some of the perimeter track still survives as does part of the runways. There is a fine obelisk memorial to the Group on the road to Beeston, which is splendidly maintained in a neat memorial garden with an adjacent car park. A Stars and Stripes flag and a Union Jack proudly fly at flagposts to mark the spot. The site of the airfield and the memorial may be discovered by taking the A47 road out of Swaffham in the direction of East Dereham and after about seven miles there is a left-hand turning to Crane's Corner and the Beeston industrial estate.

38
WEST RAYNHAM

At the time of writing it would appear that West Raynham is about to close its gates finally as an RAF station after 55 years of sterling service. The airfield first opened on 5th May 1939 and Group Captain Maskill was appointed its first Station Commander. Prior to this date the nascent airfield had been used for a couple of training exercises. During the Munich crisis of the late summer of 1938 when the RAF emergency routines and procedures were being brought into force, and many squadrons were being mobilised, both Watton and West Raynham were used for full refuelling exercises. These were to ensure that No 2 Group's Blenheim squadrons could operate over northern Germany. In March of the following year Wellingtons from No 38 squadron at Marham arrived at West Raynham to engage in a 'full war exercise', which included bombing runs over the Wash. The squadron was compelled to live in tents because the accommodation units had yet to be completed.

Blenheim I of 139 Squadron, October 1937.

On 9th May the first squadron, No 101, comprised in the main of Blenheim IVs, arrived at the airfield and by the middle of July the crews were engaged in long flights over France. These exercises had a more serious reason than purely showing the flag, they provided valuable information about the aircraft's operational range and fuel consumption. Within days of the outbreak of the war No 90 Blenheim squadron moved in, but just as quickly departed to Upwood though it would return to West Raynham in the summer of 1941. After all their long training flights over France it must have been an irritation to the Blenheim crews to find that they were solely engaged in training the Group's aircrew personnel on the finer points of the Blenheim! It was not until late April 1940 that two Training Units appeared at the airfield, enabling the squadron to prepare, at long last, for operations.

Their very first operational mission went out from the airfield on 4th July when just three aircraft were detailed to bomb an oil pipe-line near the Kiel Canal. On the following day four Blenheims were active over northern France, one failed to return and this had been piloted by the Squadron Commander – Wing Commander Hargreaves. Until mid-August the squadron concentrated on daylight raids to communication and oil targets. There was then a change in tactics when the crews were directed to enemy airfields in northern France by night. The real intention of these operations was to try to prevent the Luftwaffe's bombers from landing after their nightly raids on London. One of No 2 Group's heaviest incursions occurred on 14th November 1940 – the night that Coventry was bombed – when three squadrons of Blenheims attacked airfields at Etaples, Knokke and Amiens. Seven aircraft from 101 squadron joined a mixed Bomber Command force of over 100 aircraft that bombed Mannheim on 16th December as a purely retaliatory raid for the bombing of Southampton and Coventry. The squadron suffered very heavily on this night with Wing Commander Sinclair, the Squadron Commander, being the only survivor. West Raynham, like other No 2 Group airfields, suffered heavy operational losses with its Blenheims.

The airfield itself suffered from quite a few Luftwaffe attacks and the most serious one was on 10th July 1940 when three aircraft were destroyed as well as several more damaged. Largely as a result of this heavy air-raid it was decided to find safer accommodation for the aircrews outside the station confines and Weasenham Hall came into use. Further attacks were sustained later, especially during February and March of 1941.

No 18 squadron arrived in the middle of June 1940 and became deeply involved in attacks on enemy airfields and the long and heavy guns sited at the Pas de Calais, which were threatening the Channel shipping and Dover. In September the squadron moved to Great Massingham, the grass satellite field just a few miles away, and its aircraft continued to operate from there for the next nine months or so.

After several missions to Rotterdam, Cologne and Homberg in the early months of 1940, No 101 squadron was ordered to Manston in Kent to take part in the so-called 'Channel Stop' – a sustained operation planned to close the Straits of Dover to all enemy shipping during the day. Although the Blenheims operated with strong fighter support it was nevertheless a dangerous and most fraught exercise as most of the enemy vessels were well protected by flak ships. Actually when sufficient resources were diverted to the exercise it proved to be quite successful.

Soon after the squadron arrived back at West Raynham it was converted to Wellingtons and the crews quickly worked up to operational readiness. The first sortie – just one aircraft – left on 11th June to bomb Rotterdam docks and only two missions to the Ruhr were despatched before the squadron moved to Oakington in Huntingdonshire in early July. Later on 101 squadron became one of the most famous Lancaster squadrons of the war.

Whilst the Wellingtons, which were then the RAF's major heavy bombers, were still at West Raynham, they were joined by the Americans' famous heavy bomber – the Boeing Flying Fortress. These aircraft were unique to No 90 squadron, which was commanded by Wing Commander MacDougall, and indeed it had been specially reformed to trial the aircraft for the RAF. The Fortresses certainly created considerable interest and speculation and in theory they appeared to be able to provide a new dimension to Bomber Command's offensive – daylight high altitude bombing. All the RAF crews had been specially selected for service with the squadron – young and very fit to enable them to cope with the strains of operating at extremely high altitudes.

The press was very impressed with the aircraft, '...No one can deny that the Boeing is a good looking aeroplane. Its body is an almost perfect streamline, its wings have easy curves on leading and trailing edges, and the four powerful air-cooled radial motors are housed in well-proportioned nacelles that run back half-way across the wing...' The RAF crews were more interested in the aircraft's

Boeing B-17 Flying Fortress Is of No 90 Squadron.

interior refinements – carpeted floors, comfortable seats, padded walls, fitted thermos flasks and ash-trays, and they were quickly dubbed as 'aircraft for gentlemen'. The crews were lavish in their praise of the new bomber, the pilots were very impressed with its flying qualities and all preferred to be flying by day, '... at night you see nothing but searchlights and flak; by day you can see half of Germany from the Fortress...'

Their appearance at West Raynham brought a clutch of important visitors to the station. Winston Churchill, Air Vice-Marshal Stevenson, the AOC of No 2 Group and several technical experts from the Air Ministry arrived on 6th June. Churchill took the opportunity to address the station's crews praising their efforts and exhorting greater attention to shipping targets as he expressed his grave concern of the threat of U-boats. The Station Commander at the time was Group Captain the Earl of Bandon, who knew all about Blenheim operations having commanded 88 squadron at Watton with great verve and distinction. He later (in 1950) returned to command No 2 Group, when he had attained the rank of Air Commodore.

The early operations undertaken by 90 squadron were mounted from Great Massingham and none of them could be considered successful as there were many problems encountered with the aircraft. In fact the RAF's experience with these mighty aircraft was quite disastrous. Several accidents during training, frequent aborted sorties and some operational losses resulted in the squadron being transferred to the Middle East in late September. The interested American observers, and there were many of them, noted all the problems that had been experienced by the squadron and when the B-17s were introduced into the Eighth Air Force they were much improved versions. The American experts had always maintained that the RAF had not used the aircraft properly. For instance insufficient training had been given to the crews on the vastly different techniques required and they had been flown in small or individual sorties rather than in formation. Certainly from 90 squadron's experience it would have been difficult to imagine that the Flying Fortress or B-17 would become such an effective and powerful strike bomber with the Eighth Air Force.

With the departure of the heavy bombers the airfield was left to the old but familiar Blenheims. In July No 114 (Hong Kong) squadron had arrived from Scotland where it had been operating with Coastal Command and, in fact, during its time at West Raynham detachments periodically left for spells at several Scottish airfields. On 11th August eleven aircraft took part in the Group's famous raid on the Cologne power station losing only one aircraft on the mission. But perhaps its most important missions came in May and June 1942 with 'Operation Millennium' – the three '1,000' bomber raids on Cologne, Bremen and Essen.

For the first operation to Cologne No 614 (County of Glamorgan) squadron brought its Blenheims down to West Raynham from Scotland. It had been earmarked as an Army Co-operation squadron and as yet had not seen any action, so for two days its crews were busily engaged in training flights over East Anglia. The concept of No 2 Group's involvement in the massive operation was that certain Blenheim squadrons would attack enemy airfields along the path of the main bomber force some two hours before the main stream with the express intention of keeping the Luftwaffe's fighters on the ground. The Blenheims from West Raynham were allocated the airfields at Bonn and Twente, which were about five miles from the German/Dutch border. Twenty-six aircraft took off from the airfield and at least 16 claimed to have bombed the targets. Later photographic evidence showed that considerable damage had been wrought on Bonn but Twente was still relatively unmarked. Nevertheless it was an impressive performance especially as only one aircraft from West Raynham failed to return. On the Bremen operation further attacks were made on Twente and eight Blenheims from 114 squadron actually took part in the main bombing raid.

In September 1942 another strange American plane made its first appearance at West Raynham – the North American Mitchell. This aircraft was to be supplied to a new No 2 Group squadron – No 98. This squadron had, until July 1941, been operating with Coastal Command in Iceland. It was decided to re-activate this squadron as well as another – No 180. The two squadrons stayed at the airfield for barely two months before moving to their permanent base – RAF Foulsham. In the following April yet another new squadron was formed at West Raynham, this time with another new American light bomber – the Douglas Boston. This squadron comprised all Free French airmen and was known as the 'Lorraine' squadron with all their aircraft bearing the Cross of Lorraine emblem. The Frenchmen soon moved to Sculthorpe, West Raynham's second satellite airfield, which had opened in January 1943.

By the end of April 1943 the station was being cleared of all its aircraft as two concrete runways were to be built. When it finally reopened on 3rd December 1943 it was as the headquarters of the newly formed No 100 (Special Duties) Group until January when the Group moved its headquarters to Bylaugh Hall. West Raynham was destined to become part of the fighter arm of the new Group – quite a major change in operations.

Within a week the two new fighter squadrons had arrived. The first was No 141, the original 'Serrate' squadron, equipped mainly with Beaufighter VIs and just a few Mosquito IIs. The second, No 239, flew down from Ayr where it had been engaged on night-fighting duties. Of the four fighter squadrons in the new Group No 141 was the only one in any state of readiness for operations although it was awaiting its full allocation of Mosquitos. The other West Raynham squadron needed further training on 'Serrate' techniques and it was well into the New Year before its crews were ready for operations.

As already noted the fighter squadrons within the Group had a

De Havilland Mosquito of 239 Squadron.

variety of tasks from flying within the bomber streams, pure escort duties, intruder missions and patrolling known enemy fighter assembly points. The first Group victory was credited to 141 squadron on a mission to Berlin in mid-December when an Me110 was shot down. The other squadron had to wait until late January before it notched its first kill. By the early summer the two squadrons were well into the action, indeed by the end of June pilots from 239 squadron claimed their 25th victory and the lucky crew were given £5 National Savings Bonds! There were also some rather close calls. In June one of the squadron's Mosquitos shot down an Me110 over Paris but it flew through the wreckage, which resulted in it getting most of its tail section badly burnt, but despite this quite horrendous damage the pilot still managed to fly the Mosquito almost 300 miles back to base. A glowing testimony to the durability of the Mosquito.

One of the pilots flying with No 239 squadron recalled, '... Many low-level patrols were flown but the general opinion was that the occasional squirt at a train or truck was very poor excitement by comparison with the full-blooded thrill of an AI [Air Interception] chase terminating in the destruction of a Hun...' In fact his squadron was the most successful in No 100 Group, its crews claimed 55 enemy aircraft destroyed.

By the beginning of May 1945 the wartime operational life of the airfield was almost at an end and two months later both squadrons had left the airfield. West Raynham was passed to No 12 Group of Fighter Command and for the next 30 years or so the station would be greatly involved with fighter aircraft and the training of fighter pilots as it became the home of the Central Fighter Establishment. Flying finally ceased from the airfield in 1975 and the station closed permanently in 1994. The future of the airfield is in doubt but the present RAF station is well signed off the A1065 and is just a few miles from the village.

39
CIVILIANS AT WAR

It was perhaps inevitable that the Second World War would have a very profound effect on Norfolk and its inhabitants. From its position as the nearest coast to Germany it was right in the forefront and it was considered, rightly or wrongly, as offering the greatest opportunity for a German invasion, at least until the fall of France. Furthermore its flat landscape proved to be ideal to accommodate airfields, and more especially bomber stations. The very fact that such a large number of airfields were sited in the county made it a prime target area for Luftwaffe air attacks.

In 1939 Norfolk was predominantly a rural county. The majority of the population lived outside the two main centres – Norwich and Great Yarmouth. Norfolk was a large county with over 700 villages largely devoted to agriculture. It had always seemed to be cut off from the rest of the country; this was not solely because of its position, jutting out far into the North Sea, but also due to a cultural barrier. Its people were very conservative, strongly independent, a little stubborn to change and possessing a distinct and unique dialect. It is perhaps fair to say that in 1939 most of the county was lacking in some of the more modern facilities. Over 400 country parishes were still without any public water supply, many rural areas had no mains electricity and there were relatively few telephones, at least compared with the rest of the country. Therefore it was to be expected that this rather peaceful and somewhat secluded corner of England would be dramatically changed by the effect of 37 airfields and the massive influx of servicemen (especially the Americans) during the Second World War.

As early as 1937 serious concern was expressed in Government circles about the effect of enemy air raids and an Air Raids Precautions Act was passed. The Government's main worries were poison gas and incendiary bombs and how the public were going to combat them. In the following years 35 million gas masks were distributed to the civilian population and posters regarding their use were prominently displayed. So convinced were the Government that the enemy would use poison gas that GPO post boxes were coated with yellow gas detector paint. Also during the year air raid sirens were erected throughout the country, the digging of shelter trenches in parks and open spaces commenced and the first of the ubiquitous sandbags appeared around official buildings. In November 1938 Sir John Anderson, forever remembered for the garden air raid shelter that bears his name, was appointed to take charge of the nation's civil defence. The first 300 Anderson shelters arrived in Norwich about two weeks before the outbreak of the war. Evacuation plans were worked out and the recruitment and training commenced of a large force of volunteer workers including wardens, firemen, and first aid helpers.

The National Services Committees established under the Act first met in January 1939. In Norwich the Air Raid Precautions (ARP) headquarters was set up in Sussex Street, a training centre and central store was established and over 80 air raid warden posts were selected and agreed throughout the city. Early in the year every household in the country was issued with the National Service Handbook, which gave people details of what they could do in a crisis – demolition parties, decontamination squads, driving ambulances, fire watching or even help in the provision of hot drinks and food. The public were certainly aware that the country was inexorably being placed on a war footing and unlike previous wars the civilians were destined to play a major part.

During the weekend of 8th and 9th July 1939 there was a full dress rehearsal for the 'blackout' when 18 counties were blacked out whilst RAF aircraft flew overhead to judge how effective it was. Black material was placed at all windows, car headlights were hooded and traffic lights were deflected downwards. But because of poor weather conditions many of the aircraft were grounded so that the whole exercise was rather futile. The full blackout restrictions were introduced on 1st September 1939 and were enforced, sometimes rather officiously, by ARP wardens. At first the blackout gave rise to some annoyance and there was a marked increase in road accidents and minor injuries. Of course it had a lesser effect in the rural areas where the people were quite used to having no street lights.

Generally the public quickly adapted to the change although it was never really fully accepted and remained the biggest inconvenience of the war to most people. The restrictions remained in operation until September 1944 when it was replaced by 'half-lighting' except in coastal regions.

On Thursday 24th August it was announced that 'the country finds itself today in imminent peril of war' and the Emergency Powers (Defence) Bill was passed on the same day. This bill gave wide and almost draconian powers to the authorities; homes could be searched without warning, people could be removed out of areas, the ports and railways were taken over and bus and train services were severely curtailed. Many of the coastal areas were taken over by the military although it would be almost another year before all of the East Anglian coast was designated a Defence Area with severe restrictions on movements into and within the area.

Three days before the outbreak of the war the first evacuees from London arrived at Norwich station. Evacuation was to prove one of the major problems of the early years of the war. The decision to billet the children, and in some cases their mothers, in private houses became a controversial issue, especially when it was discovered that refusing to take in 'strangers' when ordered by the authorities could lead to a £50 fine. Compulsory billeting of these families or individual children was an emotive issue that filled endless columns in local newspapers. In the event by the end of 1939 many of the families had returned to London, though in the following year with the onset of the London blitz thousands found themselves back in Norfolk. Also, in June 1944, as the V1 rockets rained down on London many sought refuge in the county.

Perhaps one of the most obvious signs of the changes due to the war could be observed in rural Norfolk with the welcome appearance of the Land Army girls. These young women in their green jumpers, breeches and wide-brimmed hats, drawn from all walks of life, soon became an essential part of the Norfolk countryside. Although there were early suspicions of their value and worth they soon proved to be excellent workers, who gained 'generous praise from a body of men [the farmers] who did not bestow it lightly'! Indeed many of the American servicemen arriving in Norfolk during 1943/4 commented, 'Much of the farming equipment was outdated ... But many of the farms are manned by the Women's Land Army, who kept them productive whilst the men were away in the Services ...' And, of course, the Land Army girls found themselves in great demand for

The importance of air raid precautions is seen in these cigarette cards issued by WD and HO Wills.

the Saturday dances at all the many airfields in Norfolk.

The so-called 'Phoney War', which is now recognised as lasting from September 1939 to the beginning of May 1940, was perhaps remarkable for the lack of enemy air activity over England. Although the air raid sirens had continually sounded their wailing dirges no enemy aircraft had appeared and the public were becoming a trifle blasé about these warnings. But the period was not without its discomforts for civilians. Petrol rationing had been introduced in September 1939 followed in November by the first food rationing. Also the winter of 1940 was one of the coldest for over 45 years with severe frosts and heavy falls of snow, and to add to this misery there was an acute shortage of fuel.

With the invasion of the Low Countries and France and the debacle of Dunkirk the whole mood of the country changed; now the threat of invasion seemed very real indeed. From this time more positive signs of wartime Britain appeared around the countryside – anti-tank traps, concrete emplacements, barbed wire and the familiar pill boxes – many of which have survived throughout the county; recently it has been suggested that they should now be preserved as historical buildings! Road signs and the names on railway stations suddenly disappeared, as did iron railings around parks, public buildings and many houses. Maps were taken out of sale, the carrying and use of cameras led to great suspicion and censorship of letters was imposed on those people living near to the airfields, indeed the country seemed to be in the throes of spy mania. Posters such as 'Keep mum, she's not so dumb' appeared in great numbers and the message that 'Careless talk costs lives' was treated very seriously indeed. Everybody was conscious that the country had its back to the wall and the public were exhorted to support the various National Savings campaigns – in 1940 it was the 'Spitfire Fund', 1941 'War Weapons Week', 1942 'Warships Week', 1943 'Wings for Victory Week' and in 1944 'Salute the Soldier' week. Women were exhorted to take up 'war work' and other slogans such as 'Dig for Victory', 'Lend a hand on the land' and 'Is your journey really necessary?' only emphasised the seriousness of the country's position.

In May a force of 'Local Defence Volunteers' was formed with the avowed intention of defending the country from enemy airborne troops. The call went out to all available men between the ages of 17 and 65 years to volunteer and the response was instant, within a week over a quarter of a million men had enrolled for what later became named, at Winston Churchill's suggestion – 'The Home

The Cadbury's cocoa caravan – always a welcome sight in bombed areas. (Cadbury Limited)

Guard'. Almost every village had its own platoon and soon the Home Guard began to make their presence felt throughout the county. They manned most of the road blocks, inspected the identity cards of everyone passing during the hours of darkness. They stopped all vehicles and persons at night and were quite prepared to fire on those who refused to halt! The movement of civilians was quite severely restricted and the roads seemed quite deserted except for the movement of military vehicles from the many army camps and airfields. At its peak the Norfolk Home Guard comprised over 31,000 officers and men. Despite the images created by *Dad's Army* it developed into a well-trained force that was eventually used as a reserve army releasing regular units for military duties.

On 25th May 1940 the first bombs fell on Norfolk when RAF West Raynham was attacked. This air raid was quickly followed by attacks on other airfields such as Swanton Morley, Watton, Bircham Newton, Horsham St Faith and Marham, indeed the latter airfield seemed to attract the Luftwaffe bombers more frequently than the others. Although these attacks did not cause any serious damage as many of the bombs fell in open country, the raids were frightening for those who lived close to the airfields. Winston Churchill had said in June, 'Everyone should learn to take air raids and air raid alarms as if they were no more than thunderstorms'. Londoners especially, as well as the residents of most provincial cities, had ample experience of such 'thunderstorms'!

Norwich was to suffer its first air raid on 9th July 1940, before London or any other provincial city. Almost since the outbreak of the war the city's sirens had sounded almost daily and nightly. One local resident recalled, 'I remember Londoners staying here, who said that they were glad to go home at weekends to get some sleep'! But on the 9th at 5 pm no sirens sounded and the attack on the Boulton and Paul factory came without warning. In this first raid 26 people were killed and many more injured. This was just the beginning of an air onslaught which by the end of 1940 had resulted in over 260 separate raids.

It was during the series of 'Baedeker' raids of 1942 that Norwich received its heaviest bombardment. On 27th April, just about a half-an-hour before midnight, a large enemy force approached Norwich. The railway station was the first building to come under attack and because it was mainly constructed of timber, it quickly erupted into flames making it an ideal marker for the following streams of bombers. Whole areas and streets were devastated and all the emergency services were at full stretch. The raid lasted about one and a half hours leaving 158 people dead and another 161 seriously injured and not a single enemy aircraft was destroyed.

The response from the authorities was immediate and Norwich became 'a gun defended area' with the speedy transfer of heavy and light anti-aircraft batteries; hitherto most of the AA defences had been sited around the RAF airfields. On the following evening many women, children and older men left the city with just a few belongings to sleep outdoors on the outskirts of Norwich. This 'trekking', as it was called, was a feature of all the air-raids on provincial cities and towns. The Government considered such activity as 'a symbol of lowered morale' and decided not only to ignore it but to actually refuse to acknowledge that it did go on! 'Trekking' was really the only positive action people could take as a response to the collapse of their lives on a quite unprecedented scale. Many expressed the utter horror of the raids and they were described by one resident as 'living nightmares'.

No enemy raiders appeared on the evening of 28th April but they did return the following night although not in such great numbers, but Norwich did sustain quite severe damage and 68 civilians were killed. The overnight destruction of a lifetime of solidarity came as a special form of shock, and the sudden loss of familiar streets and buildings had far more impact on people than the greater damage over a wider area. This feeling of despair was mirrored in the raids on other provincial cities and towns. Quite miraculously the cathedral with its splendid spire managed somehow to survive, even during the raid on 26th June when the roof was struck by incendiaries. The city suffered its last air raid on 6th November 1943; during the raids a total of 1,400 civilians had been killed or seriously injured with some 4,700 houses destroyed or seriously damaged. Great Yarmouth had to wait until June 1944 before its residents could breathe a sigh of relief and although the town suffered more raids and a greater weight of bombs than Norwich there were fewer fatalities and less damage.

For almost three years from 1940 to 1943 the county, along with the rest of England, suffered one of the biggest construction programmes ever undertaken in the country – the building of airfields. It was a project on a massive scale and it has been estimated that almost £1,000 millions was the ultimate cost! At the end of 1939 there were just seven operational airfields in Norfolk, by the end of the following year this figure had more than doubled and two years later there were 37 airfields either in operation or awaiting occupation. Scores of contractors, both large and small, were involved and armies of workmen (mostly Irish) along with an armada of heavy plant machinery moved in to turn the requisitioned farmland into airfields. Millions of tons of concrete were needed to construct the runways, perimeter roads and hard standings. Most of the cement was brought by heavy steam-powered lorries and the narrow and winding lanes became choked with cumbersome traffic. Many of the local people who suffered this major disruption to their lives considered it the worst inconvenience of the war.

Then came the servicemen to fill the completed airfields and although the RAF had the largest number (only just) in Norfolk – 19 – the biggest impact on the county was undoubtedly made by the arrival of the Americans, which has been aptly called 'The Friendly Invasion'. The first US airmen made their appearance in late 1942 and by the following year the trickle had become an avalanche. Soon Norwich and the small market towns like Thetford, Diss, Wymondham and East Dereham echoed to the sound of American accents as their streets became crowded with GIs (Government or

'The narrow and winding lanes became choked with cumbersome and heavy traffic.'
(John Laing PLC)

General Issue) along with their own military police, who were dubbed 'snowdrops' because of their white helmets.

It certainly proved to be a clash of cultures. The Americans were foxed by the local dialect – 'From what I've heard they don't even speak English here'! The locals' early impressions of the Americans were not that favourable, they were considered boastful, brash, ill-mannered and slovenly – the famous saying 'overpaid, oversexed and over here' was quite a common view with, at times 'overfed and overbearing' added for good measure! There is no doubt that there was much local resentment at their extra money, the scarce goods they could obtain from their PX (NAAFI) stores, their attraction for the young women and for their general assertion that the USA was 'God's own country'.

It was probably at the local public houses that the two cultures met most frequently and although the Americans complained regularly about the warm British beer they nevertheless drank it in great quantities which in itself caused some problems. For most of the war beer was strictly rationed and when the 'No Beer' signs went up the Americans invariably moved to another pub, much to the chagrin of the genuine locals! There were regular 'Liberty runs' to Norwich where the cinemas and public houses were crowded with US servicemen. The Samson and Hercules house in Tombland was a favourite place for the Americans, at least until it was badly damaged by fire in March 1944. However, many American air bases provided in-house entertainment with their American Red Cross clubs and most supported their own dance bands and US trucks (Passion Waggons!) brought local girls to their Saturday night dances.

The friendly and generous nature of most American servicemen soon broke down the local reserve and antipathy and generally a very good relationship was established. Many Norfolk families welcomed the Americans into their homes and most airbases organised Christmas parties for local children, they distributed gifts and gladly shared their rations. Many air bases became deeply involved with children's hospitals and local orphanages. There are still many fond memories of the American 'invasion' of East Anglia as was evidenced by the most successful and well-attended 'The Reunion 1942-1992' to celebrate 50 years since the first American airmen arrived in England. Also there are very many local people who still keep alive the memories of those brave American young men who sacrificed so much during their relatively short time in Norfolk.

Another contentious matter for the locals was the number of prisoner-of-war camps in the county. This was especially so with the Italian prisoners, who were allowed considerable freedom, a policy which came under very strong criticism locally. Although they were required to work on the farms, they could be seen wandering around towns without very close supervision. Furthermore it was strongly felt that both German and Italian prisoners received better rations than the locals and the hatred of 'these damned Fascists' was very near to the surface.

The sheer number of airfields in the county meant that the Norfolk skies were hardly ever empty of aircraft. By day hundreds of American heavy bombers filled the sky and then by night there was the constant and continual throb of RAF bombers passing overhead, only for them to return again in the early hours of the morning. The time during any lull in operational traffic was taken up for innumerable training flights frequently at low level. During late 1944 over 4,000 flights were being mounted daily with the attendant risks of mid-air collisions and there were some unfortunate accidents which resulted in the loss of civilian lives as well as incidents of 'friendly' bombs landing on the county. Indeed more Allied aircraft came to grief over Norfolk than any other English county.

With the coming of D-Day most civilians felt that their long trial was coming to an end. But during the next six months certain areas of Norfolk would suffer a bombardment from the German unmanned rockets. The V1 rocket or 'Flying Bomb' caused relatively few problems for Norfolk. The first one fell on 10th July and the last and

A V2 rocket erected in Trafalgar Square after the war.

13th landed in January 1945. It was the more deadly and frightening V2 rocket that caused most of the rocket damage in Norfolk. These 45 foot streamlined projectiles flew faster than sound and gave no warning of their approach, the noise was only heard as an echo when the sound of the explosion had died away and the blast covered a very wide area. The rocket took only about five minutes from launch to impact and it travelled too high or too fast to be tracked.

From 8th September 1944 to March 1945 115 V2 rockets were fired at England with almost half falling on London and of the rest 29 landed in Norfolk. Norwich was, of course, the target but they were not particularly accurate and rather fortunately none landed directly on the city – the closest fell at Hellesdon golf course when over 400 houses within a two mile radius were damaged. The heaviest period of attack lasted from 26th September until the middle of October 1944 when the countryside around Norwich received one, if not more, rockets daily. Many fell harmlessly on farmland with no loss of life and mercifully few injuries but there was considerable damage done to property. It was not until 10th November that the Government admitted to the V2 rocket attacks! The last V2 rocket fell at Mundesley on 15th January 1945.

By now most civilians felt that the end of the war was in sight. They had survived the air raids, the rockets, war work, shortages of all kinds and just come through a hard and freezing winter. There had been some slight increase in the weekly rations, ice cream had suddenly appeared again, the strict black-out restrictions had been eased, the Home Guard had been stood down, coastal resorts could again be visited and the ban of place-names had been revoked – it almost seemed as if life was returning to some normality.

When VE-Day (8th May) came there was a great national outburst of relief and joy as well as thanksgiving for the end of nearly six years of war in Europe. As we have already seen most of the airfields closed very quickly and many of the servicemen just as swiftly left Norfolk. But the remains of the airfields took many more years to disappear. Fifty years later little is left of the majority of the wartime airfields except for the discreet memorials dotted about the countryside to remind coming generations of the part Norfolk played in the Second World War.

BIBLIOGRAPHY

Air Ministry, *Bomber Command*, HMSO, 1941.
Ashworth, Chris, *RAF Coastal Command: 1936–1969*, Patrick Stephens, 1992
Bishop, Edward, *Mosquito: The Wooden Wonder*, Airlife, 1980.
Bowman, Martin, *Fields of Little America*, Wensum Books, 1977.
Bowyer, Chaz, *Beaufighter at War*, Ian Allan, 1976.
Bowyer, Michael J.F., *Action Stations: 1. Military Airfields of East Anglia*, P. Stephens, 1990.
Bowyer, Michael J.F., *History of 2 Group RAF*, Faber, 1974.
Bowyer, Michael J.F., and Sharp, Martin C., *Mosquito*, Faber, 1967.
Brandon, Lewis, *Night Flyer*, W. Kimber, 1961.
Cooper, Alan, *Air Battle of the Ruhr*, Airlife, 1992.
Cooper, Alan, *Bombers over Berlin*, W. Kimber, 1985.
Crosby, Harry, *On a Wing and a Prayer*, Robson Books, 1993.
Frankland, Dr Noble, *The Bomber Offensive against Germany*, Faber, 1965.
Franks, Norman, *RAF Fighter Command: 1936–1968*, P. Stephens, 1992.
Freeman, Roger A., *The Friendly Invasion*, T. Dalton, 1992.
Freeman, Roger A., *Mighty Eighth War Manual*, Arms and Armour, 1990.
Freeman, Roger A., *The Mighty Eighth*, Arms and Armour, 1989.
Harris, Sir Arthur, *Bomber Offensive*, Collins, 1947.
Hastings, Max, *Bomber Command*, M. Joseph, 1979.
Johnson, J.E., *Wing Leader*, Chatto & Windus, 1956.
Jones, R.V., *Most Secret War*, Hamish Hamilton, 1978.
Kinsey, Gordon, *Aviation: Flight over the Eastern Counties since 1937*, T. Dalton, 1977.
Longmate, Norman, *The Bombers*, Hutchinson, 1983.
Moyes, Philip J.R., *Bomber Squadrons of the RAF*, Macdonald & Janes, 1976.
Rawnsley, C.F. and Wright, Robert, *Night Fighter*, Collins, 1957.
Rawlings, John, *Fighter Squadrons of the RAF*, Crecy Books, 1993.
Richards, Denis, *The Royal Air Force: 1939–45*, HMSO, 1953.
Scutts, Terry, *Lions in the Sky*, P. Stephens, 1987.
Streetly, M., *Confound and Destroy: 100 Group & the Bomber Support Campaign*, Janes, 1985.
Turner, John F., *British Aircraft of World War II*, Sidgewick & Jackson, 1975.

RAF SQUADRONS

9   91-2, 102
18   137–8, 189, 268
19   152
21   60–1, 110, 169–170, 191, 252–6
23   150–1
34   252–3
37   156–7
38   266
42   52
56   167–8
57   103
66   71–2
72   164
75   103–6
82   60–1, 253–6
85   229–31
88   43, 191
90   267–70
98   111, 120, 270–1
101   267
105   138–40, 159–62, 232–5
107   118–9
109   162
114   136, 189, 270
115   94, 147–8, 157–9
118   72–3
133   70
137   165–7
139   136, 159, 162–3, 266
141   271–2
144   146
149   172
157   229–31
167   154
169   121, 148
171   174–5
180   111–13
192   115–6
195   154–5
199   174–5
208   51–2
214   99–100, 172, 192–4, 205–6
218   84–8, 159
220   53
221   81
222   165
223   192–4
226   36, 235–6
229   168
233   54
235   53, 81
236   190
239   271–2
242   67–9
255   70–1
257   69
264   135
278   72, 168
279   57
280   57, 143
303   74
311   92
316   74, 146
320   46, 55
342   201–2
403   82
407   55
415   55
451   231
453   168
458   145–6
462   115–6
464   106, 110, 170–1, 202–4
487   202–4
489   145–6
514   113–4
515   148–51
571   90
602   155
603   155
610   152–3
614   270
616   68
623   87
635   88–90
815 (FAA)   54
1401 (Met) Flight   82–3
1 A/A Flight   143

USAAF GROUPS

25 Bomb Group   258
36 Bomb Group   192
44 Bomb Group   215–21
56 Fighter Group   140
92 Bomb Group   113
93 Bomb Group   122–28
96 Bomb Group   33, 222–8
100 Bomb Group   238–44
319 Bomb Group   45, 140, 215
352 Fighter Group   59, 62–5
359 Fighter Group   91, 94–8
386 Bomb Group   223
388 Bomb Group   108–10
389 Bomb Group   129–34
392 Bomb Group   259–65
445 Bomb Group   245–51
448 Bomb Group   207–14
452 Bomb Group   75–80
453 Bomb Group   183–8
458 Bomb Group   140–2
466 Bomb Group   46–50
467 Bomb Group   195–200
491 Bomb Group   180–2
492 Bomb Group   176–80
36 Bomb Squadron   257–8
408 Bomb Squadron   257–8
3 Strategic Air Depot   257–8

INDEX

Airfields 39-42, 43-272
Airspeed Horsa 201
Airspeed Oxford 237
Alconbury 113, 123
Armstrong Whitworth
  Whitley 11, 12
Attlebridge 43-50, 141, 196, 197, 199
Avro Anson 29, 52, 53, 57, 144; *Manchester* 15, 89;
  see also *Lancaster*

B-17 see *Boeing*
B-24 see *Liberator*
B-26 see *Martin Marauder*
Barton Beamish 84
Bell Aircobra 165
Bentley Priory 22
Biggin Hill 137, 153
Bircham Newton 29, 39, 41, 51-57, 72, 81, 82, 83, 143, 253, 278
Blackburn Botha 29
Blenheim 11, 12, 14, 23, 31, 44, 53, 54, 57, 60, 61, 81-83, 135, 189, 201, 233-234, 252-258; *IV* 43, 117-119, 136-138, 266-272
Blickling Hall 189, 190
Bodney 58-65, 95, 111, 255, 257
Boeing B-17 18, 33, 34, 36, 47, 57, 75-80, 113, 119, 123, 131, 134, 140, 179, 192-194, 205-206, 216-218, 222-228 *passim*, 238-244, 258, 268-270; *B29* 206
Bomber Command 9-21 and *passim*
Boston see *Douglas Boston*
Bottisham 48, 96
Boulton Paul Defiant 24, 25, 70, 135, 136, 137, 148
Bourn 163
Boxted 223, 265
Bristol Beaufighter 26, 29, 31, 57, 70-73, 120-121, 144-146, 150, 189-190; *Beaufort* 29;
  see also *Blenheim*

Castleton 154
Catalina 31
Cheddington 177
Cheshunt 264
Church Fenton 74
Coastal Command 28, 29-33
  and *passim*

Coltishall 11, 23, 41, 42, 55, 56, 66-74, 93, 146, 152, 153, 155, 164, 165
Cranwell 8, 9

DB-7 see *Douglas Boston*
Debden 70
De Havilland see *Mosquito*
Defiant see Boulton Paul
Deopham Green 75-80
Diss 280
Docking 72, 81-83, 146, 173
Douglas Boston III (DB-7) 44, 111, 119-120, 171, 190-191, 201-202, 235-237, 271
Downham Market 84-90, 159, 205, 252
Dunsford 113
Dunstable 83
Duxford 66-70 *passim*, 102, 135, 152, 154

East Dereham 259, 280
East Wretham 91-98, 202

Fairey Albacore 53, 72, 146; *Battle* 11, 14-15, 24, 44, 60, 84, 96, 202; *Hendon* 156-157; *Swordfish* 30, 54, 55, 144, 146, 166
Feltwell 11, 12, 39, 41, 99-106, 169, 170, 252
Fersfield 107-110
Fighter Command 9, 22-29
  and *passim*
Flying Fortress see *Boeing B-17*
Focke Wulf 190 26, 27, 58, 74, 79, 98, 140, 167-168, 170, 184, 209, 229, 249, 263
Foulsham 111-116, 120, 147, 173

Gloster Gladiator 82-83; *Meteor* 28, 68
Grafton Underwood 38
Gravely 90
Great Massingham 117-121, 150, 202, 269
Great Yarmouth 72, 264, 273, 280
Griston 257

Halesworth 140
Halifax 15, 28, 57, 87, 115-156, 174-175
Halton 9

Handley Page Hampden 11, 12, 61, 145; *Harrow* 99-101, 156-157 see also *Halifax; Hurricane*
Hardwick 122-128, 129
Hartford Bridge 45, 192
Hawker Henley 143; *Tempest* 28; *Typhoon* 26, 46, 154, 166-168
Hawkinge 181
Heinkel He111 72
Hethel 125, 126, 129-134, 184, 246
High Ercall 71
High Wycombe 200
Hingham 75
Honington 100, 101, 102
Hornchurch 137
Horsham St Faith 11, 23-24, 45, 135-142, 189, 196, 215, 235, 278
Hunsdon 205
Hurricane 22, 23, 24, 25, 26, 67, 69, 70

Junkers Ju88 70, 93, 150, 167, 212, 224, 228, 255, 261

Kenley 153
King's Cliffe 140
Knettishall 108

Lakenheath 172
Lancaster 15, 17, 58-59, 86, 87, 88-89, 94, 106, 113-114, 147, 148, 217; *Mark II* 113; *Mark VI* 90
Langham 83, 143-146
Leuchars 145
Liberator B-24 35, 36, 46-48, 57, 63, 64, 74, 93, 108, 122-128, 129-134 *passim*, 140, 141, 142, 176-182, 184-188, 192-200 *passim*, 207-221 *passim*, 223, 243, 246-251 *passim*, 257-265 *passim*
Lincoln 90
Little Snoring 121, 147-151
Little Staughton 163
Little Walden 249
Lockheed Hudson 29, 52-57, 81, 83, 189; *Lightning P-38* 150; *Ventura* 61, 106, 111, 169-171, 191, 192
Ludham 152-155, 242
Lysander 96

Madingley 38, 39, 108
Manston 131
Marham 11, 12, 39, 41, 42, 84, 85, 100, 140, 156-163, 278
Martin B-26 Marauder 36, 44, 45, 122, 140, 223
Matlaske 23, 69, 72, 154, 164-172, 231
Messerschmitt 109 55, 67, 70, 96, 101, 102, 129, 130, 133, 177, 206, 240, 263, 219; *110* 150, 166, 170, 210, 246, 254, 272; *163* 97; *262* 79, 98, 142, 155, 214
Metfield 257
Methwold 46, 103, 106, 169-172
Middle Wallop 71
Mildenhall 93, 94, 100, 101, 159
Miles Master 61, 257
Mitchell B-25 46, 110, 111-113, 120, 122, 236-237, 270-271
Mosquito 10, 17, 19, 27, 28, 32, 37, 57, 71, 74, 83, 90, 93, 110, 116, 121, 138-140, 148-150, 159-163, 175, 201-205, 229-231, 232, 234-235, 271-272
Mundesley 284
Mustang P-51 36, 37, 48, 63, 64, 65, 74, 79, 95-98, 110, 133, 142, 146, 150, 181, 182, 242, 249

Narborough 156
Neaton 257
Newmarket 105
North Coates 145, 190
North Creake 173-175
North Pickenham 176-182
North Weald 153

Norwich 66, 70, 72, 135, 196, 197, 215, 273, 274, 275, 279, 280, 281, 284

Old Buckenham 80, 183-188, 246, 248, 249
Oulton 118, 136, 189-194, 206

P-47 see *Thunderbolt*
P-51 see *Mustang*
Portreath 219

Quidenham 227, 228

Rackheath 141, 195-200

St Eval 258
St Faith's see Horsham St Faith
Saffron Walden 265
Saunders Roe Lerwick 29
Sculthorpe 192, 201-206
Seething 207-214
Shipdham 129, 176, 177, 215-221
Short Stirling 15, 84-88, 147-148, 156, 158-159, 174; *Sunderland* 29, 32
Snetterdon Heath 222-228, 239
Spitfire 20, 22, 23, 24, 26, 28, 32, 54, 66, 68, 70, 74, 82-83; *I* 67; *II* 22, 152; *V* 72-74, 152-155; *IX* 74, 168, 231
Stansted 135
Steeple Morden 233
Swaffam 259
Swannington 229-231
Swanton Morley 17, 36, 42, 43, 46, 114, 138, 159, 190, 191, 232-237, 278

Syerston 220

Tangmere 131
Tempsford 258
Thetford 91, 156, 169, 224, 280
Thorney Island 235
Thorpe Abbotts 225, 238-44
Thunderbolt P-47 36, 37, 59, 62, 94-95, 140, 241
Tibenham 184, 245-251
Torpedo Armed Beaufighters (Torbeau) 145

United States Army Air Force (USAAF) 15, 20, 33-39 and *passim*

Vickers Warwick 57; *Vildebeeste* 29, 52, 140 see also *Wellington*
Vultee Vengeance 202

Waterbeach 148
Watton 11, 12, 39, 41, 42, 67, 135, 181, 252-258, 266, 278
Wellington 11, 12, 31, 55-56, 57, 91, 92, 94, 100-106, 115, 146, 157-159, 268
Wendling 176, 220, 259-265
West Malling 153
West Raynham 11, 12, 19-20, 39, 42, 111, 114, 117, 119, 121, 202, 266-272, 278
Westland Whirlwind 165-167
Weston Longville 43
Weyborne 143
Wick 145
'Wimpy' see *Wellington*
Woodbridge 90, 108, 180-181
Wymondham 134, 280
Wyton 88, 162